W9-CDT-502

CRIMEA

• Metracha

Cherson •

B L A C K   S E A

Dristria •

• Anchialus

Phasus •

TH   R   A   C   E

• Sinope

Edirne •
ADRIANOPLE

Istanbul
CONSTANTINOPLE

Trapezus •

• Nicomedia

IRMAK

• Nicaea

• Troy

ASIA MINOR
ASIA

C   A   P   P   A   D   O   C   I   A

• Pergamus

• Caesarea

LESBOS

• Edessa

CHIOS

• Smyrna
• Ephesus

• Iconium

EUPHRATES

DELOS

Attaliya

• Circesium

• Antioch

RHODES

• Myra

NEAR

Kia

CYPRUS

• Tripoli

• Palmyra

TE

S   E   A

• Heliopolis
• Damascus

Sidon •
Tyre •

P
H
O
E
N
I
C
I
A

EAST

Jaffa •

• Jerusalem

Alexandria •

S   Y   R   I   A

C

• Petra

Memphis •

E   G   Y   P   T

NILE

THE BYZANTINES AND THEIR WORLD

THE BYZANTINES

ST. MARTIN'S PRESS   NEW YORK

ND THEIR WORLD

PETER ARNOTT

Wingate College Library

Copyright 1973 by Peter Arnott
ALL RIGHTS RESERVED
First Printing

Library of Congress Catalogue #72–89423 *7-11-77*
Manufactured in the United States of America
No part of this book may be reproduced without
permission in writing from the publisher.

St. Martin's Press
175 Fifth Avenue
New York, N.Y.10010

AFFILIATED PUBLISHERS: Macmillan Limited, London
—also at Bombay, Calcutta, Madras and Melbourne

CONTENTS

070875

INTRODUCTION

This book, the third in a sequence on classical civilizations, has been without doubt the hardest to write. Not, Heaven knows, for lack of material—Migne's endless *Patrologia Graeca* burdening the library shelves testifies to that—but because the humanity of the Byzantines, as distinct from their official posture, proves so elusive. It is this formidable public image that has made the people so remote. A class of schoolboys reading "Sailing to Byzantium" proves never to have heard of Byzantium. A learned and accomplished colleague insists that he cannot regard the Byzantines as people, only as shapes petrified in mosaic. A student is advised by his parents, professors both, to avoid Byzantine history as "too frivolous." And yet we are talking of a civilization that lasted as long as the Roman; that began when Romans still commanded Britain and ended when Columbus had already taken his infant steps; that withstood for centuries the pressures of the emergent and angry East, and allowed Europe to grow up in its lee; and shaped, for Catholic and Orthodox alike, a major part of Christian doctrine. There is a major gap of popular understanding here, and I hope this book will go some little way to fill it.

In pursuit of the Byzantines one runs up against early difficulties. Who were they? At what point did they acquire a national identity? When did their empire begin? There are no easy answers. Other peoples thought of them as Greeks and used this as a term of abuse. In the mélange of peoples gathering around Rome's carcass, we find the extraordinary spectacle of Goths sneering at Italians because they are willing to let themselves be governed by Greeks, a race of dilettanti and poseurs. But the Byzantines, although their common language was Greek, thought of themselves as Romans, legitimate descendants of the Roman Empire; and there are still parts of the world where *Romaioi* means *Greek*. Patrick Leigh Fermor, in his book *Roumeli*, has fruitfully explored this etymological confusion.

The beginnings of the Empire are equally ambiguous. Some would date it from the foundation of Constantinople as a separate, Eastern capital. The present book takes this position. Others would begin with the reign of Justinian; still others, with the final breach between East and West marked by the coronation of Charlemagne at Rome. And then there are the problems of the people themselves. It is a difficulty rather analogous to the study of the Etruscans, whom we think of as obsessed with death because we have nothing to inspect but their tombs. By the same token, we think of the Byzantines as obsessed with religion because there is nothing left to look at but their churches. Secular architecture, apart from Mistra, the Istanbul waterworks and a few remains of private houses in the Near East, is almost entirely lacking. In Pompeii and Ostia we can see how Romans lived from day to day. There is no Byzantine equivalent, though it is very easy to find out how the people worshipped. The literature is similarly biased. Most of it is concerned with things spiritual, argued with such humorless pedantry as to deter the most hardened researcher. It is virtually obligatory to preface a book on Byzantium with the admission that one has scarcely scratched the surface of Migne. I hasten to add my own confession to the pile.

And yet there must have been more; and it is the task of this book, as with its Greek and Roman predecessors, to try to indicate what this might be. One cannot avoid the religiosity, for it was a major part of life. It was admitted that you could not so much as ask the time of day in Byzantium without being treated to a discourse on the Trinity. But one can at least try to place this in a human context and talk not of doctrine, but of St. Theodore's mother and of what it meant to be an active Christian in her time. Though the book is roughly chronological, it makes no pretensions at completeness. It merely tries, as its predecessors, to give a taste of things—of city-building, war and travel; of life at both ends of the social scale. Byzantium was a jeweled mirror that, unchanging, reflected a changing world, and so other cities must have their place in this story, particularly Rome, with its several declines and falls, and Venice. And so, inevitably, must my own preferences and predilections have their place. It will soon be apparent to the reader, for instance, that I am fascinated by saints, their works and deeds, their comings and goings, both dead and alive. I have tried to allow the ancients to speak in their own words. If this book seems overburdened with quotations, my excuse is that many of these passages, to my knowledge, have never ap-

peared in English before. All translations are my own,
with the exception of that of Benjamin of Tudela. Having no Hebrew, I reproduce the charming version of A.
Asher, first published in 1840.

My debts of gratitude are many. To the Director and
Secretary of the British School at Athens, for their kindness to one who has long ceased to have any legitimate
claim on their attention; to Ann Bergren, for assisting
me in tracking down material; to Barbara Ropes and
George Biris, for their help with knotty points of medieval French; to my wife, as usual, for typing. Yet, as I
look back, I think my main debt must be to the two
anonymous black-swathed ladies that I met by chance
in Thessaloniki. I lost my way here in the Old Town one
gray morning and came by accident across the tiny
church of Holy David—which is, perhaps the only way
to find it. I stopped there for a while to look and rest,
and the two ladies, who were sitting on the porch, expressed great concern about the condition of my face
and hands. (For someone with a professional interest in
the Mediterranean, I am absurdly sensitive to the sun.)
They had a sure cure, they informed me proudly; I had
only to wash in the *nero Christou*, the water of Christ.
Out of politeness I assented, thinking to be presented
with a stoup of holy water from the church; no such
thing. The ladies, emerging with a censer and a huge
iron key, signaled me to follow. Through the narrow
streets we went, with the incense purifying the way
before us and a small procession forming behind ; it was
evidently a familiar spectacle. Finally, after many
twists and turnings, we arrived at a large door in a rock
wall. Unlocking it, the ladies ushered me inside. I found
myself in a dark grotto, with water trickling down the
wall and collecting in a pool at the base—the *nero*

Christou, and in all probability a healing shrine centuries before Christ was heard of.

The walls gleamed with icons. Some, as far as I could make out in the half-dark, were of considerable antiquity, others merely picture postcards. At my guides' insistence I lay down and plunged face and arms into the stream. At this moment, with uncanny timing, the heavens opened. The rain which had been threatening all day cascaded down, and coatless, hatless, we were trapped. For two hours in that cave we talked, while the storm roared outside; and it was clear there was only one permissible subject. Why was I interested in the church? Was I perhaps an *anthropos theou?* No, I replied apologetically, I was not a man of God. But surely I was a Christian? Yes, indeed, Protestant, of course. A murmur of pity here. Did I believe in the saints? Well, yes and no. Did my priest wear a beard? No, I said, trying to imagine one on my Episcopalian minister in Massachusetts, he did not. And so it went on, till the rain stopped; and then we walked back together to the church and went our several ways. As I left them, it seemed to me that, in spirit and in presence, I had come as close to Byzantium as I was ever likely to get.

It would be pleasant to record that the *nero Christou* worked. It did not, alas; perhaps it benefits only those who believe in the saints and whose priests wear beards. But the memory of those two ladies, for whom St. Demetrius and all the rest were as alive as I was, will remain with me for a long time; and it is to them that this book is really dedicated.

CHRONOLOGICAL
CONSTANTINOPLE

324–330	Constantine builds New Rome, Constantinople.
337	Death of Constantine
361–363	Julian the Apostate briefly restores paganism.
527–565	Reign of Justinian I. City-wide building program, including Haghia Sophia; codification of Roman law.
534	Byzantine reconquest of Africa.
537	Byzantine reconquest of Italy.
602	Military insurrection: accession of Phocas.
610	Accession of Heraclius inaugurates Heraclian dynasty (610–711).
668–685	Years of palace revolt.
717	Moslem siege of Constantinople. Accession of Leo III inaugurates Isaurian dynasty (717–820).
726	Promulgation of iconoclastic decrees.
765	Active persecution of icon-worshippers.
787	Empress Irene re-establishes cult of images. Second Council of Nicaea called to discuss controversy.
813–842	Persecution of icon-worshippers renewed.
843	Triumph of icon-worshippers: restoration of images.
867	Basil I inaugurates Macedonian dynasty (867–1081). Important military advances under Basil I (867–886), Leo VI (886–912), Constantine VII Porphyrogennetus (912–959).
976	Accession of Basil II, "the Bulgar-killer." Revolts in Asia Minor put down.
1025	Death of Basil II.
1057–1081	Disruption of Macedonian dynasty amid years of anarchy in Constantinople.
1054	Schism between the Eastern and Western Churches: under the leadership of Constantine IX, Eastern Orthodoxy disassociates itself from the Pope in Rome.
1081	Accession of Alexius I inaugurates Comnenian dynasty (1081–1185).
1204	Fourth Crusade sacks Constantinople. Latin Empire established, to endure until 1261. Scattered Greek states remain in Trebizond, Epirus, Nicaea.
1261	Michael VIII retakes Constantinople from Latins, restores the Byzantine state, and inaugurates the dynasty of the Polaeologi. Some Latin possessions in Greece seized, including Mistra. Unsuccessful attempts at reconciliation with Rome. Empire torn by social and religious quarrels.
1453	Mohammed II takes Constantinople.

CHART
ABROAD

313	Constantine and Licinius promulgate Edict of Toleration, decreeing freedom of Christian worship.
325	First Council of Nicaea: condemnation of Arian heresy.
409	Decay of Roman Empire in West. Britain abandoned to invaders.
410	Capture of Rome by Visigoths.
476	Deposition of Romulus Augustulus, last Roman emperor.
610	Loss of Egypt, Jerusalem, Near Eastern territories to Persia.
629	Heraclius secures sweeping victories over Persia, temporarily restores Byzantine prestige.
632	Death of Mohammed.
640–and after	Moslem conquests of Alexandria, Cyprus, Rhodes; attacks on Constantinople.
680	Bulgars appear on world scene.
668–685	Carthage falls to armies of Islam.
750	Centre of Moslem power shifts to Bagdad.
751	Capture of Ravenna by Lombards: effective end of Byzantine power in Italy.
800	Coronation of Charlemagne as Holy Roman Emperor, St. Peter's, Rome.
843	Spreading menace of Arab piracy in Mediterranean.
864	Byzantine conversion of Bulgars to Orthodox Christianity.
961	Byzantines recapture Crete.
969	Byzantines recapture Antioch.
976	Revolts in Asia Minor put down.
1014	Resounding and brutal victory ends war with Bulgars.
1054	The Normans appear in Italy. The Turks predominate in Asia Minor. Turkish dominion extends to shores of Sea of Marmara.
1096	First Crusade begins; captures Nicaea, Antioch, Jerusalem, Tripoli, Edessa.
1147	Normans invade Greece.
1185	Normans sack Thessaloniki.
1342–1349	Triumph of Zealots in Thessaloniki establishes city as independent republic.
1421	Sultan Mured II attacks Constantinople, takes Thessaloniki.
1439	Council of Florence seeks reunion with Rome.
1446	Turks take Athens. Turks invade Morea.

1. A WORLD DYING

The teeming heart of Venice is St. Mark's, shaken by the daily rush of tourists who come to stare, to wonder and to photograph one another; and one of the favorite backgrounds for their pictures is a sculptured group on the south wall of the Basilica, at the angle of the Treasury looking out across the Piazzetta toward the Grand Canal. It is one of the most familiar sculptures in Venice, for there is a stone bench under it, where tour guides stand to harangue their charges before plunging through the archway to the Doges' Palace. Yet probably not one visitor in a thousand realizes that, like most of the ornamentation of the south wall, it came to Venice by an act of plunder, the rape of the East by the West, or that it represents a crisis of history, one of those decisive moments when the face of the world suddenly changed. Of red Egyptian porphyry, it shows four figures standing two and two, each dressed in the style familiar from Byzantine illustration, with tunic, cloak and jeweled belt and scabbard. Their faces wear the studied impassivity proper to all, and particularly to Roman, imperial portraiture. Who are they? A popular

Venetian tradition considers them to be marauding Crusaders who attempted to rob St. Mark of his treasure and were turned into stone for their pains. There is this much truth in the story: that pillage was a favorite activity of Crusaders; it was the prospect of pillage that eventually led them, as we shall see, to Constantinople. But no, say some historians; the figures represent the Basileus of the East and the Emperor of the West, the conjoint rulers of Byzantium and Rome, petrified in perpetual amity. If so, this would be not much less of a fiction than the other; when the Roman world divided into two, there was no love lost between the East and West. But most historians cry no to this also. They claim, with reason, that this stone depicts a moment somewhat earlier in history, that it shows the quartet who after 293 A.D.divided the Roman Empire among themselves: Diocletian, Maximian, Constantius Chlorus (The Sallow) and Galerius, the four rulers of the world, the Tetrarchs. Their Eastern dress is accounted for by the adoption at court of Asiatic costume and ceremonial, indicating the elevation of the ruler to the status of an oriental despot and foreshadowing the temporary eclipse of West by East. The long swords in their elaborately carved scabbards betray the necessity, accepted by these men, of fighting to retain what they possessed. Diocletian was the last of those "soldier emperors" whose activities retarded the process of decay and prolonged for a while Rome's illusion of eternity. Where the sculpture originated is not known, but like so many of Venice's treasures it seems to have come from abroad. A missing foot, recently rediscovered in Istanbul, suggests that the group resided for a while in the city of Constantine. But sculptures like it must have been familiar in many parts of the Roman Empire towards its end. Such a monument probably stood in the Roman Forum; we can see it in the carved scenes which decorate the Arch of Constantine. There was another, appropriately, in Diocletian's palace at Split. The Tetrarchs meant to be remembered.

And perhaps, if these were indeed the Tetrarchs, the unknown sculptor sculpted better than he knew. The figures stand as they were paired by title; two Augusti and two Caesars, names which had once been personal and had now become badges of rank. The arm of each Augustus is thrown around the shoulders of his subordinate Caesar, in an attitude intended to express comradely affection. Is it only hindsight that suggests an undertone of fear and shows us not so much brotherly love, as a huddling together for mutual protection? Two by two they stand, and back to back, as if afraid that someone might jump on them from behind; and though each has one arm draped about his colleague's shoulder, the other hand is tensed on the hilt of his sword.

There was room for apprehension, for the world that these Tetrarchs ruled, the moribund Roman world, was open to attack from every side. Pressure came particularly from the north. The Emperor Gallienus, who came to the throne in 253, saw the frontiers crumble virtually before his eyes. Roman power, which over the centuries had gradually spilled across the great rivers into the wilderness, was rolled back to the Rhine and the Danube. A passing remark by a late historian evokes the spirit of the time; he talks of the great, lonely Roman guardships endlessly patrolling the icebound rivers, vigilant to prevent the barbarians from crossing or, more often, to harass their columns when they sought to return. In 258 the tribe of the Alemanni succeeded in pushing through the Alps to the Po valley. The pleasant northern towns, Verona, Comum, Aquileia, felt the cold wind and ravaged their ancestral tombs to build themselves walls. Ten years later the Juthungi, Alemanni and other tribes had advanced to within seventy miles of Rome. Aurelian was Emperor then; both a general and a builder, he not only drove the barbarians away, but fortified the capital against their return. "This was the first time," remarked the historian Zosimus, "that Rome had walls."[1] There had, of course, been walls before, but they had been un-needed, outgrown and forgotten. Aurelian's construction fitted the timidity of the times. Begun on the advice of an apprehensive senate, the walls were rushed to completion by forced labor exacted from the Roman guilds, who were permitted thereafter to call themselves "Aurelians." It was a formidable undertaking. The finished circuit was some twelve miles long and had 371 ordinary turrets, forty-nine fortified turrets, 6,900 bastions, fifteen gates and fifteen postern gates. Embraced within the system of fortifications, the mausoleum of Hadrian, now the Castel' Sant' Angelo, began its second life as a fortress. Its great drum shape was admirably suitable for a castle; the stone statues which still plentifully decorated the summit were to prove their worth as missiles before many years had passed.

From this point Roman history begins to resound with exotic names. Some foreigners of course were old acquaintances, though sometimes newly dangerous. We hear of the pugnacious Gauls, clean livers but hard drinkers, whose womenfolk were even more formidable than the men:

One Gaul is more than a match for a whole crowd of foreigners, particularly if he invites his wife to join in the fight. In Gaul the women are deadlier than the male. Their eyes shine with a strange wild light; with a great grinding of teeth, and a swelling of veins on her neck, the wife flexes the muscles of her pale and brawny arms and lets fly with such a hail of kicks and blows that you feel you are under fire from a catapult. There is no withstanding such an assault.[2]

There were the Franks, who fought with axes and who, together with the Saxon pirates, offered a constant menace to the coasts of Britain, Spain and Gaul. There were the various German tribes, old enemies, for the Romans had never been completely successful beyond the Rhine. There were the Erulians, originating from beyond the Danube, who practiced the systematic elimination of the old and unfit and encouraged ritual suttee. There were the Goths, and behind the Goths a menace as yet still distant, the Huns, who seemed to Roman observers like vegetable creatures from a sub-human world, with lumpish faces and pinhole eyes; whose cheeks were scarred at birth: who ate meat still half raw and wild roots, and looked like gnarled roots themselves; who wore round caps, never changed their clothes, and bound their legs and feet with goat skins; who were almost glued to their horses, and could eat and sleep in the saddle.

In the East were other enemies, more civilized but no less dangerous. There were the Parthians, fighting Indian style, accompanied by their elephants carrying iron howdahs full of archers. There were the law-abiding, highly moral Persians, riding on the crest of their resurrected empire, who had caught a Roman emperor and held him to ransom; who were wrapped in shimmering, iridescent robes, covered in chains and necklaces of gold, studded with the pearls that were their greatest treasure. There were the Saracens, a warlike people, perched half-naked on their racing camels, so nomadic in their habits that "a woman might get married in one place, give birth in another, and raise her children in a third, without the right or opportunity to settle down."[3] There were the Sarmatians, who "make better brigands than they do honest soldiers; who have spears longer than one usually sees, and cuirasses made of plates of polished horn, fastened like scales to a linen shirt."[4] All these people, in their different ways and in their own time, surrounded the aging, faltering colossus that was Rome, and probed or waited.

The division of the Empire was Diocletian's idea, a practical recognition of the fact that it had grown too big for one man to govern. It was a wide world, that at its fullest extent had stretched from the black northlands of Britain to the deserts south of Egyptian Thebes, from the mines of Spain to the caravanserai-cities of Damascus and Palmyra, recipients of the growing trade with the Orient. Diocletian's measure cut this world administratively in two, gave him an equal partner, and allotted to each of them a second-in-command and heir-apparent; it set a limit to the reign of the two Augusti, himself and Maximian, and insisted that the two of them resign together and hand on their power to their respective Caesars, as they did on May 1, 305. Diocletian was quoted as saying that "of the many decisions he had taken for the public good, this one had been far and away the best,"[5] and perhaps the most surprising thing about it was that for a while it worked, despite the fact that the Tetrarchs were men of widely different dispositions and in no real sense a cohesive body. Julian the Apostate, in his burlesque vision of the unrolling pageant of Roman history, depicts them as inseparable, all for onè and one for all, skipping and dancing eternally in a merry foursome. But it is historical fact that Domitian and Maximian met only once during the latter's reign, for a brief conference at Milan. It is clear also that the Tetrarchs reserved the right of interpreting important decisions according to their individual standards and inclinations. Diocletian's persecution of the Christians, carried out mercilessly in some parts of the Empire and in others not at all, is a case in point.

The division of rule was an acknowledgement of the fact that the Empire had already begun to divide itself. Rome remained the nominal capital, the repository of centuries of tradition, but for practical purposes the Tetrarchs chose other administrative centers more convenient for the new mechanics of government. A brief survey of these places shows how diverse the Empire had become and how the old blanket assumption of Roman standards was succumbing to a new regionalism. Diocletian was in Rome for a few weeks only during the twenty-two years of his reign. He preferred Nicomedia, on the northwest coast of Asia Minor, while Maximian chose Mediolanum (Milan). This city first enters history in the fourth century B.C. as a Celtic settlement; its ancestry is remembered in its name. After the Roman occupation in 222 B.C. it grew and flourished. In the early years of the Christian era it was still only a city of the second rank, but the increasing pressure of the German tribes gave it a new importance as the bastion of the north. Ausonius, rhetorician and occasional poet, composed in the fourth century a verse catalogue of noble cities. The city of the Caesars, of course, begins the list, but is dismissed with an obligatory, perfunctory couplet:

> The first of cities and the home
> Of gods, the golden city, Rome.

But it is the *arriviste* cities that clearly claim Ausonius' attention:

> Milan is full of wonders and delights,
> Of stately homes, of men with sparkling tongues
> And shining faces. See the double walls
> That give it space and splendor, and the cheering
> Thousands in the circus, the majestic
> Precinct of the playhouse, row on row. . . .
>
> These brick and mortar mountains, rearing high
> To top each other, nor are they inclined
> To genuflect towards their neighbor, Rome.[6]

It was the Emperor Aurelian who had wrapped Milan with walls at the same time that he fortified Rome. Once established as an imperial capital, Milan embarked on that long rivalry with Rome which is still in evidence today; the parvenu city was to grow into an industrial giant, threatening the ancient repository of culture and tradition. Some of Maximian's Milan may still be seen, though not much; the walls were not strong enough, there have been too many sacks, too many sieges. Yet in the quarter southwest of the Duomo traces of the original rectangular plan are still apparent, and the visitor can see patches of the early fourth-century walls, of Maximian's circus and of his amphitheater.

Constantius Chlorus, the Caesar of the West, took Treveri, now Trier to the Germans; the French preserved the original name in Trèves, in all fairness, for it was theirs to begin with. Named after one of the most powerful tribes of the Belgae, conquered by Julius Caesar in 36 B.C., the city was coeval with the Roman Empire. Augustus had consolidated, fortified and rechristened it; as Augusta Treverorum, it served first as a center for the brief, abortive Gallic independence movement and later, in Diocletian's reorganization of the Empire, as the capital of the whole diocese of Gaul. A military seat of strategic importance, it was still for a while a civilized place to live. There are the remains of an amphitheater, southeast of the modern town, built by Trajan or Hadrian to accommodate some 20,000 spectators; there were enormous public baths, the inevitable concomitant of Roman occupation.

Beside the Rhine

And pillowed on the breast of peace, Trèves lies,
The nurse, the tailor and the armorer of empire,
Whose walls sprawl over the surrounding hills.
Down to the wide Moselle, whose tranquil stream
Bears produce from all corners of the earth.[7]

It was not always a tranquil city. In 271 it was attacked by the Franks, and it was after this, according to some historians, that the walls went up, together with the monumental *Porta Nigra*, Black Gate, that still provides an entrance to the city. Others would argue that the walls had been in existence long before this time; but the more romantic view alleges that, when the barbarians came too close for comfort, the scaffolding was hastily removed and the masons took shelter inside their newly-built walls.

Other cities acquired a similar new importance. One was Sirmium, a military outpost on what is now the River Sara in Yugoslavia. Another was Thessaloniki in Macedonia, already a city of distinction, which had sheltered Cicero during his exile and whose inhabitants had been harangued by St. Paul. Holding a commanding position on the coast, it was at the same time linked to Italy by the Via Egnatia, the main highway to the East. It was now chosen by Galerius, the Caesar of the East, as his place of residence. Archaeology has uncovered some portions of the city as the Tetrarch knew it. As this book is written, work is proceeding on the ancient agora, just north of the square where the modern buses assemble. A fragmentary colonnade has come to light, and a huddle of shops. Nearer the waterfront stand the relics of the triumphal arch erected to Galerius by his citizens when he returned from his eastern victories in 297. It is of brick faced with stone, and straddles the modern Egnatia Street, which preserves the name, though probably not the route, of its ancient counterpart; its reliefs show Galerius as warrior and priest, offering sacrifice, haranguing his soldiers from the rostrum and standing triumphant over the kneeling representatives of the peoples he had conquered.

In its time this arch, still impressive in ruin, was merely the center of an imposing complex of buildings. To the north, a columned street led to the great rotunda which Galerius may have constructed for his own mausoleum. The rotunda still stands, though long given over to Christianity. To the south was the hippodrome, now overlaid by modern buildings, and an immense palace, of which a few uninteresting lumps remain. There are traces of the main hall and a mosaic floor; an octagonal building, its purpose unknown,

stands a little apart. A richly decorated marble arch
from this building is on view in the Thessaloniki Archaeological Museum. It is carved with grapes and foliage,
with images of Dionysus and Pan; on one side is a portrait of the Tyche, the Fortune of the city, on the other
a grimly smiling Galerius. It is ostentatious without
grace or charm; like the palace that housed it, it represents the last efflorescence of a troubled paganism, the
last time in the Roman world when a man could be god
and house himself as such. Galerius, claiming descent
from Hercules as Diocletian did from Jupiter himself,
inspired the persecutions out of which Christianity
emerged as the new official religion of the Roman state.

As in Macedonia, so in Gaul, where Arelate (Arles)
served as an occasional seat for emperors and eventually as the capital of the prefecture. Already graced
with a number of buildings from the early Empire, it
acquired new importance in the fourth century by the
addition of a mint and, within the next hundred years,
extensive public baths. The Roman world was diversify-
ing. Here and there, beneath the ancient map, one can
see the modern starting to thrust through. Places which
had not long before been primitive settlements were
starting to acquire distinct personalities. From the Emperor Julian in the fifth century we have a description
of a European township whose cheerless surroundings
seem to have appealed to his austere temperament.
The town, he writes, is on a small island lying in a river.
It is protected by a circuit wall, and wooden bridges
give access to the banks on either side. The water of the
river is clear to the eye and pleasant to the taste; the
weather is fairly mild, though Julian spent one winter
there when the ice came down the river like blocks of
marble—he refused to light a fire to draw the damp

from the walls, because he thought the discomfort would be good for his soul. However, the natives managed to grow a good kind of wine there and even figs, by preserving the plants in straw against the cold. The city was Lutetia and would in time be Paris. Julian was living on the Ile de la Cité. There was little gaiety as yet; for the real "gay Paree" of the late Roman world one had to look to the Near East, to Antioch, the pleasure capital—Rome could not claim even that title then —packed with dancers and flute players and more mimes, as Julian grumbled, than ordinary citizens. But Julian had a grudge against the people of Antioch because they laughed at his beard; they had no time for philosophers. And of course there was another city near Antioch destined to be even more distracting: Jerusalem, to which earnest pilgrims would soon write gazetteers listing the distances to be traveled and the best places on the imperial road system to stay. Rome was being displaced; it was no longer in the center of things. But we must return to Trèves, for the man who ruled there had already fathered a son who would displace Rome even more.

The boy in question, Constantine, was born into a precarious world, but one in which, for him at least, the omens were good. His father, Constantius Chlorus, was a distinguished military man whose life was a continued demonstration of his ability. His mother, Helena, came from a humble background, and Constantius Chlorus was eventually compelled, in the interests of his career, to divorce her. Constantine himself was born about 274 in Naissus, the modern Nis in Yugoslavia. When Constantius was elevated to the rank of Caesar, he put Helena aside, made a diplomatic marriage with Theodora, the daughter of his Augustus, Maximinian, and went on to justify the high hopes placed in him by the reclamation of rebel Britain.

This damp and gloomy province, lying on the western limit of Roman rule, had been hard to conquer, difficult to administer and impossible to defend. It was too close to the wild fringes of the world, the savages whom even the Romans thought it more prudent to ignore. When Diocletian and his colleagues ruled, there were particular dangers. The urgent restlessness of the Teutonic tribes had communicated itself to the seas around Britain, and that island's shores, together with the adjacent coast of Gaul, were being harried by Saxon and Frankish pirates. It is at this moment that the British navy first enters history. The Romans created—or as good as created, for there can have been little enough before—a sizable and disciplined fleet to restrain the pirate menace. As admiral they appointed Marcus Aurelius Carausius who, though a Gaul by descent, has been described as the first British sea-king; he soon took advantage of his position to feather his own nest. Rumors began to circulate. Carausius, it was hinted, was worse than the pirates; he was turning a blind eye to their activities so that he could appropriate their booty for himself. When charged with disloyalty by Maximian, he promptly revolted, setting up his headquarters at Gesoriacum (Boulogne) and using his mastery of the sea to laugh in the Romans' faces. Maximian and Diocletian were compelled to compromise. Carausius was confirmed in his possession of Britain, given command of the Gallic shore of the Channel and recognized as a colleague. At least, he so announced himself on coins—struck at his own mints in London and Rouen —which boasted a triple portrait labeled "Carausius and his brothers."

Wingate College Library

Carausius ruled Britain successfully for the next
seven years. But the two Augusti clearly had no intention of adhering to so humiliating an arrangement.
With the appointment of the new Caesar in 293, the
offensive was resumed. Constantius advanced through
Gaul and with some difficulty captured Gesoriacum.
Carausius himself disappeared from the scene, murdered by his treasurer, Allectus; and though the latter
held on for a while, he was soon outmaneuvered by a
combination of superior skill and bad weather. Constantius sent out his own fleet, which slipped past the
enemy in a dense fog. A land battle was fought somewhere west of London, the usurper was defeated, and
Constantius was hailed as the restorer of civilization,
redditor lucis aeternae. A medallion was struck to celebrate the liberation. It shows on one side Constantius as
Caesar, dressed in armor and a laurel wreath, and on
the other the entry into London, with the general on
horseback and a galley full of armed men rowing up the
Thames. They are welcomed by the allegorical figure of
London, forerunner of the Britannia of modern coin-
age.

This period in the administration of the West has left
its monuments, and they show the same architectural
schizophrenia that we notice elsewhere in the late Roman world. As the walls grew, of necessity, stouter, the
cities they protected burst forth into new prodigies of
engineering and construction. In Rome, Aurelian, at
the same time that he built the walls, erected the gigantic Temple of the Sun, as though hoping by increasing
ostentation within to distract attention from the encroaching dark without.

It was the same at Trèves, the same dichotomy of
grandeur and defensiveness. The rulers profited from

the disaster of 271 to establish their own building program. Where the Frankish invasions had reduced the
town to rubble, Constantius Chlorus took the northeast
corner for his palace. Some traces of it still remain. The
palace lay where the cathedral and the Church of Our
Lady now stand; and indeed, by the end of the Constantinian age, there were already churches on the site,
rising on the foundations of the ruler's private apart-
ments. There were new baths too, opening out from
the forum through a big gateway shaped like a triumphal arch. There was an ornamental fountain and a
palaestra where the patrons could take exercise. The
actual bathhouse was contained in vaulted rooms ad-
joining the palace on the eastern side, with the usual
progression of chambers from cold to very hot; there
were massage rooms and a library. It was a striking
building, constructed as a cluster of apses with arched,
recessed windows striated in red and white. When the
Romans started to vacate their subject territory and
took the habit of bathing with them, the building continued to serve in other functions. The *caldarium,* the
warm room, was quickly turned into an audience chamber. The whole complex was used as a fortress in the
Middle Ages and later as one of the gateways to the city.

After the defeat of Allectus, Constantius had spent
much time in Britain, reorganizing, building, mending
fences: he fortified the town of Eboracum (York) and
rebuilt Hadrian's Wall in the north where the barbarians had smashed it down. And on the southeast coast
Constantius—or it may have been Carausius before him
—erected a chain of coastal defenses, the "forts of the
Saxon shore," stout towers, with walls from nine to fourteen feet thick, strong to keep pirates out, and linked
by warning posts and signal stations whose traces Brit-

ish archaeologists are slowly and painstakingly recover-
ing. Their ruins mark the ancient waterline, lost har-
bor-mouths and silted estuaries. Some have nearly vanished, like Lympne, lost among the marshes, or
Reculver, licked by the encroaching sea. Others were
left stranded as the sea receded. In Suffolk the walls of
Burgh Castle enclose a field of waving grain. At Pevensey the solid land extends a mile or more beyond the
ramparts. You reach the castle now by a twisting railway line from Eastbourne, the staid holiday town which
in Roman times provided from its quarries the green
sandstone of which Pevensey was built. In those days
Pevensey was a peninsula standing high and dry above
the surrounding marshes. In the bay beyond there was
safe anchorage for shipping; a Roman road led inland
from the shore. The Romans laid out their walls in a
great oval, surrounding them with a ditch. They laid
out barrack huts inside and dug a well. Long after the
Romans had gone, the walls were still strong and useful.
When the Normans came—the battle of Hastings was
fought ten miles from here—they built their own keep
in a corner of the Roman walls, enclosing it within an
inner moat. During World War II, the Roman walls
held modern gun emplacements.

At Portchester, near Portsmouth on the Hampshire
coast, one may see a Roman fortress more nearly as the
Romans saw it, for the sea is still close. The plan is
rectilinear, with the same combination of wall and
ditch as that at Pevensey. Within the wide enclosure
there is room for a medieval keep in one corner and a
church in another; from the roof of the keep one can
look out to the lines of small boats on the water and see
in them the craft of long ago, moored in the embrace
of Rome's long arm. But even on a bright day there is

something sinister about these fortresses—Pevensey's, aptly, has a ghost, and Portchester has done duty as a prison—and when the skies are gray and rain falls dully on the jagged battlements and worn gray stone, the castles seem most aptly to sum up their time: solid, graceless, functional, built solely to keep people out.

In 305 Diocletian, his term of office having run its course, abdicated. If we are seeking architectural metaphors for the state of the world, we can hardly do better than to consider the palace where the former Augustus spent his declining years: a private residence which, like the cities, showed the same uneasy mélange of ceremony and fortification. It was at Salonae, Diocletian's birthplace, near the Yugoslavian coastal town of Split, a short boat journey from Venice. Eroded by time and encrusted with houses, the palace still reveals the magnificence and the fear which attended its conception.

Built in 300, the palace spread over eight acres. The defensiveness of the age is apparent in its plan, reminiscent of the traditional Roman camp, solid and foursquare, with a gateway at the midpoint of each wall and two principal roads crossing at the center. One wall, seven feet thick, fronted onto the sea; the others, facing landward, were protected by turrets, ramparts and watchtowers. They were dressed with what appear to be decorative niches; every other niche was in fact a loophole. Yet if the palace was, in one aspect, an armed camp, in another it was a combination of theater and temple. Within the walls it was designed to impress. The visitor approaching from the north—through the principal entrance on the landward side, the *Porta Aurea* or Golden Gate—would pass down a long, colonnaded street, between great blocks of red-tiled buildings, to a pillared courtyard open to the sky. Through the columns he could see a temple, probably that of Jupiter, Diocletian's adopted ancestor, and the emperor's *memento mori,* the pyramidally-roofed, octagonal mausoleum containing Diocletian's purple-draped sarcophagus; the mausoleum was large enough to be used as a church in the Middle Ages. At the far end of the courtyard the visitor could see a facade designed as an elaborate frame for the Emperor's public appearances. A central arch flanked by two smaller doors reinforced the impression of a Roman theater. So did the niches which originally contained cult statues. But the central opening above the main door was reserved for Diocletian himself. There he would manifest himself in person like a god in a tragedy—or like the image of a god in the state religion; for the structure of the facade also recalled the conventional arrangement of a shrine, with the divine inhabitant framed by a vault signifying heaven.

Diocletian's palace was the extension in architecture and the tangible summation of his life—the life of a soldier for whom religion and politics were once more fused, as they had been in the earlier days of Rome's imperial greatness, and who insisted that he be adored as a god in his lifetime. The rigid ceremonial that Diocletian established was to be inherited by his Byzantine successors, just as his administrative reforms were to provide a basis for the operation of the Christian Church. The theatrical religiosity of Split may have had its seeds in the posthumous deification of Augustus, but it also looked forward to the ruler of Constantinople, who would be revealed by the rising of a curtain to his adoring subjects.

This, then, was the world in which the young Constantine grew up: a shifting and uncertain world in which the old values were more and more coming into question. About his boyhood we know little except that he spent most of it at Diocletian's court, possibly, implicitly, as a hostage for his father's good behavior; the Augusti could not afford another Carausius. He rode, he hunted, he saw some military service and he was at his father's bedside when he died. Constantius had returned to Britain and to York, the town he had fortified in 306. Dead, the old Augustus was declared a god. His son, very much alive, was hailed by his father's troops as Emperor.

It was an election that was bound to offend, for there was another claimant. In 305, when Constantius had been promoted to Augustus, Galerius had become his colleague for the East and two new Caesars had been chosen: Flavius Valerius Severus and Maximin Daia, Galerius' nephew. Maximian had abdicated, only to find his own son, Maxentius, overlooked, and with a place now open, the latter hoped to seize an appointment for himself. But, as so often in the history of Rome, the army's voice was too loud to be ignored. Galerius, far away in Serdica (modern Sofia) was forced to accept the young Constantine, though only as Caesar.

Constantine settled in his father's former capital of Trèves, where he contributed heavily to the building already described. Maxentius, in Rome, secured the support of the Praetorian Guard, the traditional prop of emperors, and of his father, Maximian, who had emerged from grumbling retirement to see his son given justice. Diocletian, from his own fortified seclusion, watched and worried. The years of fighting and shifting alliances that followed saw the deaths of three

contenders and the emergence of a fourth. Severus'
death removed him, a nonentity, early from the scene.
Maximian died in Massilia (Marseilles), aged, embit-
tered, strangled at his own request. Galerius too died,
but not before he had appointed Valerius Licinianus
Licinius as Eastern Emperor. In 312 Maxentius was in
Rome, adding extra feet to the wall Aurelian had built,
when Constantine swept down from the north. He
came through the Mont Genèvre pass, and the cities of
the north came over to him one by one: Susa, Turin,
Milan, Brescia, Verona, Modena, Ravenna, Aquileia, till
finally Constantine stood within grasping distance of
Rome. And here occurred the event that was to change
the course of world history.

The story that has become a vital part of the Christian
tradition receives its first brief mention in the works of
Lactantius, a professor of rhetoric from Africa who was
to end his life as a tutor to Constantine's son; it is told
for the first time in detail in the version that was accepted as authoritative as part of the *Life of Constantine* by Eusebius, a native of Palestine who was one of
the first great scholars of the Christian Church.
Eusebius' biography is a fulsome work, written by one
who had good cause to hate the opponents of Christianity and to praise its champions; he had lived through
Diocletian's persecutions and seen his own friend and
master, Pamphilus, beheaded. When he wrote, therefore, of Constantine's conversion to his own beloved
faith, he was liable to err on the side of enthusiasm,
particularly since the fashionable style in which he
wrote was addicted to flights of fancy, extravagant
superlatives and vivid dramatic contrasts. We are presented with a picture of the two contenders for the
throne. Behind the walls of Rome is Maxentius, adulter-

ous, tyrannical, slaking his lusts on the wives of noble Roman senators, but apparently having no luck at all with Christian women, who preferred death to dishonor; reducing the capital to beggary, and its armies to starvation; and above all, practicing black arts, disemboweling human sacrifices and conjuring up demons to help him win the war. Outside is Constantine, driven to the conflict only by the failure of his elders, chivalrous, self-sacrificing, accepting it as his appointed duty to rid the world of a tyrant—and being confirmed in his crusade by a vision of the Christian God.

Eusebius presents us with a Constantine who was already toying with Christianity; who had surveyed the history of Rome and concluded that those who believed in many gods were doomed to disaster. Given this, why should Christianity in particular have seemed attractive? History offers certain answers without the assistance of Eusebius. The sect, originally small, had rapidly grown larger. An accurate estimate of numbers, of course, is impossible. None the less we may venture some informed guesses. It has been conjectured that by the end of the first century there were about 100,000 Christians in the Empire, with a proportionate strength roughly equivalent to that of the Mormons in the United States today. (The comparison is a happy one; claiming a separate divine revelation, indulging in unusual social practices and having a considerable nuisance value in the eyes of their contemporaries, the followers of Brigham Young had much in common with the followers of Paul of Tarsus.) By A.D. 250 there were perhaps half that number in Rome alone. Fifty years later there may have been as many as ten million in the Empire, one-quarter of the total population. Christianity was clearly the wave of the future. Persecution had not crushed this dangerous sect. On the contrary, it had strengthened it. Not that the persecutions had been systematic. They had occurred sporadically from the reign of Nero on, sometimes for political, sometimes for personal, rarely for religious reasons. It was not until the reign of Diocletian that a systematic attempt had been made to persecute the Christians throughout the length and breadth of the Empire on an organized scale; and even this attack largely failed, because the Tetrarchs were by no means wholeheartedly in agreement on the subject. The Christians died like flies in Diocletian's East, but Constantius Chlorus would not touch them in his division of the West.

Eusebius suggests that it was by studying his father's example that Constantine veered toward Christianity himself. He writes feelingly of the effects of the persecution where it did take hold: of the mass butchery in Nicomedia, where, as we might expect, the pogrom was cruelest, the city later claiming 26,000 martyrs; the burning of churches; the wholesale imprisonment of clergy. "In every city, prisons built originally to hold grave robbers and cutthroats were now so crammed with bishops, deacons and elders of the church, with readers and exorcists, that there was no space in the cells for condemned criminals."[8] He writes of the martyrdoms in Phoenicia and Palestine, many of which he must have seen with his own eyes:

> To see them was to wonder: these shining lights of Christendom, God's champions on earth, flogged and beaten till the mind lost count, but bearing all with courage and restraint. Then, fresh from their flogging, they were thrown to the wild beasts; to lions falling on them to devour them, to bears of every size and color, to wild

boars, to bulls maddened with burning irons; and each of them in turn their victims faced with miraculous endurance. We saw these happenings with our own eyes. We saw the holy strength of Jesus Christ in them—yes, that same Jesus Christ of whom they testified. We saw the revelation of that strength to these, the martyrs. For a long time the ravenous beasts did not dare approach them. Rather than touch the flesh of those beloved by God, they turned upon the others posted round the cage, supposedly to urge them on. And though God's champions stood naked and defenseless, and with their own hands beckoning the beasts toward them (for thus their jailers had commanded them to do), they were the only ones that were spared. Now and again the animals would make a rush toward them, only to be held back by some divine power and turned in their tracks. As they watched this happen again and again, the spectators were filled with great wonder. Beast after beast was let loose against the same martyr; and each in turn failed.[9]

A man who had seen such things and who could write so movingly of them was not likely to write objectively and dispassionately of an emperor's espousal of the faith for which those martyrs died.

And so the history of these years is written, for obvious reasons, in deepest black and purest white. Constantine was the soldier of Christ; his opponents ministers of the devil, who perished in sinister and appropriate ways. Galerius, according to Lactantius, died of an obnoxious disease. Maximian, as previously noted, was buried at Marseilles. In the eleventh century his coffin was exhumed, and still, apparently, possessed its potency for evil: when it was thrown into the sea, the waters seethed and bubbled. It is in such a context that we must see Eusebius' description of the vision of Constantine. We must see it, too, against a long background of mythic, literary and religious tradition. Pagan rulers before Constantine had been shown manifestations of divine grace. It was only seemly that a Christian emperor should have the same opportunity. Nor was this the last such revelation. Julian the Apostate, who later in the fourth century was to lead a brief reversion to paganism, wrote that he was granted a vision of his own, which he found no less convincing than that of Constantine—though he coyly refused to tell us what he saw.

But what, if anything, did Constantine see? The answers tend to cast more light upon the scholars than on the problem. They range all the way from unquestioning acceptance of the tradition to the assertion that the vision was a fiction, politically inspired and cynically promulgated. The truth probably lies somewhere between the two extremes. While it is no longer possible for us fully to evaluate the religious and psychological factors that conditioned Constantine's change of heart, there are several reasons why it should have appeared politically expedient. Constantine, given the ambiguity of his constitutional position, may well have desired a clean break with the past. Or he may have wished to confirm the allegiance of the Christians in his army. There must have been many such. Diocletian had tried to purge them from the fighting forces, but this would have had no effect in the territories ruled by Constantine's father. Whatever the source and nature of Constantine's conversion (and it was not of course a complete conversion: the Emperor was not baptized till just before his death), such factors must have weighed with him. Nor does there seem much doubt that the original form of the story was expanded and exaggerated by later writers for propaganda purposes. It is the only reasonable explanation of why Lactantius, one of Christianity's foremost apologists, made so little of it, and Eusebius so much.

But however we choose to interpret the vision—as a literary or rhetorical device, as fact, symbol or political expediency—there can be no doubt that it was accepted by Christian tradition, along with the conversion of Paul, as one of the turning points of the history of the Church. It was not long before another tradition, of equally dubious authenticity, was coupled with it: that of the so-called Donation of Constantine, cited in the Middle Ages as the foundation of the temporal power of the Papacy.

Eusebius had no qualms, no doubts, no reservations. He tells us that he speaks on the sworn authority of Constantine himself. There had appeared a sign in the sky, a luminescent cross above the sun, with the inscription "In this sign, conquer." Later, after nightfall, as Constantine slept, there came a second vision, a sort of divine explanatory footnote. Christ himself appeared to Constantine and ordered him to copy the sign for use as a talisman. The next morning Constantine had a copy made in precious stones and metals: the familiar chi-rho monogram. Eusebius tells us that the Emperor wore the badge on his helmet; Lactantius, that his soldiers had it painted on their shields. The device became known by its technical name, *labarum,* to which the dictionary adds the additional mystery "etymology unknown."

For Constantine, it proved highly effective. The crucial battle took place near the Milvian Bridge, twelve miles up the Tiber, still standing under its local name of Ponte Molle. Maxentius had constructed a bridge of

boats beside the stone foundation. When this broke—
Eusebius talks vaguely of an "engine" which "collapsed"—the defending army was pitched into the
river, and many, including Maxentius, were drowned.
Eusebius makes the appropriate comparison to the
crossing of the Red Sea.

Constantine entered Rome in triumph. His procession followed the route ordained by tradition,
through the *Porta Triumphalis* in the southwest corner
of the city by a winding road that debouched ultimately
upon the Sacred Way and so down into the Forum,
Rome's primitive core and summation of its past. Every
stone was steeped in history, every inch of the way
replete with memories of ancient shrines and glories. It
is appropriate to try to reconstruct the city that Constantine would have seen, for this procession brings an
era to a close: no ruler was ever again to make such an
entry into a Rome that was the sole capital of the civilized world.

The Forum to which Constantine's route took him
was by this time only one out of eleven that adorned the
city, but to all Romans the most important, the kernel
and the showplace of their Empire. It was framed by
triumphal arches celebrating victories of the past. That
of Titus, on the high point of the Sacred Way, was
ancient history by now; it commemorated with appropriate designs the conquest of Jerusalem and the sack-
ing of the Temple in 70 A.D.. At the other end, toward
the Capitol, rose the arch of Septimius Severus, a mere
century old, dedicated to him and to his sons Caracalla
and Geta for their victories over the Arabs and the
Parthians. As Constantine saw it, perhaps for the first
time—we do not know if he had been to Rome before
—it was surmounted by a great six-horse chariot, stud-

ded with shields and other ornaments in bronze. Between these arches lay a string of buildings ranging
from austere to ostentatious, each recalling a man, a
mood, a time. We do not need to rely upon our imagina-
tions entirely to reconstruct the imperial progress.
Summer visitors to Rome can see the buildings picked
out in light, while recorded trumpets and the noise of
marching feet evoke the grand processions of the past.
The show of *son et lumière* affects to recall the triumphal entry of Julius Caesar, a dubious pretense at best,
for most of the buildings were not standing in the dic-
tator's time. It does very well, however, recall the
march of Constantine.

Fire had scarred the Forum twice in recent years,
and the rulers had seized their chance to build or rebuild. Constantine may have winced at the monuments
left by Maxentius, the man he had just defeated: the
Temple of Venus and Rome damaged by fire and recently restored; the great, bulbous basilica at the Capitol end that Maxentius—planning a monumental coun-
terbalance to the republican basilicas—had left
unfinished at his death; the temple of the divine Romulus, with its handsome rotunda and fine bronze door,
dedicated to Maxentius' younger son, who had died in
307. Then came buildings that may have had greater
appeal. Past the temple of Antoninus and Faustina,
with its colossal statues of the couple who presided over
the Indian summer of the Empire. Past the Senate
House, that austere and dignified dead letter, soon to
become the center of an amusing Christian-Pagan tug-
of-war. And so to the brilliant bulk of the Capitol itself,
the temples of Jupiter, Juno, Moneta and Minerva,
called "golden" because of their wealth of dedicated
treasure and gleaming ornament. The roofs were tiled

with thickly-gilded bronze, the doors with gold; when
Domitian, long ago, had embellished the roof of the
temple of Jupiter, it had cost him 12,000 talents. It was
a prodigy, a marvel, "so far surpassing all things else as
things divine surpass the things of earth."

Gilded statues stood sentinel round it. Perhaps Constantine was conscious of, more than anything else,
those silent, impassive faces, the pagan gods and the
glorious dead, watching his procession. For Rome had
a population of statues sufficient for a good-sized village. The ancient traveler must have felt in Rome as his
modern counterpart does in Venice, that he was under
constant scrutiny from stone eyes. In Rome at this time,
we are told, there were eighty statues of the gods in
gold and seventy-four in ivory. In all the *fora* and in
every street the silent faces looked down on the living
ones cheering from the flat roof-tops of the houses. In
the Forum of Augustus stood the great figures from
Roman history. In the Forum of Nerva, Alexander
Severus had set up colossal statues of all the emperors
who had been deified, with bronze columns listing their
achievements. The Forum of Vespasian held not only
the Temple of Peace, but a piazza which was an open-
air museum of Greek art. This silent population had its
own caretaker, the *curator statuarum*. Constantine
would have been acutely conscious of his predecessors,
for they had left their works and images behind.

On his left rose the Palatine, the hill that had been
the official residence of emperors since Augustus first
built a humble house there. It was a city in its own right,
capable of housing not only the imperial family, its suite
and guests, but also a vast staff of administrators and
palace servants, a staff so large that the palace cooks had
their own private hospital. Rodolfo Lanciani, the Italian

archaeologist, compares it aptly to the Vatican Palace. Like the Vatican, too, it was capable of being tightly defended, and in spite of its enormous bulk could be sealed shut and protected by a handful of guards. With the growth of new administrative centers outside Rome, the Palatine had lost much of its importance, though it was to remain in use as an occasional imperial residence well after Constantine's time.

Ringing the cluster of imperial *fora* were the pleasure palaces, the theaters, amphitheaters and circuses. Some of these were now museum pieces in their own right and were falling into neglect and disuse. The Colosseum was in good shape still. It represented a more popular form of entertainment. So was the Circus Maximus, where a third of the population of Rome could sit at one time to watch the chariot races and cheer for the Reds or the Whites, the Greens or the Blues.

And, ringing these, were the public baths. The building emperors had competed here, as with their palaces: first Trajan, then Caracalla and finally Diocletian, who, living in an age when magnificence had become obligatory, added his own enormous contribution to those already present. These baths were, in the words of an awe-struck observer, "like whole provinces." Diocletian's were, according to the dedicatory inscription, furnished with every refinement of luxury. To build them he had torn down a meeting hall, a temple, a portico, a paved court and numbers of private houses; a labor force of 40,000 is said to have worked on them, and they could accommodate 3,000 bathers at one time, twice the capacity of the Baths of Caracalla. They were built of concrete faced with brick, which was covered in turn with stucco painted to imitate marble. A gaudy sham, but an impressive one; the *surviving* fragments cover an area of some five city blocks and house within their ruins a church, a cinema, a parking lot, several gardens, a museum and a waxwork show. And even the Baths of Diocletian would have been dwarfed by other imperial projects, had they but come to completion. Rome was studded with monumental follies left abandoned by rulers whose dementia increased as their reigns grew shorter—unfinished basilicas left by Alexander Severus and Gordian the Younger, a portico begun by Gallienus and a colossus started by the same emperor more than twice the height, as projected, of Trajan's column.

The walls of Aurelian enclosed an area of some four square miles. At its greatest, the population of Rome numbered between 800,000 and 1,000,000; the people lived, most of them, in high-rise tenements or, for the richer classes, single-family dwellings: a contemporary gazetteer counts 46,602 of the former in Rome and 1,790 of the latter. Between the mass of city streets and the Aurelian walls there ran a green belt of gardens, parks and private estates; the guidebooks for pilgrims of the Middle Ages still comment on the network of basilicas and green spaces that surround the city. Close to the barracks of the Praetorian Guard, the king-makers, was a zoo, the Vivarium, where animals awaited slaughter in the arena. The zoo was surrounded by a moat and had an amphitheater attached in which the beasts were trained. Small wonder that both residents and visitors alike found Rome to be a city of marvels. When Constantine's son had his first sight of Rome a few years later,

he looked about and saw the limbs and body of the city and its suburbs, rising as the land rose or prone upon the plain, bounded by the summits of the Seven Hills. Each sight in turn impressed him as the best: the sanctuaries of Tarpeian Jupiter, beyond comparison, as things divine are to things mortal; the huge bulk of the amphitheater, set and framed in Travertine stone, that strains the human eye to see its summit; the Pantheon, a segment of the living city vaulted over with a splendid roof; the towering columns pierced with stairs and galleries, and bearing likenesses of emperors past and gone; the Temple of Venus and Rome, the Forum of Peace, the Theater of Pompey, the Odeum, the Stadium, and all the other adornments of the Eternal City in between. . . . Bewildered with the sights that he had seen, and lost in admiration of their many wonders, the Emperor remarked reprovingly, "Fame must be either incompetent or jealous. Everything else it exaggerates. But when it comes to describing what there is in Rome, Fame is a shoddy witness.!"[10]

2. A WORLD BORN

The city now belonged to Constantine. The Empire was not to be solely and undisputedly his until 323, when the other claimants had been driven off; but in Rome at least he could behave as an emperor should, and this meant to build. Constantine's monuments in Rome are scanty, perhaps through the lack of available land, perhaps because he already had his eyes on a more distant site. Some of this building was conventional, almost, indeed, obligatory. North of the Forum of Trajan Constantine erected his baths. They stood in appropriately monumental surroundings. In the Colonna Gardens, on the west slope of the Quirinal, is the corner of a gigantic pediment from what must have been Rome's largest temple—Aurelian's Temple of the Sun, perhaps, or the Temple of Serapis built by Caracalla before him; and nearby the visitor can still see the brick foundations of an enormous double staircase which led to the temple and the neighboring, now vanished, Baths of Constantine. Vanished, too, in great part, is the reconstruction of the Basilica of Maxentius, pushed through to efface a hated rival's name and rechristened the Basilica of Constantine by an obsequious senate. It was hardly a building that Constantine could afford to ignore. The biggest hall in the ancient world, it had a central nave 262 feet long, 97 feet wide and 114 feet high. Modeled on the great rooms in the thermae of Caracalla and Diocletian's bathhouse architecture, it took these inspirations and inflated them to giant proportions. In function it balanced the republican basilicas at the other end of the Forum and was intended, like them, to serve as a meetinghouse, stock exchange and tribunal for the hearing of commercial cases. In grandeur of conception it obliterated them. Its central nave was split by three cross vaults, each in itself eighty-five yards long; these rested on eight elaborate Corinthian columns, there for decoration merely, as the thrust was taken by the six barrel-vaulted spaces of the side aisles. The last of these columns to survive, still standing in position, was re-erected by Pope Paul V in 1611 before the Church of S. Maria Maggiore. Festooned with cables and dwarfed by high-rise buildings, it still contrives to dominate the square.

At the east end of the basilica, as Maxentius originally conceived it, was a long entrance hall, and at the west end a semicircular apse housing the judges' platform. Constantine's changes were ponderous, abrupt and less concerned with commerce than with self-glorification. The judges' platform was swept away to a subsidiary nave on the north side. The empty western apse was filled by a statue of Constantine himself, ten times life-size. Fragments were found among the ruins of the basilica in 1487: a nine-foot head, two feet, the bent left knee, the right hand holding a staff. Carved and painted glories shielded this colossus in its original home. The roof of the basilica was tiled in bronze; in-

side, the walls and floor were veneered in marble, with
painted plaster rising from the second tier of windows
to the ceiling, the whole washed in the rich Roman
sunlight that came flooding in above each arch. Even in
ruin it was one of the joys of the Forum, going under
many names as successive generations forgot who the
original builders were; when Bramante came to make
the barrel vaulting for the new St. Peter's it was to this
building that he turned for inspiration. It has served as
warehouse and as riding school; when Mussolini restored the Forum and its environs in the 1930s, it became—as it still is—a concert hall, with chairs set underneath the ruined vaults, the north apse serving as a
band shell, and Mussolini, who did not deign to enter
by the common way, rising like a specter from the
center of the floor.

Other examples of official monuments to Constantine
survive. An equestrian statue was erected in the Roman
Forum near the site of an earlier and similar statue of
Domitian. The brick core of the base is still there; it was
originally covered with slabs of marble. Another statue
has been found in the Forum, in what may have been
the offices of the Water Board. Roman piety probably
placed such an effigy in every government bureau,
much as the photograph of the President hangs in every U.S. Post Office. At the foot of the Sacred Way, near
the Colosseum, the Senate erected in 315 a triumphal
arch, interesting not merely because (like Constantine's
basilica) it is the last of its kind in Rome, but because of
the ambiguity of its architecture and its inscriptions. It
is a patchwork thing, employing portions of earlier
monuments to Domitian, Hadrian and Marcus Aurelius
—perhaps through necessity and the poverty of invention and materials, perhaps designedly, as a sign that

the new regime was concerned not merely with preserving the past, but with dismembering and remold-
ing it. Its shape is modeled on the Arch of Septimius
Severus. It bears eight medallion-like reliefs from the
time of Hadrian, mostly showing the Emperor hunting
wild game and offering trophies to the appropriate pagan deities—Silvanus, god of the wild woods; Artemis,
the huntress; Hercules. Another sequence of reliefs
comes from the arch of Marcus Aurelius, erected in
173. On the sides are extracts from a frieze showing
Romans fighting against Dacians, which once stood in
Trajan's Forum. Trajan's portrait is transformed into
that of Constantine. And then the contribution of the
new regime: a frieze showing the progress of the recent
war, from Verona to the Milvian Bridge, together with
scenes of the Emperor presiding over the distribution
of largesse to his people and delivering a speech from
the rostrum. Critics have found in these reliefs the
quintessence of late Roman art, which at the same time
reveals the face of Roman society: the individual subor-
dinated to the pattern, just as under Diocletian every
Roman was bound to his caste and occupation; the concept of an orderly society, stratified rank by rank with
the emperor at the apex; the hieratic, oriental quality
of the whole conception, recalling the orientalizing
tendencies of Diocletian and foreshadowing the trans-
fer of power to the Eastern portion of the Empire. And
then the inscription: "To the Emperor Caesar Augustus
Flavius Constantine Maximus Pius Felix Augustus, who
through the inspiration of the deity and in the greatness
of his own mind took up arms to avenge the common-
wealth, and at one blow defeated both the tyrant and
his supporters, this triumphal arch is dedicated by the
Senate and people of Rome."[1] The precise nature of the

deity is—probably deliberately—unspecified. How Christian, at this point, did the emperor want to be? Eusebius tells us that Constantine

> gave orders for the symbol of our Savior's Passion to be placed in the right hand of his statue, and commanded a Latin inscription to be engraved as follows: "By this sign of salvation, the true badge of courage, I saved your city from the yoke of the oppressor and set it free; I set free the senate and the Roman people, and restored them to the fame and splendor of the days of old."[2]

He is referring presumably to the colossus in the basilica, as he talks of "Rome's most public place"; but time has removed the evidence, so that we can no longer tell whether Eusebius told the truth or was allowing fervor to triumph over mere accuracy; whether the object in the great stone hand was indeed the labarum or, as pagan tradition would have dictated, the small winged figure of a Victory.

More convincing evidence of Constantine's religious affiliations comes from his donations to the Christians. Before his time there had been no monumental Christian building in Rome; it is with Constantine, architecturally, that paganism ends and Christianity begins. The reign of Diocletian had seen the last known pagan temple, the one that adorned his own palace in Salonae; the reign of Constantine sees the first buildings officially and purposely designed as places of Christian worship. In 313 Constantine had persuaded Licinius, then ruler of the Eastern Empire, to join with him in proclaiming the Edict of Milan. It insisted on tolerance and the right of freedom of worship; it spelled an end to the persecution of Christians and demanded that their property be

restored to them. The Christians, who had their own
definition of tolerance, promptly laid their hands on
pagan property. When Julian the Apostate came to the
throne and for a brief space restored the old gods to
their former glory, he found that many of their places
of worship had been pillaged and reduced to ruin. In
Caesarea three fine temples were destroyed by Christians. In Daphne, a suburb of Antioch, the temple of
Apollo had been desecrated and its pillars stolen for
Christian purposes, while a Christian church was
erected opposite. In Rome itself new houses of worship,
of a new shape, rose alongside the old.

The Christian Church had been well organized, but
had never, for obvious reasons, been inclined to advertise its presence. Each town had its bishop, each bishop
his deacons and elders to assist him; there was, so far,
no sense that the Bishop of Rome enjoyed superior
status. We are given hints, too, that the bishops were
often less than imposing in their personal appearance;
we are continually reminded that Christianity was
originally a lower-class religion. In Rome as elsewhere,
the meeting-places of the early Christian communities
were in private homes (tradition has greatly distorted
the nature and function of the catacombs) known as
domi ecclesiae or *ecclesiae domesticae,* domestic
churches. We cannot be certain that any of these buildings survive, though it is likely that they do. One possible site is the substructure of the Church of SS. Giovanni e Paulo, on the Caelian Hill. Here the extant
church is built above a private residence, or rather a
whole series of houses or shops, built in the late second
or early third century and at some subsequent date
assimilated into one large structure, possibly for the
purpose of Christian worship. Some of the surviving

frescoes are argued to have Christian themes, notably the so-called *orans,* a hooded man in prayer. The house contains graves, perhaps of the very John and Paul who are the patrons of the church—Christian officers who flourished under Constantine and refused to recant under Julian.

On the Via Appia stands the Church of S. Sebastiano. Under it, among the catacombs, is a structure which is recognizably a Christian cult center. It has a little roofed veranda, a courtyard and another room leading off it; the walls are covered with graffiti honoring Peter and Paul. One view would have it that this, and not the Vatican, is the actual site of St. Peter's tomb; another that this was the saint's original residence in Rome, and thus the first papal palace. In any case this must have been a center of the faith, perhaps a place to which the faithful came to study the sacred texts—we know there were such places, though the first Christian library proper was not founded until the time of Pope Damasus, that is, after 366. In the case of S. Sebastiano at least the Christian affiliations are obvious, but in the other supposed *ecclesiae domesticae* final proof is lacking. The association of these houses with churches later built on the same sites certainly suggests that the Christians were giving monumental forms to known places of worship; but we cannot be sure.

Although Constantine's own religious beliefs at this time must remain as ambiguous as the inscription on his triumphal arch, his partiality toward the Christian Church is attested not merely by the Edict of Milan, but by his gifts of land and buildings. Medieval Christianity was to enlarge this generosity into the legendary Donation of Constantine, the supposed authority for the temporal rule of the pope in Italy. According to the story,

Silvester, who was Bishop of Rome from 314 to 335, had cured Constantine of leprosy. In gratitude the Emperor bestowed on him the whole of central Italy, including Rome itself. In the eighth century there even appeared a document purporting to be the official record of this transaction. A palpable fraud, it was none the less happily accepted by church and laity alike as documentary evidence of what most people already believed. The forgery was not exposed for another seven hundred years.

Constantine's actual benefactions, though less generous, were still generous enough. The Lateran Palace was made over to the Christian Church. It had originally belonged to the Laterani, a rich patrician family who had been suspected—as many were—of complicity in one of the conspiracies against the Emperor Nero. Confiscated from them, it had become imperial property, passing through the hands of, among others, Annius Verus, the grandfather of the Emperor Marcus Aurelius. Constantine had received it from his bride. It was now presented by him to Melchiades, or Miltiades, the Bishop of Rome. Beside it, over the remains of the Severan barracks of the *equites singulares,* the private bodyguard, Constantine built the first of the great Christian basilicas, that of St. John Lateran, S. Giovanni in Laterano; and beside it again, over what had originally been part of the palace bathhouse, he constructed the baptistery, originally octagonal in shape and surrounded by a dome. The sequence of the building is uncertain, particularly since the baths seem to have doubled for both sacred and secular purposes. Pope Melchiades had already convened a synod in the baths in 313; after this synod the first service of baptism was held; and some time after this, Constantine built his baptistery on the site. Yet as late as 326 it was still being used for grimmer purposes, the domestic tragedy of Constantine's reign and a reminder of how Christianity was still tempered by the demands of imperial paranoia. Fausta, the daughter of Maximian with whom Constantine had made a diplomatic match, brought capital charges against Crispus, his son by his first wife, so that her own sons would be free to inherit. Fausta was subsequently tried and convicted herself and, according to tradition, suffocated in the hot room of the self-same bath.

Legend has in fact heavily colored the history of the Basilica of St. John (as it is now; it was originally dedicated to Christ the Savior). One story had it that Constantine was himself baptized here, by the same pope who cured him of leprosy. According to another, Christ himself was present at the coronation ceremonies. This, scholars argue, may be a back-formation from a mosaic that perhaps stood in the original basilica, portraying the head of Christ presiding over Silvester and Constantine—probably the first time that Christ had been depicted in a public monument in Rome. Among the many other tales which surround the building is the legend that the Basilica preserved the simple wooden table on which St. Peter celebrated Mass, now supposedly contained in the papal altar, along with the heads of St. Peter and St. Paul. The Lateran Palace was for a long time the center of Christian administration in Rome and housed five synods of the Church; it was gradually superseded in importance by the Basilica of St. Peter in the Vatican, and the old basilica and palace were largely destroyed by fire in 1308. Near the baptistery some shreds of the original Roman fabric still remain; and the modern visitor who follows the crowds

into the cavernous gilded interior of the present-day
Basilica of St. John may reflect that he is walking over
one of the earliest official sites of Christendom.

Constantine inaugurated other buildings. Over the
supposed tomb of St. Paul, on the road to Ostia, he
erected a small church, which was replaced in 386 by
a larger, five-aisled structure. He is said to have encased
Paul's body where he found it, in a double sarcophagus
of marble and bronze. Excavations have shown that the
church does, indeed, lie over a cemetery in use from
the first to the third century A.D. More systematic studies might produce results as exciting as in the case of St.
Peter's. The church was damaged by fire in 1823, but
was restored; it remains the outstanding surviving example of fourth-century basilical architecture.

And then there is the church which Christian centuries have elevated to the highest place: the basilica
erected over the supposed tomb of St. Peter himself, on
the Vatican Hill, and which, by virtue of the peculiar
sanctity of the site, superseded the Lateran Palace as
the papal seat. Begun in 322 by Constantine, it was
completed fifteen years later by his son. Excavations
have shown the tradition of the foundation to be based
on truth. There is indeed a pagan cemetery beneath
the papal altar; there was, indeed in that cemetery a
tomb of particular sanctity; and there seems no doubt
that, whether it actually held the martyr's body or not,
it was regarded as so doing from early times. St. Peter's
was of course rebuilt during the Renaissance, but the
walls of the old apse still survive behind the papal altar,
and of the six spiral marble columns presently to be
seen, four originally supported a canopy above the
shrine of St. Peter, a boxlike marble and porphyry
structure enclosing an earlier monument.

The churches of St. John, St. Peter and St. Paul have been so changed and embellished over the centuries that it is hard to imagine them as they were. Between ourselves and Constantine there rise the formidable figures of the Renaissance popes. There is a church, however, in which one can come closer to the spirit of the fourth century and catch the excitement of Rome's transition from a temporal to a spiritual capital. It is the little church of S. Clemente, halfway between the Colosseum and St. John Lateran, in the valley between the Coelian and Oppian hills. The present structure, standing at ground level, dates only from the twelfth century, but the foundations, systematically excavated since the 1850s by the Irish Dominicans who administer the church, reveal a history of building going back to the reign of Nero.

There were originally private houses on the site, some sixty feet below the present ground level, in what was then one of the most populous quarters of Rome. The neighborhood of S. Clemente, somnolent now, would have been a great deal noisier then, with apartment houses towering above the narrow streets, loud with huckster cries and shouts of draymen, teeming, raucous, flamboyant, malodorous. Then disaster: in 64 A.D. the valley was a sea of flame as Nero's fire laid waste whole quarters of the vibrant city. Nero cast greedy eyes on the good building land thus forcibly vacated and seized many of the properties nearby to erect a palace for himself, the notorious Golden House. But he spared the S. Clemente site, and in the course of time private homes began to rise again. In the lowest level under the church some rooms of these houses still survive. There were apparently two buildings, separated by a narrow alleyway. One was an apartment house, the kind of tenement into which the greater part of Rome's population was crammed. It held a little temple for the worship of Mithras, the Persian god who was so popular in the later Empire: some forty men could pack into the hall around the altar with the bull motif and sit in sweaty darkness through the exotic rites.

Across the alley was a more palatial building, later in date and owned by a householder of more substance. The vaulted rooms still seem cramped and low-ceilinged to us; by Roman standards they would have seemed capacious. Their floors are neatly tiled, the walls picked out in ornamental brickwork; a scattering of vases in the rooms hints at the life that once filled them. There may even have been running water on the ground floor, tapped from an underground stream or nearby aqueduct. A luxury then, it has proved a considerable embarrassment now and had to be drained off before the excavations could go deeper. The visitor who stands, shivering slightly, within these rather gloomy rooms, may hear the trickle of the water kept at bay and banished down a specially-dug drain to the Colosseum. And in this house the Christians kept their worship, competing with the Mithraists across the street, as long as official hostility confined the new religion to the safe obscurity of private homes.

In the great Christian building program after the Edict of Milan, the whole structure was taken over and converted into a church. The courtyard of the *palazzo* was filled in, to become the floor of the nave; a rectangular building was erected, with arched walls (the tops of which may still be seen peeping into the twelfth-century church) and colonnaded entry. Eventually there was added an apse behind the altar, which encroached upon the area of the Mithraic temple. After a period of coexistence, Mithraism ultimately retired defeated, banned by the authorities in 395. The new church was dedicated to St. Clement, whose picturesque career, alive and dead, is woven into the fabric of the Byzantine Church and will appear later in these pages.

As the years passed, S. Clemente was adorned and embellished. There was a fine stone choir and pulpit—which we can still see, because it was transferred to the later church—carved with the early Christian symbols of fish, dove and vine. On the walls, successive ages added frescoes and occasionally repainted old ones. A painting of Justinian's Empress, the questionable Theodora, seems to have been given a new lease on life as the Madonna; two ladies of her court are adapted into Saints Euphemia and Catherine. We see a portrait of Pope Leo IV, whose reign began unpropitiously with an earthquake, so that brickwork had to be added to support shaky columns. We see scenes from the life of St. Alexis and of course from that of St. Clement, whose remains were returned to Rome in 867 in circumstances that inspired a whole series of frescoes. Suffering from age and act of war, the fourth-century church was eventually superseded by another, placed in turn above it and retracing its outline, though in smaller compass: the church of S. Clemente that has stood from about 1100 till today.

S. Clemente hides modestly from passers-by. Its columned portico is now barred off, its only entrance a plain wooden door in a gray stone wall. Yet in its narrow space it offers a cross-section of Roman history and a fascination that outbids more loudly-touted monuments. In the intertwining of its stairs and corridors the centuries meet and mingle; time is lost, and two steps down may take you back two centuries. In the older church, although the plaques have crumbled and the paint has largely faded from the walls, it is still possible under lamplight to imagine what it must have been; to see the sun come streaming in to light the altar and surround the worshiper with warmth and color as Christianity emerged from the cellar into the light of day.

The form these Roman churches took was that of the basilica. This was a Greek word originally, meaning "royal"; for us, it has come to mean a church or cathedral possessing special liturgical privileges. There are seven such allowed to be designated in Rome, and others elsewhere. But for the ancient Romans "basilica" denoted an architectural style, a type of building associated theretofore with purely secular purposes. The Basilica of Maxentius demonstrates this function perfectly, though architecturally it differed somewhat from the customary construction. It was intended as a stock exchange and meeting-place, to provide a venue for business transactions and the hearing of commercial cases. Rome's earliest basilica had been built in 184 B.C. Constantine himself had built one during his residence in Trèves; it still stands, with its walls, originally plastered and painted over, now raw with the redness of brick. It was a building designed for show and comfort, where the moneyed classes could spend their business hours in surroundings calculated to flatter their success. The forecourt and the nave were honeycombed with black and white. Geometric patterns of multicolored marble and gilt glass covered the walls as far as the second tier of windows. Within the brickwork ran a network of pipes, and there was space beneath the floor for the cirulation of hot air. At one end stood the semicircular apse with its throne and dais, decorated with gold.

It was this kind of structure, as the Basilica of Maxentius shows, that provided a marvelous showplace for the glorification of the ruler. It was the same kind of structure to which the Christians turned for the glorification of God. To an extent we can read their minds and follow their reasoning. They must have turned to a secular model, rather than a sacred one, from a natural desire to disassociate themselves from the building styles of a discarded religion. In addition the Christian edifices were intended to perform a different function from that of the sanctuaries of Jupiter and Minerva, Venus, Isis and Hercules. The Greco-Roman temple was a house for the deity, a gilded cage to entice and entrap him into staying, not a place for collective worship. When the people celebrated their deities, they normally did so out of doors, en masse, with community festivals and processions. (Indoor worship in Rome was *ipso facto* suspect, carrying connotations of unspeakable orgies and nameless rites: hence the odium that fell on early Christianity.) But the Christian church had different needs, partly because of its basis in rabbinical teaching and group discussion, partly from the necessity of indoor worship forced upon a church that had not cared or dared to advertise its presence. Thus the basilica, the most familiar kind of enclosed public meeting-place in the Roman world, was adapted to serve as a Christian church. Such were the buildings we have seen in Rome. St. John Lateran, St. Peter's, St. Clement's had the same basic form: an oblong hall divided down its length into aisles, sometimes five, sometimes three, with an apse protruding from the altar end, flanked perhaps by two protruding chapels, and, origi-

nally, a pillared forecourt. This was to remain the customary pattern until the Byzantine East introduced a
rival design.

Our first literary description of such a building comes
from Eusebius. It is worth quoting at length, if only to
show that the old Roman ideal of architecture as a visible manifestation of the guiding principles of the state
had not vanished with the new faith.

He fortified the outer enclosure with a circuit wall, the
better to protect the whole; and before the gate he built
a porch with arms spread wide and towering high to
greet the morning sun, so that even those who stood far
off from the sacred precincts were not grudged a view
of what lay within. It drew the eyes, even of those who
were strangers to the faith, to where one first entered
the temple, so that even the most casual passer-by might
be struck to the soul by his memory of the desolation that
had once been, and this miracle that now, against all
expectations, stood in its place. It was the builder's hope
that this spectacle alone would lure the awe-stricken
traveler toward the gates. But once inside, he is not left
to trample with profane and unwashed feet on holy
ground; a more than ample forecourt greets his eyes, and
on each side a handsome colonnade, two this way, two
that way, bounding a square, as it were, with a fence of
columns. The space between the columns is filled by
lattices to an appropriate height. But the central square
has been left open to the sky, fanned by the breezes,
glowing in the sunlight. And here too, facing the temple,
the builder has provided fountains—water being the
outward and visible symbol of cleanliness and godliness
—in whose bountiful streams the pilgrims may wash
themselves before they cross the holy threshold. This is

the first halt on their way. It gives grace and splendor to
the building as a whole and, to the uninstructed, a place
to pause and wonder.[3]

The visitor then passes to the main doors, three in
number. The central door is larger than the others, rich
with bronze and decorative ironwork. Inside the
builder has created beauty that beggars description.

He adorned it with high thrones, for the greater honor
of those placed in authority, and benches set in ranks
throughout, as was fitting. And more than these, he has
set the altar, the holy of holies, in the midst of them, and
built a fence about this too, to keep the multitude from
trespassing, carved and fretted by the finest craftsmen's
hands. And everyone that looked upon it marveled.[4]

The altar stood at the junction of apse and nave; it
was, as Eusebius states, regularly screened off from the
public, as it continued to be in the Byzantine, though
not in the Roman, rite. Eusebius goes on to attribute a
mystical significance to this erstwhile prosaic structure,
and to see in it a microcosm of God's universe. As each
element has its place in the basilical complex, so each
Christian has his divinely appointed place in the
scheme of things. Some fortify God's church with a wall
of faith. Some are "gateways to the temple" and serve
to usher others in. The four lines of pillars in the forecourt represent the Four Gospels, strong to sustain the
faith. The great central door is God Almighty, the flanking doors the Son and Holy Ghost. And in the temple
itself are seats and benches without number,

as many as the souls on which the gifts of the Holy Ghost
come to rest—yes, that same Spirit which in time gone
by appeared to the blessed Apostles and those with

them, in the shape of forked tongues as of fire, which sat
upon each one of them. . . . But as to the great altar,
unique, aloof, revered by all, what might this be but the
immaculate Holy of Holies, belonging to Him who is the
priest for all mankind? Standing beside it, on the right
hand is the high priest of the universe, yes, Jesus, God's
only begotten son; and He receives from all the sweet-
smelling sacrifices, without blood, without substance,
even, as they are offered up in prayer; and His face
shines with a pure joy, and He holds His hands on high:
and He sends the sacrifices on their way to God in
Heaven, the Father of all mankind.[5]

Such were the benefactions of Constantine. The
buildings and the occupants were supported by endow-
ments and other privileges. Roman emperors had enjoyed their own hunting and game preserve at Lauren-
tum, on the coast. This estate was now made over to the
Church. Ecclesiastical dignitaries were allowed the
right of free travel over Roman roads, using the post-
ing-stations normally reserved for government business. This privilege was abused to such an extent that
after Constantine's death the whole system nearly
broke down. The roads were clogged, we are informed,
by prelates traveling from one synod to another, urged
and encouraged by a monarch whose interest in theological hairsplitting was intense.

Up to this point,, however, we are still talking of an
ambiguous Rome, poised uneasily between paganism
and Christianity, under the jurisdiction of a ruler who
acted like a Christian in fact, though he was not yet one
in name. Then suddenly, history provides us with one
simple declarative statement: Constantine abandoned
Rome to found a new capital elsewhere.

The site he chose was one of the great junctions of the
world, the confrontation of two continents across a strip

of water. Where Europe reaches out to Asia lies the Sea
of Marmara, pinched between two narrows. The south-
ern-most of these, known as the Hellespont in antiquity
and the Dardanelles today, leads into the Aegean; here,
on the Asian side, the city of Troy had been founded
centuries before, to control the waterways and levy
tolls on ships bringing grain and ore from the Crimea.
The northern, shorter passage was the Bosphorus,
opening into the Black Sea and offering similar advantages. This was famous in Greek legend as the "cow's
crossing" which gave the straits their name, the route
of poor demented Io, half-girl, half-heifer, as she fled
across the world before the wrath of Hera. The Bosphorus and Hellespont were barriers as well as waterways. Over the latter Xerxes flung a bridge of boats
when he moved to attack Greece; but it was a feat
which had the richest nation of the world behind it. The
Bosphorus had been bridged only once, by Xerxes' father, Darius. As this book is written, this feat is being
repeated: a colossal road bridge is inching across the
water, just below the narrowest point. But the Bosphorus will never lose the strategic and commercial
importance it has always had. In places less than half a
mile across, it is still deep enough for larger vessels to
anchor close to shore. The Turks still guard it, like the
Byzantines before them and the Romans and the
Greeks before them; the little ferryboats which ply up
the coast do not go far beyond Sariyer, for the northern
reaches are a military command.

On the European side, where the Bosphorus opens
out into the Sea of Marmara, a tongue of water carves
into the land. This is the famous Golden Horn—"horn"
from its shape; "golden" according to some, because of
the wealth unloaded from the ships here, or according

to others, from the shimmer of the morning sun across
the water. This may have been true once; today the
Horn is golden only in the sense that the Danube is
blue. On the promontory thus formed, the wedge of
land bounded by three waters—the *burnu,* as the
Turks call it—the nose, Constantine built his city. It was
already a developed site. In primitive times there had
been a fishing village here at Lygos, on the tip of the
peninsula. The first Greeks in the area had been colo-
nists from Megara, who built Chalcedon on the Asian
side. Seventeen years later, about 658 B.C., had come
one Byzas from the same city. A prophecy had commanded him to build "opposite the blind"; he interpreted this to mean the Chalcedonians, for only blind men
would have failed to see the advantages of the western
shore. So Byzas settled on the unclaimed land and built
the city named for him, Byzantium. The two settlements are now engulfed and united by modern Istanbul. Ancient Chalcedon is now the suburb of Kadikoy,
the terminus of the railway from Asia; and the country
has now presumably been restored to the blind, for of
Istanbul's three-million population, one million live on
the European side and two million on the Asian, crossing daily by ferry till the bridge is built.

Byzantium was a small town. Its early walls enclosed
only the tip of the promontory and the first hill, on
which Topkapi Palace now stands; the Greek acropolis
occupied the site of the seraglio. It appears in history as
a typical Greek city, insular, protective, safely on the
fringes of great events, though sometimes caught up in
them against its will—it barred its gates to Xenophon
when he struggled back from Persia with the remnants
of his ten thousand. We are given a glimpse of a little
seamen's town, with a long jetty running down into the

sea and triremes moored to slide into the water. In 340
B.C. the city was besieged by Philip of Macedon. The
moon betrayed a night attack, and in gratitude Byzantium, in common with other cities in the area, adopted
the horned moon of Hecate as its symbol—the same
crescent that would later grace Islamic banners. In 196
A.D. it was besieged and captured by Septimius Severus
and became thenceforth a truly Roman city. The conqueror destroyed and then rebuilt. Flanking the old
acropolis were new constructions in the imperial style:
a theater and an amphitheater, a stadium for foot races,
an army drill ground, splendid porticoes and—pointing
ominously to the future—a hippodrome where the
population gathered for the chariot races.

For Constantine, however, the city's virtues lay in its
site rather than in its history. Diocletian's administration had shown that, while Rome might continue to be
regarded as the traditional capital, other cities had
more practical advantages. Given the shape that the
Empire had now assumed, Byzantium was geograph-
ically and politically more suitable than Rome had ever
been. Also, by and large, it was a more pleasant place
in which to live. It did not have Rome's fetid summers
or damp, miserable winters; it was not built, like Rome,
upon a marsh. It did suffer, however, from the usual
pest of watery environments; hence the poem spoken
fancifully by a mosquito net.

> I catch no vicious jungle beast, no fish within my snare,
> No flying birds, but only men, and they come willing
>   there.
> I guard you at siesta time, and like a city wall
> I keep away the stinging flies that persecute you all.
> I bring you undisturbed repose, and to your slaves I say,

"You can save yourself the trouble; I will keep the flies away.[6]

The change of center also signaled decisively the arrival of a new dispensation. Byzantium was a capital created by political expediency, like Canberra, Ottawa, Brasilia and Washington, rather than by natural evolution; but unlike those places, it did retain some earlier traditions, which had to be reckoned with. It was a place whose native language was Greek, not Latin; and lying on the borderline of Asia, it partook deeply of the Asian spirit.

For propaganda purposes Byzantium, New Rome, was set before the public as the facsimile of Old Rome. The historian Zosimus, a man of transparently pagan sympathies, thought it indecent that such a venture should be undertaken without due prompting from the gods. Roman tradition abounded in prophecies concerning the foundation of the old capital; where were the corresponding omens for the new? Searching in desperation, Zosimus could only find:

Soon their rule will pass
To men who inhabit the domain of Byzas.
Thrice-blessed Hellespont, walls built by gods for men
. . . at divine command.[7]

Other parallels have the same air of contrivance. Old Rome had seven hills; so did the new—or rather, it had six, where valleys cut across the promontory, and, by a stretch of territory and imagination, a seventh. These are the hills now crowned with mosques and minarets that give the city its distinctive skyline and greet the traveler arriving by water. Rome had fourteen *arron-*

dissements; so did Byzantium (if you included one across the Golden Horn, in the modern banking district of Galata). Rome's Forum held the *miliarium,* the milestone to which all roads led, which marked the distance to the cities of the Empire; Byzantium had its corresponding *milion,* in gold. Noble families were induced to emigrate. There was a duplicate Senate and duplicate consuls, as useless as the ones they left behind. There were other, more sinister parallels. Both cities were subject to earthquakes—the series of shocks which have made Haghia Sophia a buttressed travesty of its original self, and brought periodic devastation to large areas of Turkey. And soon after its foundation Byzantium, like Rome, was overcrowded; the population built out into the harbor.

Zosimus again:

Constantine built a circular forum, which he surrounded with two-storied arcades. Intending to expand the city, he enclosed it with a new wall some fifteen furlongs beyond the old one, cutting off the entire promontory from one shore to the other. The city thus encompassed dwarfed its predecessor. In it he built a palace, hardly smaller than the one in Rome, and a hippodrome decked out with every conceivable kind of finery. Part of this he turned into a shrine of the Dioscuri; their statues may be seen to this very day, standing in the porticoes of the hippodrome.[8]

Constantine's city, as it was soon to be called—Constantinopolis, Constantinople—was about four times larger than its predecessor. The new walls, running from the Sea of Marmara to the Golden Horn, have long since been destroyed. There is, however, still one landmark of Constantine's Forum: a column on the second hill originally crowned with a statue of Apollo changed to bear Constantine's face. Under the base is buried what must be the most intriguing "time capsule" of all time—for it is presumably still there—the Palladium, the ancient image of Athena supposedly brought from Troy and replanted in Constantinople as another link with the distinguished past; the ax with which Noah made the ark; loaves from the Miracle at Cana; a stone from which Moses drew water; and the alabaster box from which Mary Magdalen anointed the feet of Christ. Perplexed, perhaps, by this uneasy congruence of pagan and Christian relics, the statue toppled during a storm in 1105 and was replaced by a cross. In 1779 the column itself was practically destroyed by fire. Its blackened remains, hooped with protective iron (hence the Turkish name *cemberlitas*, the burnt column) stand in a small grassy square which is the last vestige of Constantine's Forum, hard by the Covered Bazaar.

A few other traces of Constantine's foundation survive. From the burnt column one may follow the modern road which cuts through the heart of the city and follows, more or less, the *mese*, the Middle Road, of antiquity. The first hill remained in use as the acropolis. Nearby, on the site of a pagan temple, Constantine built a small basilica, the forerunner of Haghia Sophia. It was a further point of resemblance with Rome that Constantine's palace has been lost in the welter of building that was soon to rival the Palatine, but the foundations of the hippodrome are still in evidence.

And a stone's throw from Haghia Sophia, just inside the outer walls of Topkapi Palace, is a church that Constantine would recognize, though it was restored somewhat and enlarged after his time. This is St. Irene, Constantinople's most important church before the building of Haghia Sophia and, for some time afterward, joined to it by a common courtyard. It stands forlornly now, bypassed by the crowds which stream through to the bejeweled splendors of Topkapi Palace, while taxis and buses jostle for a parking place outside. To enter, you descend to find a side door: the ground level has risen round it. A few steps down, along a darkened corridor, and you find yourself in the wistful quiet of the cool, gray church, with no other company but the cooing of birds in the dome. The shape of St. Irene is the now-familiar basilica, with three aisles and a protruding apse; inside the apse, around the altar, are tiers of benches for the faithful. A passageway runs under them, with little windows looking into the body of the church. No one knows what they are for; spy-holes, perhaps, to allow the accurate timing of the church processionals. Apart from this, the church is blank. In the courtyard behind and on the patchy grass outside, one may still see rows of tarnished cannon, for the church was used for years as a military museum (unlike most of the Christian churches, it was never turned into a mosque); and in one dark corner of the cloisters is a bell said to be that of Haghia Sophia. But even in its barren and neglected state, St. Irene serves as a reminder that Constantine was on this hill before the Sultan Mohammed; and if one wanders incautiously away from the church in the direction of the sea, one has another forcible reminder, in the shape of an indignant Turkish sentry, that this was once a fortified place.

This was the epicenter of the Constantinian world. A Christian city, it set a new pattern for town planning: henceforth, the physical and spiritual center is the church, set on a height to reach to God. Yet some of the pagan memories endured. The old gods survived, if only as decorations. The statue of Priapus, a fertility god of immemorial antiquity, gazed benignly on the vessels sailing into harbor. In the senate house stood statues of Jupiter and Athena. Some years later, when St. John Chrysostom was preaching hell-fire and destruction in the city, the building was destroyed by earthly fire. The statues were miraculously preserved—a sign, people said, that the old gods still extended their protection, even to the unfaithful. And pagan practices survived, as well as pagan books. When Constantine died, it was merely as God's regent; but he was buried with a pomp that Diocletian, who was a god himself, would have approved.

Eusebius records the funeral of Constantine. It is worth reporting, for it reveals the style of the new age. The Emperor died at Nicomedia, Diocletian's city. Shortly before this, he had been baptized, wrapping himself in white and declaring that he would never wear the imperial purple again; his wish was overridden when he died. The death occurred at noon on the feast of Pentecost, and the news provoked a spasm of public grief. Constantine's soldiers came in crowds to mourn him. Lifting the body into a golden coffin, they began the slow journey to Constantinople. Once arrived the body was laid out on a dais in the palace, surrounded by candles burning in golden candlesticks. Attendants watched it day and night. Soldiers and courtiers kept up their visitations, as if the Emperor were still alive. When the news reached Rome, the baths, the markets and the shows were closed; on both sides of the Adriatic a nation mourned. When at last Constantine was buried, coins were struck showing him ascending

to heaven. If Diocletian left this earth as Jove's descendant, Constantine died convinced that he was *isapost-
olos*, the equal of the Apostles. There was a place reserved for him in heaven too.

The shift of power was not felt everywhere with
equal weight. For those far from the seats of the
mighty, life continued more or less unchanged. The
voices of simple men are not heard often enough in
Roman history. In the years after Constantine's death,
however, we may listen to one or two. With the army
in Egypt, Flavius Abinnaeus goes about his duties as
generations of officers have done before him. He is
quartered in a fort of standard military pattern, the
utilitarian, unimaginative design which crops up everywhere in the Empire: the sort of fort on which Diocletian's palace was modelled, solid and foursquare,
with stout towers at the corners. He probably still wor-
ships pagan gods, for in the army, tradition dies hard.
One such Egyptian fort, vacated and picked clean by its
garrison, was found on excavation to hold one thing
only, a statue of Nemesis. Abinnaeus himself we know
through his correspondence. We see his days pass in the
mindless drudgery of military routine. Troops must be
provided to assist in the collection of taxes, an unpopular task, for the villagers resent the soldiers whose
needs they must supply. A decision must be reached
about a soldier who is drunk and presumably AWOL,
and making a nuisance of himself in the village. Illegal
traffic has been reported in goods controlled by the
imperial monopoly: this must be suppressed. A recruit
petitions for discharge on compassionate grounds. The
priest Mios, jocularly Christian, sends a present of a
hyena skin. Complains come from a farmer that while
he was sleeping, someone sheared his sheep. The rou-

tine of provincial administration had hardly changed
since Augustus' day. But Abinnaeus had his day of
greatness. In a letter to Court he requests that his appointment be ratified and recalls his meeting with the
Emperor face to face:

> To our sovereign lords in perpetuity,
> Constantius and Chlorus:
>   Providence has given you the opportunity to demon-
> strate your continued favor and indulgence toward your
> soldiers, particularly those who have served in your
> bodyguard—those, I mean, who have done their duty
> zealously, and have a claim on your good will. I was
> posted to the Parthian Archers stationed at Diospolis, in
> the Upper Thebaid. After thirty-three years' service I
> was detailed by Senecio, formerly Count of the March of
> that same province, to escort refugees of the Blemyes
> tribe to your most revered and sacred feet in Constan-
> tinople. We arrived with envoys of the aforesaid tribe
> and the Count of the same March, and presented them
> to your indulgence; whereupon Your Divinity ordered
> me, in my rank of *ducenarius,* to adore the sacred pur-
> ple. . . .[9]

Things moved slowly on the frontier; all the more
reason for an officer to remember that red-letter day
when he had been in Constantinople, seen the Emperor in person and enjoyed the envied privilege of
kissing his robe. Or there was the old man of Verona
memorialized by Claudian, for whom a trip to town was
an adventure:

> Happy, with two acres and one house
> To live his life in; where his limping age
> Trod paths of babyhood, where four walls held

So long a history. He was not plagued
With fortune's sudden storms. A stay-at-home,
He never drank from streams beyond his ken,
He had no ships, so never feared the sea;
The trumpet blew for others, not for him.[10]

The old man's tranquillity was soon shattered. By the turn of the century the Goths rampaged around Verona. But Claudian, in any case, was more concerned with princes. Alexandrian by birth, court poet by profession, he reveals a world of pomp and protocol, of gossip and intrigue, in which plain soldiers are ill-matched against scheming politicians. We may see the face of this new Rome in the sculpture room of the Istanbul Archaeological Museum. Here is a line of traditional Roman heads: a confident Hadrian, a saintly Marcus Aurelius, a brutal Diocletian—and then suddenly, following them, the head of the Eastern Emperor Arcadius, with wide, staring eyes and a woman's face. It was in his reign and that of his Western brother, Honorius, that Claudian wrote.

The poet is scornful of what he sees. He compares the council to a theater, where the performers posture for applause, while off duty they dine on peacock and parrot.

Their passion's scented silk, their one ambition
To earn a giggle by a witless jest.
And from their painted faces rouged lips cry,
"This silk's too rough, it chafes my skin!" When Huns
And Sarmatians beat on the city doors
They will all be watching the play.[11]

An imperial marriage is staged like a grand ballet, with the army dressed in white and pelting their gen-

eral with purple blossoms. By pandering and conniv-
ing, a disgusting eunuch wins his way to high places.

> The palace was flung open to the world;
> The senate rubbed shoulders with men of the streets
> While the Law and the Army shook in their sandals
> And fought for the honor of falling before him
> And planting kisses on his wrinkled hide.
> "Defender of justice, our Emperor's father!"
> They call him. The court kowtows to a slave.[12]

A conservative, Claudian distrusts the new fad of
Christianity. He writes a little poem to a presumably
Christian friend, invoking so many saints' names that it
reads like a parodic litany. He hungers for a once-famil-
iar world where Rome was the center of all things.
Indeed the Emperor now hardly visits Rome at all:

> How long shall monarchy be exiled, and
> The seats of power be empty? Why
> Should this, the father of all palaces,
> Be left untenanted to waste and die?
> Is this no more a place from which a man
> May rule the world?[13]

But when the monarch condescended to come, the
spirits quickened:

The robes, the uniforms we saw, the fabulous parade,
When through the streets of Italy you made your way,
arrayed
In the toga of your fathers, yet more splendid than before
Among your soldiers wrapped in white, the chosen ones,
who bore
Your godly burden on their backs, and carried it with
pride.

Thus go the gods of Egypt forth, to view the countryside.
The image issues from the shrine; it seems a little freight
But many groaning priests beneath bear witness to the
weight
And testify to god in sweat.[14]

So moved the Emperor now, in West and East alike,
a jeweled effigy, not a man. He bent his head while
passing through the gates, in token of his stature; but
apart from this he made no motion, looking neither to
right nor left nor showing any sign of life. He signed
himself Divinity, Eternity; the troops that followed him
waved dragon banners woven out of purple thread,
bound to the gold and jeweled tops of spears.

Amid the dazzle of the red and purple, it was hard
to see the dissolution of the Empire as a reality.
Claudian has been happily compared to Kipling, singing the praises of a power whose end was already imminent. While the lesser breeds without the law, shortly
to become the law, were massing on the frontiers,
Claudian could compose an allegorical picture of the
provinces assembled to pay tribute. First Spain, her
hair wreathed with the gray-green olive, Minerva's
tree, and sparkling Tagus woven in her robe; then Gaul,
a Valkyrie with a necklace round her throat and a spear
in either hand; Britain, dressed in beast-skins from the
Highlands, her cheeks tattooed, wrapped in a cloak of
ocean blue; Africa, her face bronzed with the sun, an
ivory comb and wheat-ears in her hair; Italy, crowned
with ivy leaves and vines, treading plump grapes
beneath her feet.

But Rome was dying, almost unawares, a dinosaur
that had not yet realized that its heart had been cut out.
It was a city of flagrant contrasts, whose historical testi-

mony echoes the nightmare place that Fellini conjured up for his *Satyricon.* We see it through the eyes of Ammianus Marcellinus, a plain soldier and a good Christian, later in the fourth century. His picture is not a happy one. Foreign wars and difficulties of transport play havoc with food supply. There has already been one wholesale expulsion of foreigners from the city, the natives feeling that they have not enough to feed their own. The people are rioting because of the lack of wine. News from other cities is as bad. Carthage has run short of grain. In Antioch in 354 the starving masses set fire to a mansion and tore the owner limb from limb. Five years later there were similar atrocities in Rome. In 365 the prefect of the city, Lampadius, had his house near the Baths of Constantine attacked by an incendiary mob. A pitched battle ensued, with Lampadius' friends hurling missiles from the roof-tops. In 366 there were massacres throughout Rome.

Nor did Christianity bring surcease. On the contrary, the Christians, engrossed with their internecine squabbles, were often the worst offenders. In Rome the Christians held their assemblies in the Basilica of Sicinius, now S. Maria Maggiore. During the rivalry between Damasus and Ursinus for the papacy in 365, thirty-seven corpses were found in this basilica. The statue of Victory, defiantly pagan, moved in and out of the senate house as the winds of religious favor shifted.

It was a teeming city, with an acute housing shortage and a perpetually empty belly. By 367 there had been so much private building around the sacred structures that the ground had to be forcibly cleared. In 374 the Tiber flooded as it had often done in the past, inundating the slums in the low-lying sections of the city; food had to be distributed in rowboats. Constantly the gap between rich and poor increased. There was still a vogue for monumental building. Ammianus writes of an Egyptian obelisk brought with enormous difficulty from the Nile to the Tiber, hauled through the Ostia Gate on sleds and erected in the Circus Maximus:

> A number of tall beams were brought in and stood on end; a forest of derricks. On these were festooned miles of heavy ropes, a vast cat's cradle blotting out the sky. To these in turn the monument was fastened—no, not a monument, a mountain with a legend carved upon it. Inch by inch it was hoisted up into the great void of the sky. For an eternity it hung dangling, while men in thousands set their shoulders to the wheels, like millstones going round and round; then it settled in the middle of the Circus and a gilded globe of bronze was clapped on top.[15]

The golden orb was promptly struck by lightning; a divine admonition, perhaps.

The obelisk looked down on streets jammed with the chariots of the rich, with covered litters rushing back and forth, with fashionable idlers attended by armies of slaves looking for the day's amusement.

> The libraries are shut up tight as tombs; they spend their time constructing hydraulic organs, and autoharps as big as coaches, and flutes and huge instruments for actors to posture to. . . . And wherever you turn your eyes you can see gangs of women with their hair in curls who might have produced three children by this time had they married, sweeping the pavement with their feet till they drop with fatigue, and pirouetting through the innumerable convolutions of the ballet.[16]

Meanwhile the indigents sleep in the empty theaters when the crowds have gone. They spend their days in the wineshops, in playing dice or

in the universal passion—from dawn to dusk, rain or shine, discussing in minute detail the good or bad points of horses and their drivers. It is an extraordinary thing to see this huge crowd worked up to a kind of frenzy, hanging on the outcome of a chariot race. Because of this and similar things, nothing serious or memorable can be done at Rome. Let us return then to our subject.[17]

3. CONSTANTINOPLE

As the voices of Old Rome turn sullen, whimper and die, those of New Rome become louder and more insistent. Some are censorious, like that of St. John Chrysostom castigating the vanities of the flesh, or his contemporary, Gregory, complaining that the feasts of the Church have grown too self-indulgent:

> See here, you martyrs of our God,
> How the gluttonous have made
> Orgies round your sepulchers
> And your austere rites betrayed.
> Banquets brought your lives no joy,
> Cooks and spices you could spare,
> Now the worshipers adore you
> With a belch and not a prayer.[1]

But most are celebratory, praising the triumph of Christianity and the growth of a city. Constantinople was rapidly becoming, as Rome had been, the showplace of the world.

A century after its foundation it had expanded to its fullest extent. Constantine's walls had long since been outgrown. Theodosius I built his triumphal arch about a mile and a half outside them, to the west, close to the Sea of Marmara. Erected in 388–91, it was three arches in one, adorned with the exploits of pagan heroes— Prometheus, Hercules—and crowned with a statue of Theodosius and four bronze elephants. It was still standing in the eighteenth century for travelers to see, though by that time it had been built into the Turkish fortress of Yedikule. Twenty years after it was built, this Golden Gate was assumed into a panic wall, erected in twelve months by another Theodosius after the news of Rome's fall. The early fortifications went up so fast that cemeteries were trapped between the old walls and the new, flouting the ancient hygienic taboo against burial within the city limits. As late as Justinian's time, the dead were still being interred in the old places.

The new walls were built of brick and stone, perhaps too quickly. Shaken by an earthquake in 447, fifty-seven towers collapsed. It was an embarrassing moment, for Attila the Hun was then advancing on Constantinople. Rapid rebuilding threw up an outer wall and a moat. These had greater success, and for most of its length, the wall of Theodosius may still be seen.

Apart from minor adaptations—principally to enclose the Palace of Blachernae near the Golden Horn, the Versailles of later emperors—the new walls defined the city for the rest of its existence. They still do. The traveler driving through the gray and undistinguished suburbs from the airport knows, when the line of stone comes into sight quite suddenly and he passes through the magnificent Topkapi Gate, that he is indisputably in Istanbul. Contantinople had its suburbs too; they must have been more picturesque. Blachernae, the favored residence of emperors, has already been mentioned.

Hebdomon, about three miles west of the Golden Gate, was where a number of emperors were invested in the purple before the massed troops. It was also the place where people fled to avoid earthquakes in the city. Across the Bosphorus was pleasant too; there was beautiful countryside for those who had to live or work there. We have a somewhat conventional lament from a young man forced to study law on the Asian side while his girl lived on the European:

> The country wears its new green clothes to please,
> And there is beauty to be seen among
> The branches. Underneath the cypress trees
> The mother birds sing softly to their young.
> The finch pipes treble, while the turtle dove,
> Clutched in its cage of thorns, makes heavy moan.[2]

All this means nothing to Agathias without his love. His friend Paul writes a testy reply to this deficient Leander.

> So, my pensive friend, be merry;
> You at least can take the ferry.[3]

The ancient city too must have had its commuters.

But all that was important in the city lay behind the walls which kept it safe. Their length can still be walked, from the Sea of Marmara to the Golden Horn. It is not always a pleasant journey. At the southern end the walls lose themselves in Yedikule, the Castle of the Seven Towers (four Byzantine, three Turkish) which is in turn inextricably interwoven with a railway station. Once inland, the walls are more exciting. It is possible to follow them from a distance, as one follows Hadrian's

Wall in England, and see how proudly they rise and swoop along the contours of the land. Here the towers are still magnificent; the wonder is that they ever surrendered. For a good part of its length the wall is bounded by dark cypress trees which conceal Mohammedan cemeteries. Once past the old Adrianople Gate, the wall's highest point, it is literally and metaphorically downhill all the way. A broken concrete road follows the walls outside, a serpentine path inside, through slum streets and dingy alleys down to the waterfront of the Golden Horn. Holes in the wall hold shacks and lumberyards. The turbaned gravestones run riot, spreading round the wall like weeds. Perhaps the traveler should make this his first journey—it will at least give him a foretaste of how the Turks treat their antiquities.

The walls now surrounded six of the hills. These were precious to the resident, for the high places promised a breath of air, and a good view, on a sultry day:

> "Hard work is more than virtue," says the god.
> He must have known this house, old Hesiod.
> I stumble panting up the endless stair
> With aching feet, sweat streaming from my hair.
> To find this gorgeous prospect of the sea.
> A good room is its own reward for me![4]

The houses clustered round the city's public places. Constantine's Forum had by this time multiplied itself. The open squares that successive emperors had built were not grouped as in Rome, but strung out along the *mese* like beads on a necklace. The traveler arriving by the Golden Gate would pass from one to another. And of course some public places were more populous than

others. One voice we have from this time is that of an
inn:

> Between two monuments I take my place;
> On my right, the Hippodrome, and on my left
> Zeuxippus' dulcet waters. See a race
> In one, swim in the bath till noon and then
> Take your pleasures at my table. When
> Lunch is over and they shout "They're off!",
> You will be almost on the spot. Your room
> Is but a stone's throw from the Hippodrome.[5]

The Baths of Zeuxippus were one of the great showplaces of the city, a reminder of how much of the Roman spirit lived on in grandeur, hygiene and decoration. Dressed with the statues of famous men, the baths
summed up the history of the Greek and Roman cultures that met and mingled in Byzantium. There were
figures from Homer, Deiphobus, Pyrrhus who

> cast his eyes on high
> As one who gazed to windswept Ilion.[6]

There was Homer himself, and Vergil too. There were
the gods of pagan antiquity—Poseidon, Apollo, Aphrodite in bronze:

> Her breasts were bare,
> Her dress was drawn above her rounded thigh,
> And in her hair a golden handkerchief.[7]

Elsewhere stood another Aphrodite, all gold. There
were politicians and generals, Pericles, Demosthenes,
Isocrates, Pompey, Julius Caesar; there were those who
recorded their deeds, Thucydides, Xenophon; there

were the tragic and the comic poets, philosophers and
seers.

There were other baths besides those of Zeuxippus,
such as the one near the Aqueduct of Valens—perhaps
that one of whose sexual discrimination the poet coyly
writes:

> Love lives next door, but love's locked out
> Behind the impenetrable gate.
> Procrastination breeds delight;
> Love's sweeter, when it has to wait.[8]

Baths, in fact, rank second only to the Hippodrome as
a subject of poetic tribute. In one of them, we are told,
the waters were so sweet that Venus won the golden
apple from Paris by bathing there.

But it was the Hippodrome, not far away, to which
everybody went. Severus had built it; Constantine had
enlarged it; subsequent rulers had adorned it. Vestiges
can still be seen; it does not take much imagination to
flesh them out with the roar of crowds and the thunder
of horses. What is left of the Hippodrome has been
turned into a long, narrow public garden, At Meydani
Square, roughly reproducing the outline of the original
double track, near Haghia Sophia. It was some four
hundred yards long and seventy yards wide; thirty to
forty tiers of seats surrounded it, and estimates of its
capacity vary from forty thousand to a hundred thousand people. There was a central barrier to divide the
race tracks, and a watercourse known as *euripus*—both
a barrier and an adornment, something that was to be
copied throughout Europe in the lists built for the medieval tourneys. The supporting arches of the whole
huge structure are still visible—you can see them

clearly if you approach on the lower level, from the coast road—but the enclosing tiers have been blotted out by later buildings, the Blue Mosque on one side, an economics institute on another.

Three monuments still stand along the old center line. One was planted there by Constantine: the serpentine column, originally branching off into three snakes' heads, which was pilfered from the Temple of Apollo at Delphi. It had been erected by the Greeks to celebrate their victory over the Persian navy at Salamis. Centuries later Constantine brought it to Byzantium as he looted so many of the treasures of the pagan world, to beautify his new capital. It survived the pillaging Crusades and the Islamic invasions, and sixteenth century Turkish illustrations show it still intact. But by 1700 the heads had cracked off and were lost; today only the tortuous stump remains, green with verdigris and half underground.

The second monument came from Egypt and made the Greek look like a newcomer and an upstart. A granite monolith, it was originally erected by Thothmes III in 1515 B.C., probably at Heliopolis. The Emperor Constantius, Constantine's successor, had been the first to conceive the purpose of having it transported to his city. A freighter was built—the Romans were by now experienced in such matters—but Constantius died before the project could be completed. Unseated and forgotten, the obelisk lay for years neglected on the beach at Alexandria, attracting official attention only when its shelter was appropriated by a commune of monks, who squatted round it and made it their barren home. Julian finally had it shipped, but a wind blew the vessel off course, and the obelisk ended up at Athens. Finally Theodosius I had it brought to Constantinople and the Hippodrome.

The Emperor Theodosius undertook
To raise this column. Long years it had lain
A burden on the earth. The task was given
To Proclus, and in two and thirty days
So great a column stood up straight and tall.[9]

As seen today, the column is chiefly remarkable for the carvings on its added base, showing Theodosius, his court and soldiers, and the royal family in the imperial box, with the Emperor waiting to bestow a wreath on the victor. (In the Archaeological Museum we can see the contender's view of the contest—stone tablets erected to the men who won, carved straight and proud in their chariots, holding back their snorting four-horse teams.) Where the imperial box, the *kathisma*, stood in the Hippodrome is doubtful; it may have been near the fountain presented to Istanbul by Kaiser Wilhelm II of Germany.

The date of the third ancient column is similarly mysterious. Commonly ascribed to Constantine Porphyrogennetus, it may have been made far earlier; originally covered with sheets of bronze, it is now bare, the precious metal having been stripped from it long ago by looters.

Another, more famous, decoration of the Hippodrome is still extant, though in Venice. It is the group of bronze horses standing high above the main door of St. Mark's. Originating in Hellenistic Greece, the group was taken to Rome, where it adorned Nero's triumphal arch. After several moves within the city, it went with Constantine to Byzantium (another version is that Theodosius II brought it from Chios) and remained in the Hippodrome until the Crusaders removed it in 1204.

The Hippodrome was of course more than a place of

entertainment. On the one hand, it was a symbol of a way of life. When the emperors attended the races no less assiduously then their subjects, it is hardly surprising that the Hippodrome became associated with the ruling figure almost as much as the wearing of the purple. When King Chosroes of Persia, revolting against the Byzantine domination of Asia Minor, captured the city of Apamea, the first thing he did was to organize chariot races in the Hippodrome. He backed the Blue team, and when the Greens were seen to be winning, ordered the race stopped so that they could be held back. And this perhaps suggests the second great importance of chariot-racing to the Byzantine world. Backing one's favorite team offered an opportunity for contest and rivalry that everyday life no longer admitted. Identifying himself wholeheartedly with the riders of his choice, the spectator could vicariously strive and struggle, jockey for position and snatch triumph from the jaws of defeat—all the things that an increasingly authoritarian society otherwise forbade him to do. Consequently the passions engendered by these encounters were intense:

> In this way they develop a fierce and rancorous partisanship which is as irrational as it is ineradicable. It turns husband against wife, brother against brother, friend against friend. . . . they are deaf to divine commandments or the voice of the law; all that matters is whether their side wins. Sacrilege, blasphemy, murder, robbery, treason, all are condoned by this overwhelming passion. They may be starving, and they do not care; they may be persecuted, and they do not notice. If all goes well with the Blues or Greens, then all goes well with them. . . . It is a cancer of the soul. I have no other name to call it.[10]

Thus the Blue and the Green became much more than colors, as at other times and in other societies the Green and the Orange have done, or the Blue and the Gray—though in Byzantium it was with less reason. In time the factionalism of the Hippodrome became the approved outlet for other disputes. A man cheering for his team might also be cheering for his sect in the innumerable theological quarrels that plagued the Byzantine Empire. To this the modern world has no real parallel to offer, unless it be the conflicting religious doctrines embodied in a Glasgow Rangers versus Glasgow Celtic game in Scotland, or the ardor of those who follow Notre Dame football in the United States. In Constantinople the phenomenon was taken for granted. Undoubtedly the authorities approved. Like other regimented and rigidly hierarchical societies, notably Japan, Constantinople recognized the value of a safety valve for pent-up emotions which might otherwise explode in more sensitive areas. Over the years the Hippodrome became a licensed place in which things could be said and done that would not be lightly received elsewhere. Perhaps the spirit of the place is best summed up by a statue of the Emperor Anastasius that stood there: made in iron, the inscription said, because that metal best symbolized his brutality.

This was all very well as long as the partisans contented themselves with shouting at each other. If they should once join forces, the union would be catastrophic. In 532 such a union came about, provoked apparently by common resentment against police brutality toward rioters. The subsequent furor turned into an orgy of destruction that lasted for days, and came near to achieving a political revolution. Some of the most beautiful buildings of Constantinople went up in flames; the Emperor Justinian was on the verge of escaping by sea; and a pretender to the throne was cheered wildly in the imperial box beneath which the revolution had started. Ultimately the revolution was put down by Belisarius, Justinian's ablest general, who waited till the rioters were packed in the Hippodrome, surrounded them and advanced through various gates to the slaughter. When the damage was assessed, it was found that the Church of the Holy Wisdom was destroyed, together with portions of the Great Palace and the colonnade leading to the Forum of Constantine. The Baths of Zeuxippus were no more. Many of the wealthy had lost their homes and treasure; and all round the Hippodrome there was little to be seen but black and smoldering ruins.

Justinian, however, soon recouped his losses. Like Nero before him and Charles II of England long after, he profited from the disaster by building a more splendid city. As a direct result of the riots, Constantinople became the wonder capital of the world.

If the city was Roman in its hills, it was Greek in its proximity to and dependence on the water. Under Justinian's hand the coastline was enclosed and beautified. Along the Sea of Marmara shore now stretched a line of harbors great and small—Eleutherios, Kontoskolion, Sophia, Boukoleon, the latter taking its Greek name from the statue of an ox and a lion which adjoined the jetty. This was a small, private, royal pier reserved for the Emperor's use and serving Justinian's palace, also called Boukoleon, which stood at the shore: one of the gates still visible, now some distance inland, was originally a watergate. Of the palace itself a few fragments survive: traces of marble window frames, part of the original marble staircase, and a private entrance in the form of an arched door. Justinian kept ships here, and a reserve fund in case he should be forced to leave the city hurriedly; during the Hippodrome riots he came near to doing so. The arsenal of Constantinople was along this coast too. All traces of this maritime activity have now been lost. The sea, which until recently washed the foot of the ancient walls, is now kept some distance off by the modern coast-road. On the way to Yedikule, where the sea takes a semicircular bite out of the shore, there a few fragments jutting out into the water; and running down toward the point, a stretch of the original Constantinian walls reminds us that the sea defenses were once as impregnable as those on land. But the only trace of boating now on this side is the activity of the ferries around the point, under the shadow of the old acropolis, plying across the Bosphorus to the Asian side, and north towards the Forest of Belgrade and the Black Sea.

On the far side of the city, down the Golden Horn, it is easier to reconstruct the past, for although the ancient buildings have vanished, the pattern of life remains unchanged. Every kind of vessel is moored there, from barges and lighters to the sleek gray warships of the Turkish fleet. There are two bridges now across the Golden Horn; scholars disagree as to whether there was even one in antiquity. In time of war the entrance to the Horn could be closed with a huge chain, a segment of which may still be seen in the Naval Museum. This idea was not peculiar to Constantinople—Venice employed it too—but was particularly effective there. Permanently in position under water, the chain could be raised by a winch to block the Horn completely and make impossible any seaward attack from that side.

There were of course sea walls along the Horn; the city was completely enclosed. These have vanished

now, but the ceaseless activity of a busy port remains.
The shore is lined with sheds for boatbuilding and kin-
dred trades. Great piles of timber lie at the water's
edge. Along the cobbled street they stretch rope or
wire cables. Occasionally there are little parks, oases of
cool and quiet. Toward the point, the markets predomi-
nate. Small Turks stagger under huge loads, bent double under towers of boxes. The flower and vegetable
sellers spill from the warehouses into the street. Vener-
able Turkish bazaars and modern corrugated iron mix
without incongruity, for they serve the business which
has occupied the Horn for centuries.

In Justinian's time the coastline was a place for pleasure as well as trade. The historian Procopius testifies to
the Emperor's penchant for seaside architecture.

> He also saw fit to pour money into waterfront construc-
> tion: he was trying to stop the unstoppable, to put a
> brake upon the wind and water. There was no end to it:
> stone piled on stone and mole annexed to mole, inching
> the shoreline outwards, throwing down a challenge to
> the tides and opposing to the violence of the water all
> the resources of his wealth.[11]

But the extravagance was not without results:

> As you sail up the Sea of Marmara toward the east side
> of the city, you will see a public bath on the left hand.
> There, in the suburbs, the Emperor laid out a piazza. If
> you care to take a stroll there or drop anchor for a while,
> it is always open. The same sun that washes it with light
> at dawn leaves it pleasantly shaded as it moves toward
> the west; and round about there winds the tranquil sea,
> flowing from the Pontus like a river. So the strollers can
> have conversations with the crews as they go sailing by.

. . . Both the ground level and the upper tiers are covered with columns of outstanding beauty. The sun's rays reverberate from them, pure, intense, their radiance virtually undimmed. And there are statues too, some bronze, some polished stone. . . .[12]

Among the other buildings erected by Justinian along the shore was a home for fallen women (although in this case, according to his detractors, his motives were anything but altruistic); and the rich were not far behind, seizing the locations that commanded a splendid view:

> About my firm foundations rolls the sea,
> Licking the land's edge with its salty tongue.
> Many are happy to lean out of me,
> For every way they some new treasure spy,
> Trees, houses, ships, sea, city, earth and sky.[13]

Sea and shore merged into a lovely and harmonious whole; on the Golden Horn "when a ship is at anchor, the stern rides on the sea, the prow rests on the shore, as if the elements were rivals to render their city the greatest service."[14]

> The land is water, and the water land,
> The ocean blossoms, ships sail on the sand.[15]

And the happiest houses in Constantinople were those that had both the benefits of a high situation and a prospect of the water.

> I look from three sides on the sparkling sea;
> From every side the sunlight washes me.

Once Dawn has wrapped me in her amber light,
She has no yearning to go home at night.[16]

This sense of the enjoyment of the sea is something
that has almost vanished, under pressure of circumstances, from modern Istanbul; though on a summer
Sunday, when the entire population of the city seems
to spread along the promenade, when the open-air res-
taurants do brisk trade on the sand and the little yachts
are out on the water, you can still recapture the spirit
of the city that was.

In the center of the city the Hippodrome was restored, and opposite, the Great Palace was repaired and
enlarged. This was not one building but a vast complex
of residences, gardens and courtyards, entered by the
gatehouse known as *Chalke*, the "place of bronze"
from its massive doors. Over the doors shone an icon of
Christ. There was also a mosaic displaying the triumphs
of Justinian in Italy and Africa, with a representation of
his general, Belisarius, the captive kings of the Vandals
and Goths, and the rejoicing of the Roman senate. This
had been destroyed in the riots; Justinian now rebuilt
it.

I am the house Anastasius built, the Emperor, slayer of
tyrants.
No city upon the face of the earth surpasses the glory of
me.
Visitors come from far and wide to look on the work and
wonder.
When I was built, the architects cried, What roof can fit
such a colossus?
But Aetherius, first in the lore of his trade, knew well
what he had wrought,

And laid the first fruits of his toil before our Emperor's
feet.
So I brood over the land; and Italy offers no rival
To better my beauty and bulk. . . . For I am the house of
the dawn
And the Emperor, fresh from his conquest of the
Isaurians, made me
Shining with gold, and exposed to the wind on every
side.[17]

In the center of the city, too, stood the Augustineum,
a square on the original acropolis of Byzantium, graced
with an equestrian statue of Justinian in armor, carrying an orb and stretching out his arm to the East, the
direction from which the Persian menace had come.
The statue survives for us in a crude medieval sketch
and in the donor's inscription commemorating the Emperor's victories in the Eastern wars:

These gifts, Justinian, now the wars are done,
A City Father and the city's son
Makes bold to give: a horse for victory,
And Victory in person; making three,
Yourself, the Persians conquered, set astride
A horse that can the very wind outride.
Your might, Justinian, is set on high,
But may the Scyths and Persians subject lie.[18]

Constantinople was well-watered. Like any Roman
city of any magnitude, it depended on a system of aqueducts and cisterns. Part of the aqueduct built by the
Emperor Valens about 366, traditionally using stones
removed from Chalcedon across the water, still cuts
through the city center, bestriding the Ataturk Boule-
vard; it is merely one of several built by the Romans and

the Turks after them. Another system brought water down from the Forest of Belgrade in the north.

Once in the city the water was stored in huge cisterns, some open, some underground. The oldest now visible probably dates from the reign of Constantine; it is sixty-one by seventy yards, and its roof rests on 224 simply sculpted columns. Larger and more elaborate is the so-called Basilica cistern, Yerebatan, built by Justinian out of the remains of Haghia Sophia after he had finished the reconstruction. It was made by excavating the central courtyard of the Stoa Basilike, Constantinople's meeting-place of legal minds. Here the Great Palace drew its water. The cistern has 336 columns, and there is still water in it, though one can read from the columns how the level has gradually dropped. This extraordinary and sinister construction was once covered with houses; there have been removed now, because of their dangerous weight. Over the centuries these man-made caves acquired a dangerous reputation. Nineteenth-century travelers spoke of the folklore that had accumulated around them: stories of the shrieking of demons heard from the cisterns' depths, or of men who sailed their boats out to explore them and were never seen again. Other, open cisterns have been adapted to other uses. One, near Topkapi Gate, has been turned into a football stadium. Another, near the Church of the Pammakaristos, has gradually filled with houses, so that the cistern walls now hold a sunken village.

Most of the public and private buildings of Justinian's time have irredeemably vanished. The ancient capitol is buried under the University and Beyazit Square, where students stroll and old women squat over their little piles of goods, making small black islands in a sea of sun-reflecting stone and pigeons.

The churches, however, have survived as museums or mosques, more or less accessible, in various states of disrepair. Justinian enlarged and restored St. Irene. In the suburb of Blachernae he built a church to the Virgin Mother, later to be celebrated as a bastion of faith against the encroaching infidel.

He restored the Church of the Apostles, in which Constantine had been buried, and found three wooden coffins holding the bodies of the apostles Andrew, Luke and Timothy. Around the Golden Horn he threw a necklace of shrines and churches—of St. Lawrence, of Cosmas and Damian, of Priscus and Nicholas, the latter a favorite gossiping place for the people of Byzantium. There was the shrine of John the Baptist in Hebdomon and a whole line of shrines and harbors up the coast of the Bosphorus.

Near the sea, and associated with the Boukoleon Palace, Justinian built two churches. They were connected by a common colonnade and courtyard and shared the same entrance gates.

> To Jesus Christ, the King of all,
> Justinian this church decreed,
> Named for Peter and for Paul,
> For he who honors by his deed
> One of His servants, honors Him.
> Here are riches for the soul
> And for the eyes. So pray to win
> Your soul's desire; and from this sight
> Know beauty, wonder and delight.[19]

Peter and Paul has vanished, but its neighbor church —sharing the same luster, according to ancient notices —is still present. This is the Church of SS. Sergius and

Bacchus, erected by Justinian in gratitude for their intercession in freeing him from a suspicion of treachery when he had yet to ascend the throne. Though standing side by side, the churches differed in their style. SS. Peter and Paul was a basilica of the type with which we have become familiar in Rome, and which continued to be built in various parts of the Empire. The church of the two military saints—Christian officers who had been martyred under Maximian—was of the type we have since come to call Byzantine, with a curvilinear floor plan topped by a central dome. Outside, since its transformation into a mosque, the church has sprouted a domed portico and a courtyard surrounded by little houses that once held monks. Since Ataturk's abolition of the monasteries, these have been turned over to private families. The church has to be opened by the caretaker, who doubles as muezzin and who must be brought, with great difficulty, from his house two streets away. Inside, the church is blessedly cool, and though the lavish decoration is gone and the rising of the floor level over several centuries has changed the proportions of the building, the spirit of Justinian's construction remains. Within this rectangle pillars mark off an octagonal space which, above the viewer's head, transforms itself into a dome; from here, as in every Byzantine church, the face of Christ Pantokrator glared down upon the worshipers beneath. An upper gallery winds around the columns—the gynaeceum or women's place. The Byzantine ceremonies practised strict segregation of sexes.

But looking down on every other building, rising above the city like a watchtower and dominating it, providing a viewpoint from which every aspect of Constantinople could be surveyed, was Justinian's greatest achievement, the new Haghia Sophia. Where the old church had stood, on the first hill, was now a mass of charred rubble. Justinian spared neither expense nor ingenuity in the rebuilding. His architects were Greeks, Anthemius of Tralles and Isidorus of Miletus; according to tradition, the inspiration and even some of the construction techniques were as much Justinian's as theirs. The whole concept was an attempt to do something which had never been attempted on so vast a scale before—to mount an enormous dome over a basically rectangular structure—and, by the nature of the experiment, there were unpredictable hazards and dangers. Special precautions had to be taken against the enormous weight that the stones had to carry.

Into the gaps of the stone, where each block abuts on its neighbor,
They have laid soft sheets of lead, so the force of the block above
Should caress its neighbor below. If not, the weight of the burden
Would break the back of the block beneath. As it is, the stones lie softly
And keep the foundations safe. The pile sits sure and still.[20]

Even with these precautions the foundations were not entirely safe. The dome rested on four great arches, which were in turn supported on stone piers. While the building was going up, the piers cracked and had to be repaired. The inevitable earthquake shocks continued to endanger the structure. In major subsidences in 557 and 558,

The rim of the half-sphere shook and was rocked from its
firm foundations.
With its fall the House of God was shaken from roof to
floor.
In the city the houses heard. In their heart of hearts they
shuddered
As the earth cried out in pain. And above, in the vault of
heaven,
There were clouds and rolling dust that blazed with fire
at noon.[21]

The eastern half of the dome had collapsed, and the
wall with it. Justinian, who through all these misfortunes seems to have behaved with superhuman pa-
tience, merely remarked that it was a great tribute to
the architects' ability that more had not fallen. And the
fact that the earthquake brought no death-toll was
surely a sign of Christ's protection.

The church, once repaired, was rededicated. It was
Christmas Eve, the time of year when

The sickle is hung on the wall, still dull from toil in the
vineyard
To wait until summer comes, and the long hard days of
harvest;
And the sun rides up from the south, to shine with a
chillier light
On the sign with the horns of a goat and the tail of a fish.
The Hunter
Is desolate, eyes downcast; the shining sun has gone.[22]

The people had gathered the night before in the
Shrine of St. Plato, near the Forum of Constantine.

But then, when the urgent dawn brushed aside the veil of
darkness

And ran with a blush of pink down the lightening rim of
the sky,
Then the whole people assembled, the lords and senators
with them,
Swift to obey the behest of their Emperor, lord and
master.
Carrying gifts in their hands for the favor of Christ the
King,
Singing hymns to the Lord, they advanced to do him
service.
The candles they carried shone with a clear and precious
light.[23]

At the head of the procession came the choir with the
patriarch, who three times called for the doors to be
opened. Haghia Sophia was approached, in the regular
way, through an atrium, or forecourt, in the center of
which were placed a huge marble basin and fountain.
Beyond this were the three great doors, which provided the ceremonial entrance into the building: as the
procession reached this point, the psalms of David rang
out. Inside, across the narthex, were another nine
doors; the central one was reserved for the Emperor.
And then the full interior of the building, under the
spreading dome. On the upper floor, galleries wound
mysteriously to left and right; for the Emperor's con-
venience, they were accessible on horseback. Under-
foot was a ripple of black and white marble; overhead
the ceiling was covered with gold mosaic. All around
were columns advancing and retreating like dancers in
a chorus and walls covered with mosaic representations
of cornucopias, baskets, trees, birds. In front was the
silver *ikonastasis*, the golden altar table, the silver
tabernacle with an acanthus frieze, crowned with an
ark. At the corner stood vessels of silver bearing candles; the whole was decorated with precious stones.

The Byzantines had inherited both the gaudy color sense of the Greeks and the Roman love of flamboyance. The main impression on the beholder was of a glow of color—not merely from the gold and silver employed, but from the more pedestrian materials as well.

It would tax even Homer's tongue, the poet of thunder and lightning,
To hymn the marble pastures that the whole world brought together
To grace God's temple walls, as far as the eye could see,
And the outspread floor beneath. This green was brought from Carystus,
Fresh as the grass in spring. In the crest of the Phrygian mountains
The iron saw sank its teeth to mine this speckled marble,
Blushing and pale at once in a bloom of pink and white,
Or spangled with purple flowers in a field of silver blossoms,
A dress that a queen might envy. And here is a stone that was ferried
The length of the River Nile: a porphyry powdered with silver,
Like stars in the midnight sky. Look here, where the Spartan quarries
Have offered an emerald green; and here, where the probing iron
Explored the Iassian hills to divulge their bosom's treasure,
A marble with spiral veins that glitter and glow in the light.[24]

And if Haghia Sophia was resplendent by day, how much brighter must it have glowed at night, a phenomenon, says the poet, that words are inadequate to describe (though, being a Byzantine poet, he does not find the words wanting). Chains hung from hooks fastened to the moldings, each carrying a vessel made from silver sheet, with glass lamps in the openings. Concentric circles of light spread out from the center of the dome. On the walls were silver cups with oil lamps in them, lines of light that rose and fell in dynamic patterns, little silver ships swimming in the air.

The radiance that the ancient chroniclers talked of is now extinguished. Today, Haghia Sophia can still impress by virtue of its size, but by nothing else. Buttressed against repeated earthquake shocks, the outside is cluttered and unappealing. The atrium has dwindled to a scrubby garden, a few foundations, and lines of columns and memorials; the environs of the church seem to be in a continual state of disrepair, littered with barrows and fallen masonry. The great ceremonial doors are shut forever; entrance is now from a small door at one side. Here at least the visitor is greeted by one of the most famous mosaics of the era, a depiction of Constantine and Justinian offering the city and the Church to the Virgin Mary. Inside, the prevailing impression is one of grayness. The lavish decoration has disappeared, plastered over by Muslim divines who abominated the representation of the human form. Those mosaics that may still be seen are tucked away in the gallery. The result is that Haghia Sophia is now as cavernous and disenchanting as Grand Central Station and considerably less luminous.

There were of course shadows on the city that Justinian knew; they have not all come (despite the protestations of the Orthodox) from the Ottoman invasion. There was the ever-present threat of earthquake, still a fact of life in Turkey today. We see its effects in the patchwork exterior of Haghia Sophia; we hear them in the poetic cry of a woman trapped in childbirth:

> Earth trembled; the house around me fell,
> But the walls of my room stood true.
> I lay like a beast in my little cell
> Till I knew my time was due.
> I dreaded the shock of the shifting earth
> And the pangs of my quickening womb,
> But kind mother nature attended the birth
> And delivered us both from the tomb.[25]

There were other dangers. Constantinople was, for its time, a healthy city. Justinian had driven vice from the streets and had built a number of hospitals, one between Haghia Sophia and St. Irene, others along the seashore. But there was still the threat of plague, like the one that broke out in 542.

> And this was the year that the world almost ended, the year of the great plague. It spread destruction everywhere, without respect for persons, places or seasons. There was no local cause a man might put his finger on, simply a universal blight from which no one was safe, great or humble, young or old, man or woman . . . wherever it passed, it left death and devastation behind. The islands were not safe from it, nor the heights of the mountains, nor the depths of the earth.
> The pattern was always the same. It started on the coast, then moved inland. In the second year it reached Byzantium in mid-Spring. I happened to be staying there at the time, and this was the manner of its coming. There were reports of apparitions seen about the city, but all the witnesses agreed on this: that the man-shape

struck them on some part of their body, and that this vision was the first symptom of the disease. Death came to some immediately, while others lingered on for days or weeks. In some cases the body broke out in black pustules about the size of a lentil: these did not even live to see the night. There were many too, who for no apparent reason, vomited blood, and this immediately brought on their deaths.[26]

A more subtle Byzantine disease was already deeply implanted in the minds of its people. An authoritarian state jealously guarded its own prerogatives. Emperors brought up amid labyrinthine protocol, where the signs and symbols of office were all-important, were quick to regulate all public manifestations. Since purple was the imperial color, it was an offense to wear or even to possess purple: men could be put to death for owning such stuff illicitly. A too-successful general could be grudged a triumph. Such a society put a premium on deviousness. This was the air in which a Eutropius might thrive, and there were many such. For Justinian's reign we might consider John the Cappadocian. He was an ignorant man, knowing no Latin, and apparently took his Christianity lightly, for according to one account he used to mumble pagan incantations to himself throughout the service. Gossip enlarged this into tales of sorcery and practicing "Hellenic rites." And yet this man rose to be Prefect of the City. It seems clear that he had his eyes set on the throne. An ardent supporter of the Blues, he was tricked into implicating himself by Belisarius' wife, Antonina, who pretended to be sympathetic to his cause. Suspect by the Emperor, detested by the populace—in the Hippodrome riots the people clamored for his removal—John took religious sanctuary and was forced to become a priest. Taken to Cyzicus, he was implicated, perhaps unjustly, in the murder of a prominent and unpopular bishop. For this he was thrown into jail and beaten to extract a confession. Stripped of all his goods except a cloak, he was put on board ship and taken to Antinous in Egypt, being forced to beg for bread in every port he stopped at. Once there, he became a government spy, reporting certain prominent Alexandrians for tax evasion. John was a man who had a hand in every sort of illegality— including profiteering from the sale of bad bread to the army—and yet he returned to high position, ordering his city for a second time.

This was the basement view of the Shining City, and its language was gossip. Even today, this miasma seems to hang about the ruins; in no other city, even Rome, is the visitor laden with so much enthusiastic misinformation. One is shown the windows looking out from the subterranean walls of the Hippodrome and told, "each one held a different beast"; shapeless lumps of masonry by the railway tracks are "Byzantine houses"; a collapsed wall near SS. Sergius and Bacchus was "the palace of Theodora."

It is around this lady that most of the gossip, ancient and modern, is woven; we may see it as a symptom of Byzantine malaise. Theodora was Justinian's second wife and came to him with a spectacular past. Even making every allowance for slander and malicious exaggeration, there seems no doubt that Theodora had made her first impact on public life as a strip-tease dancer in the theater, if not an outright prostitute. (One of her "speciality numbers" involved pigeons who would eat corn off her as she sprawled naked on the floor.) Her father was a bear-keeper at the Hippodrome; she was brought up, presumably, in the mass of slums whose modern descendants still surround that structure's lower end. Having, according to repute, toured the brothels of the world, she attracted Justinian's attention and became first his mistress, later his queen. Her career was sensationally recorded by the same Procopius who elsewhere devoted eight books of sober and objective study to the history of the reign. His scandal sheet (the *Anecdota* or *Unpublished Chronicle*) was written apparently after his more serious study; it is as though his accumulated rancor had festered in the author's mind until finally it burst forth in this extraordinary document. It must have been kept a close secret at the time; our first mention of it occurs in a lexicon of the tenth century. But it is not alone. There is independent testimony to the brutal and sadistic behavior of the rulers—testimony which has caused an abiding argument as to how far the *Anecdota* must be taken seriously.

Theodora is not the only one whose reputation suffers. Justinian is shown as avaricious of his own money, spendthrift of others'; the elaborate building projects we have seen lauded above are now revealed as the symptoms of megalomania. He jealously controls the imperial monopolies and spirits away the fortunes of his nobles; he is tyrannical, irrational and controlled by the devil. Procopius relates the legends concerning him: of how he never seemed to eat or drink, but merely touched the food with his fingers; of how, when he stalked brooding through the palace, his head would be seen to part from his body; of how a hermit, come from his remote cell to lay a petition before the Emperor, looked into the presence chamber and swore he saw the Prince of Devils sitting on the throne. Theodora aided and abetted him, cowing the aristocracy with humiliating protocol and mocking them with parodies of the Christian liturgy. Even Belisarius, who is elsewhere Procopius' hero, does not escape. His wife, Antonina, is descended from charioteers and prostitutes; she is an adulteress: she controls her husband by magic. Belisarius is a cuckold, first of unimaginable stupidity, then of incredible complacency. The only ray of hope in all these sinister doings is that, in this corrupt and perverted court, the wicked batten upon each other.

Procopius' work deserves a niche in the history of pornography; no longer secret, it may be seen today between salacious covers, ornamenting the windows of the more dubious Continental bookshops. But it is far less interesting for what it says than for the state of mind that it represents. In Constantinople, as in many periods of Imperial Rome, a repressive and hierarchical state had produced a literature polarized between the adulatory and the secretly derisive. And it seems clear that the same ambivalence existed in city life; that Procopius' picture is not entirely a false one; and that Constantinople was enough of an oriental city to exhibit the violent contrasts of oriental life—the dignity and splendor of the palace and the church mocked by the squalor of the slums and bazaars. If we accept the city of Haghia Sophia, we must also accept the city where respectable ladies would expect to be molested while crossing on the Bosphorus ferry; where the young toughs of the Hippodrome, with their *outré* haircuts and padded suits, lounged about the streets and threatened the passers-by; where the five hundred prostitutes herded off by Justinian into the House of Repentance included some who injured themselves by jumping over the walls, preferring injury to forsaking their old

life. And we must see the whole age, too, as one of
continual compromise and adjustment, in which Justinian's trade controls and financial manipulations,
easily misunderstood by a Procopius, represent patchwork attempts to deal with problems that Old Rome
never had to face.

THE
BYZANTINE WORLD

300 MILES

TRM

S. Marco, Venice: the Tetrarchs huddle amid Byzantine plunder

Rome defensive: Portchester Castle, on the south coast of England

Ruins of the Lateran Palace

Church of S. Clemente

Constantinople: urban splendor, the column of Theodosius . . .

Constantinople sacred: S. Irene . . .

Constantinople: the city and the sea

. . . and urban squalor, ancient walls and modern slums

. . . and Haghia Sophia

Constantinople secular: central aqueduct

Constantinople beautiful: intricacy of Byzantine brick . . .

Ravenna of the Goths: Baptistry of the Arians

The Church of Chora

Ravenna of the Romans: shipwright's tomb

Ravenna of the Christians: Mausoleum of Galla Placidia

. . . and Mausoleum of Theodoric

Baptismal font, Galla Placidia

Christian-classical: Athens, Little Metropolis, two views

Athens, Byzantine fountain

The monastery of Daphni

Thessaloniki pagan: Arch of Galerius

Thessaloniki Christian: Basilica of St. Demetrius

Thessaloniki: Orthodox Sunday, Vlatadon Monastary

Basilica of St. Demetrius: crypt

Thessaloniki defensive: the White Tower

The destruction: Turkish castle guards the Bosphorus

Constantinople: crumbled walls, Turkish graves

Palaces in the Byzantine style, Grand Canal, Venice

The inheritors: Byzantine lions, Arsenale, Venice

Byzantine watergate, Venice

Churches in the Byzantine style, Torcello

4. RAVENNA, ROME

The most notable instance of change was Rome itself. In Paul the Silentiary's poem the older capital is depicted as looking with beaming pride on the nascent glories of Byzantium. "This," sings Paul, "is joy of parenthood."[1] In fact, when Rome had time to think of Byzantium at all, it was with envy. Most of the time she was busy with her own troubles.

The Goths—who had entered the Empire as intruders, remained as hirelings and emerged as conquerors —captured the city in 410, and a cry of dismay ran round the world. Alaric had brought Rome to her knees and exacted an exorbitant ransom—a ransom destined never to be enjoyed, for it was buried with the leader where he died, in some forgotten, blighted corner of Calabria. George Gissing, making his tortuous, fever-ridden journey round the coast in the early years of the present century, ruminates on the fate of those great riches. "Do the rivers Busento and Crati still keep the secret of that royal sepulchre, adorned with the splendid spoils and trophies of Rome? It seems improbable that the grave was ever disturbed; to this day there exists somewhere near Cosenza a treasure-house more alluring than any pictured in Arabian tale. It is not easy to conjecture what spoils and trophies the Goths buried with their king; if they sacrificed precious metal, then perchance there still lies in the riverbed some portion of that golden statue of Virtus, which the Romans melted down to eke out the ransom claimed by Alaric. The year 410 A.D. was no unfitting moment to break into bullion the figure personifying Manly Worth. After that, says an old historian, 'all bravery and honor perished out of Rome.' "[2] After the Goths came the Vandals, who, by seizing Carthage and transforming it into a naval power, sailed up the Tiber to sack Rome in 455. Carthage had avenged her defeat of centuries before. Then came more Goths, so that by the time Justinian gained the throne, the greater part of Italy was under barbarian administration. For all practical purposes the western capital moved elsewhere: to Milan for a while and later to Ravenna on the northeast coast. This city became the graveyard of Byzantium in Italy.

Ravenna today is not a lovely town. Miles of suburban blight surround and almost subdue a nucleus of antique beauty. Modern industry, in its most noisome form, threatens the atmosphere. In totality the site can have been scarcely more pleasing in antiquity. Marshy and disconsolate, it had little in the way of natural beauty to commend it. Yet this disqualification was Ravenna's guarantee of survival. Today one can still see why. Ravenna is a waterlogged town. Not as picturesquely so, admittedly, as its more illustrious neighbor; Venice has capitalized on characteristics that Ravenna did its best to conceal. Yet the water is ubiquitous and evident. It washes the mosaic threshold of San Vitale, where a bridge gives passage to the pillared entrance. It seeps through the foundations of Theodoric's tomb. It nearly fills the crypt of San Francesco, creating an indoor lake that, for a hundred lire, may be illuminated and gaped at. Where there is no visible water, its effects may be seen in subsidence. Ravenna out-Pisas Pisa; it is a whole city of leaning towers, and to spend a day there is to lose faith in the perpendicular.

In the beginning Ravenna and Venice must have been much alike. Both grew out of islands and lagoons, and both were surrounded by marshland. Ravenna knit a network of canals that tamed the water and kept it at bay. Their descendants still exist. But the marshes remained Ravenna's strong protection and made it practically unapproachable on the landward side. On the coast stood the naval base of Classis, established by Augustus and still strong. A mosaic in Sant' Apollinare Nuovo shows how it looked near Justinian's time. (Apollinaris was the first Bishop of Ravenna, with the curious gifts of liquefying rock and destroying pagan temples by the power of prayer.) Three ships ride at anchor in the harbor. One has its square sail spread; the others are bare-masted. All have arrogantly curved prows and the massive steering oar thrusting into the water. We see them between the guard-towers of the harbor. Fronting the water are more towers and massive walls; within the walls is a symphony of red-tiled roofs and rounded arches, the towers and arcades of a bustling port. On the opposite wall of Sant' Apollinare Nuovo is a view of contemporary Ravenna. We see the facade of Theodoric's palace, a row of arches poised on decorative capitals, picked out with mosaic figures and hung with curtains; above, a line of clerestory windows topped by a red tile roof; beyond, a glimpse of other domes and gables, the churches of Ravenna glowing in

honest russet brick. Framing all are the battlemented
city walls; Ravenna, like the mother city was usually on
the defensive. Protected thus by man and nature,
Ravenna doubled as fortress and market town. Traders
brought their goods to market without labor. They
loaded their wares in light boats on the coast and
waited for the rising tide to carry them up the estuary
inland. At market's end they would float out on the ebb
tide and return. Today there is still traffic from sea to
city, but the boats are huge tankers, and they make
their way into the city by canal. Ravenna's early fortifications can still be traced. A number of early gates still
stand; the crumbled walls have been tidied into a grassy
mound which runs through streets and private gardens,
defining the rectangle of the ancient town. Classis has
disappeared. The coast receded and the harbor silted
up. Sant' Apollinare in Classe, once the center of the
harbor town, was left high and dry, looking out across
the flatlands, which are in turn succumbing to suburbia.
Ravenna's chief connection with the sea is now the
marina, set among the famous pinewoods that fringe
the Adriatic coast. But in Ravenna the monuments remain, an abridged history of a perplexed and troubled
time.

In the shadow of San Vitale stands, quietly and unas-
sumingly, the mausoleum of Galla Placidia, whose life
was part of that history. Her father was Theodosius I,
who built the Golden Gate at Constantinople; her
brother Honorius, Emperor of the West; her son was
another Emperor, Valentinian III. Her first husband,
Ataulfo, was a barbarian; her second a Roman patrician.
Both, in their time, considered themselves legitimate
masters of the Empire. Galla Placidia came to rule herself, both in her own name and that of her son. Such was

the political discordance of her life, in an empire torn between Byzantine and barbarian. Inside the mausoleum's simple walls old Rome dies in a blaze of glory. We walk under a blue mosaic sky, more vivid by proximity: the floor has risen through the centuries. It explodes with golden stars, the *feux d'artifice* of an expiring universe. In the corners shine the hopeful symbols of the Evangelists; facing us are Roman senators metamorphosed into Peter and Paul. It is a place of transition. The stags and sheep, the doves, the vibrant rocky landscape, the trees and plants that decorate the walls, reveal behind their Christian symbolism a joy in the physical world per se which is essentially pagan.

From the Romans Ravenna, like most of Italy, passed into the power of the Goths. Their heavy mark may be seen on the city's outer fringes, framed unkindly by the railway marshaling-yards on one side and an arterial highway on the other. It stands amid the nodding cypresses of a designated Garden of Rest; it is squat, ungainly, and menacing; it is as German and as alien as the Kaiser's fountain in Istanbul, though of a different vintage. It is the mausoleum of Theodoric, who held court in Ravenna till his death in 526. Osbert Lancaster calls it "a corner of a foreign field which is forever Deutschland." To others it resembles a visitor from another planet or a giant war-helmet flung down on the ground. Most, however, see it as a tent in stone, the habitation of the wandering warrior's last resting place. Seen in this light, the surface decorations and appendages of this two-tiered monstrosity make sense: they are the lugs and projections that keep the tent erect and taut. Yet this tent is surely no thing of the open skies and native countryside. The most disparaging thing one can say about it is that it seems perfectly at home in its modern industrial environment.

The Goths thought of themselves as civilized, Latinized and Christian. The Romans looked on them as illiterate, savage and Arian. Hand in hand with the struggle for rule went a religious schism that was already present at the foundation of Constantinople and which typified the history of Christianity under the Byzantine Empire. There are two baptisteries from this period surviving in Ravenna. One stands next to the cathedral; like the Mausoleum of Galla Placidia, it is simple outside and ornate within. Around the baptismal basin, mosaic decoration swirls across the walls and ceilings. In the center of the cupola we see Christ being baptized by John, a bearded old man; there is a third figure present, the river-god, emerging from the water. These deities, familiar, benign and too deeply imbedded in the folk-consciousness to be lightly discarded, were the last survivors of the old paganism. In another quarter of the town stands another baptistery which, inside and out, is virtually indentical with the first. We see the same central scene, a similar river-god—fully emerged this time, green-robed and sitting on the bank, contemplating the usurpation of his powers. The same band of apostles marches its perpetual circle round the dome. Yet the first of these buildings was designed for Catholics and the second, probably in Theodoric's reign, for Arians. The fashionable religion of the Gothic court demanded its own premises.

The schism took its name from one Arius, who, when Constantine liberated Christianity, held office as a priest in Alexandria. Wrestling with the mystery of the Holy Trinity, he had propounded that Christ, being created by the Father at a fixed point in time, was a finite being who did not partake fully of the divine nature. In essence this was a Christian reawaking of an old Greek philosophical controversy. If the prime sub-

stance is eternal and immutable, how can we explain
the existence of change? God is constant, but Christ is
seen in the Gospels to change and grow: how then can
He be of the same substance? Arius' theory polarized
the ecclesiastical world and turned into a blazing controversy feeding off the mutual animosities of those
who were attempting to hammer Christianity into
shape. Forcing an issue and asserting his own primacy
in Church affairs, Constantine called the Council of
Nicaea, which in 325 placed Arianism under a final
interdict. From this Council derives the Creed named
after it and the unequivocal statement that the son is
homousion tō patri, "of one substance with the Father,
by whom all things are made." Yet Arianism was not
dead. It continued to attract distinguished proponents
and in the end attained the dubious honor of being a
persecuted religion. In the north, however, it became
the rule rather then the exception. Embraced by the
Germanic tribes, it was continually reintroduced to
Italy by successive migrations; in some parts of the Empire, Catholic persecuted Arian; in others, Arian persecuted Catholic—both as zestfully as Roman had persecuted Christian in the old days. The Goths who
conquered Italy were Arians, and this, in spite of the
fact that their administration was better than any the
people had enjoyed for centuries, was continually held
against them.

Such was Ravenna before Justinian. The visitor today
can see the churches and be impressed at least by their
number; he can see the Baptistery of the Arians, reduced now to the status of an outbuilding in the forecourt of a Catholic church; he can catch a whiff of palatial glory in the saw-toothed splendors of the so-called
Palace of Theodoric, a partial vision of the Sant' Apol-

linare Nuovo mosaic translated into three dimensions. But Ravenna's most sumptuous building belongs to the reconquest, and we must look first to the activity of Justinian's emissaries in Italy at large.

By 535, when Justinian decided to reclaim Italy for his empire, the country had settled down to something like tranquillity. He might have done better to leave well enough alone. The Goths were well-intentioned, competent administrators, decently respectful to the Emperor in Constantinople; the people of the cities, accustomed to their new masters, may have sneered at their religion, language and customs, but had to be nudged or bludgeoned into resisting. But, as Arians, the Goths were theologically beyond the pale, and in Justinian's eyes all barbarians were suspect, for the Eastern Empire was under pressure from all sides. The Persians were a constant menace. Ever nearer, too, came the Huns. In 539 the people of Constantinople saw the comet variously called "the swordfish" and "the bearded star" and whispered to one another that it was a portent of disaster. Almost at once, it seems, the Huns were in Greece, plundering as far as the suburbs of the capital and capturing Thermopylae by the same device that the Persians had used against Leonidas.

We know of the campaigns in Italy and elsewhere largely through the work of one man, Procopius, whom we have already seen as a commentator on Justinian's domestic program. Born in Caesarea, Palestine, toward the end of the previous century, he had read for the bar, coming to Constantinople while still a young man. In 527 he was appointed private secretary and legal adviser to Justinian's general, Belisarius. He serves as Boswell to Belisarius' Johnson—assiduous, adulatory, the perfect civil servant. As a chronicler he is tireless and, as far as we can judge, for the most part entirely accurate; the *Anecdota* reveal a side of the man he did not care to display in public. Though serving principally as recorder, he occasionally, as he proudly tells, offers technical advice or is entrusted with military administration. We could scarcely ask for a more informative document than his history of the wars.

Procopius' style, like his period, is full of echoes. His proem harks back to Herodotus and Thucydides. The purpose of his work, he says, is to record events "so that monumental deeds may not be eroded by the centuries for want of a historian, or consigned to oblivion and wiped out of existence as if they had never been"; in order, too, that the memory of these events might help the future "if ever time comes round again, and brings men once more to their present pass."[3] We see Herodotus in the rich allusions to Homer and the picturesque digressions; when Procopius knows a good story, he tells it. And so we have the tale of the shark who fell in love with a pearl; of the wrestling instructor in Byzantium who served as aide in the Persian campaign and practiced his civilian skills on his enemies; of the pebblework mosaic of the Gothic King in Naples which gradually fell apart and foretold the death of its subject by inches. We see Thucydides in the constant moralizing on the mutability of things and particularly in the speeches that Procopius puts into his principals' mouths; they seldom ring true, for even barbarians are made to orate with all the formal elaboration of Byzantine rhetoric. Yet for all these borrowings, Procopius is very much his own man. He gives us a powerful picture of the Byzantine army at work and of an Italy and a Rome fallen into the decay which in some regions was to endure to the twentieth century.

The army first. Belisarius' expeditionary force would have shocked Julius Caesar and dumbfounded Trajan. It is made up principally of mercenaries and foreigners. When Belisarius embarks on his Italian campaign, he brings 200 Huns, 300 Moors. The army never seemed to be large enough: one of the leitmotivs of the campaign is the perpetual cry for reinforcements. It is haphazard, undisciplined and occasionally insubordinate. Procopius records the case of an officer accused of extorting money from civilians: when Belisarius intervenes, the officer tries to stab him. The troops are no longer the impeccably drilled battalions of the Republic or early Empire. They have long forgotten how to distinguish between trumpet calls. They are at the mercy of bureaucratic paymasters who cheat the men, exact deductions and quibble over every penny. The state auditor is more to be feared than the enemy. The commanders are jealous of each other, and the more successful they become, the more suspect they are in the Emperor's eyes. Perhaps not without reason: the sense of personality cult is strong. A general sent abroad on a lengthy term of duty was for all practical purposes independent. In Procopius' account the enemy prefer to negotiate with Belisarius rather than with the Emperor and at one point even offer him the crown.

Most nobles commanded their private armies—Belisarius had a force of seven thousand drawn from his own household—and were jealous guardians of their own dignity. Small wonder that Justinian was scared and that a man who won distinction in the provinces could expect to be diminished in the capital. Though Belisarius won two triumphs for his victories, he was allowed to celebrate neither of them completely. The spirit of the officers percolated down to the men. Inefficient and underdisciplined, the Byzantine army was the army of a state that preferred negotiation to battle and would rather buy its enemies off than conquer them.

If the army has changed, so has the face of war. It is made up of situations in which Caesar's disciplined legions would have been wasted. Warfare is no longer a question of the skilled deployment of troops on open ground, but rather of massed assaults on fortified cities where the besiegers triumph by attrition or brute strength. It is already medieval warfare; it is mechanical warfare fought with catapult, ballista, onager—cumbersome devices built to fire stone projectiles or giant arrows. Covered battering-rams force open city gates; the barbarians invent a lightweight ram, its shell made of laths rather than timbers, and its head pointed for greater penetration. Boiling oil is poured down from the battlements; at the siege of Petra, the Persian defenders are burnt alive when the wind changes. Spiked wooden grilles are propped against the outer walls, to be let down *à volonté* on the enemy below. And there even is trench warfare: Procopius has a whole passage which could be translated virtually unchanged into the vocabulary of Ypres and Mons. In an age in which each city has become an island, each man has turned into a miniature, mobile, independent fortress. Instead of the adaptable infantry of the old days, we have now the *cataphractarii,* heavily armored cavalry created in response to a new kind of enemy, and borrowing equipment from him. Their armor is described by Julian in a panegyric addressed to the Emperor Constantius.

And the cavalry that you commanded—who could count them? They were like statues on horseback, sheathed in

armor molded to each contour of the human form. It
covers the arms from wrist to elbow to shoulder. A coat
of mail offers protection behind and before. The head
and face are visored, giving the wearer the appearance
of a burnished statue; for every inch of him is covered,
down to his legs, his thighs and the very soles of his feet.
These are connected to the cuirass by a fine mask, so
that, look as hard as you like, you will see no part of the
body exposed. This woven mesh protects the hands as
well, and is so flexible that the wearers can even bend
their fingers.[4]

Given all this, it is hardly surprising that the Italian
campaign is a clumsy affair. There is little evidence of
a coherent strategy, only a series of individual battles in
which towns are taken and retaken, back and forth—
the pattern of Italian warfare, in fact, for centuries to
come. There is little originality on either side; when
one has found something that works, the other copies
it. There are stupendous *gaffes* and monumental mis-
calculations. The student of strategy will find little to
interest him here. And yet the tale is fascinating for the
panorama it offers of a moribund Italy about to be lost
to Byzantium forever; of old buildings turned to new
uses, of knights in clanking armor galloping across the
remnants of antiquity; of the medieval world, in fact,
trampling on the ruins of the classical.

Belisarius arrived in Italy trailing clouds of glory. He
must have seemed the ideal commander. Procopius
tells us that he was a handsome man, of commanding
stature. Although such compliments are virtually
obligatory, his biographer adds others which distinguish him from the general run of military men of his
time. Belisarius was known for his humility and was

generous to a fault. Horses and weapons lost by his men
in battle were replaced at his own expense. (He could
afford it; he was inordinately wealthy.) A just adminis-
trator, he never permitted his men to loot grain or fruit
in occupied territory. No one had ever seen him drunk.
And to top it all, he was successful. He came fresh from
his triumphant campaign against the Vandals in North
Africa, in the course of which he had written a new
chapter in the history of Jerusalem. The sacred treasures captured by Titus in 70 A.D. had been seized
during the Vandal sack of Rome and transported to
Carthage. Belisarius had recaptured them and sent
them to Constantinople, where they remained until the
Emperor, alarmed by their aura of bad luck, returned
them to Jerusalem. From there, they eventually disappeared again, this time for good.

Belisarius brought with him a mixed force of 4,000
regulars and 3,000 others. His under-officers were Constantius and Bessas from Thrace, and Peranius from
what is now Georgia. Obeying the imperial instructions, they proceeded deviously, spreading the word
that their fleet was heading for Libya, but really making
toward Sicily. The landing was trouble-free, and
Belisarius was able to subdue Catana, Syracuse and
other cities without interference. Only in Panormus
(Palermo) did the Goths put up a fight. This Belisarius
ingeniously and rapidly quelled by sending his fleet into
the harbor, filling the small boats with archers and
hoisting them to the masthead. Towering above the
walls, these improvised floating turrets scared the
Goths into submission. It happened to be the last day of
Belisarius' consulship—an office which by this time had
become entirely honorary—and he celebrated by riding through Syracuse and scattering gold coins to the
crowd.

Leaving garrisons to hold Syracuse and Palermo, Belisarius crossed the Straits of Messina. His army marched through Bruttium and Lucania, with the fleet sailing close inshore in support, and together they arrived at Naples. This plainly was to be no Syracuse. Naples was a well-protected city with a large Gothic garrison. While the fleet dropped anchor where it could command the harbor, Belisarius seized a fortress in the suburbs and opened negotiations with the populace. Naples was, as it always has been, a cosmopolitan city; people came from all over the world to set up businesses and trade. There was a Jewish colony, as in most important cities of the time—in Rome, the Jews lived in Trastevere—and representatives of otherEastern nations. The man with whom Belisarius chose to negotiate was one Antiochus, a Syrian, a prominent shipper and a long-time resident of Naples. Though mixed in race, however, the populace was one in mind: they wished no part of Belisarius. We shall find this pattern repeated throughout Italy. For those contented with Gothic rule, there was no reason to change.

Belisarius, under orders to make them change, laid siege to Naples. He began in a way that was to become *de rigueur* in this kind of warfare: by cutting the aqueducts that fed water into the city. One does not perhaps fully realize the importance of an organized water supply to Roman civilization until this period, when the cities began to be deprived of it. The aqueducts had been built for cities that were certain of their countryside. Now the unity is broken, the cities are driven in upon themselves, and the surest way to reduce a stronghold to submission is to deprive it of its water. If the citizens are lucky—as are the Neapolitans on this occasion—they have other sources of supply, wells within the walls. If not, they must surrender or die. And so the most desperate battles take place to protect the water supply, and the most resourceful ingenuity is employed to hide it. Elsewhere Procopius records the siege of Petra, where the Persian defenders cheated their besiegers by burying three pipelines, one beneath another. The top one left an obvious trail, so that the Romans quickly cut it; then they were unable to comprehend how the besieged could still get water. Finally they deduced the presence of the second and cut that, but they never dug deep enough to discover the third. The Neapolitans were not forced to this extremity. Their aqueducts undid them in the end, though for different reasons.

It dawned on one of Belisarius' men that one of the aqueducts would make an ideal entrance into the city. It was blocked, but the obstruction could be cleared; it was big enough for men to scramble through; and above all it was covered, not only outside, but for a considerable distance within the walls, "being carried on a high arch of baked brick." A double plan of assault was therefore evolved. One party was to wriggle through the aqueduct and attack the defenders from the rear, while another, larger force rushed the wall with scaling ladders. Both plans were nearly aborted by the extraordinary inefficiency which characterized the whole campaign. The scaling ladders, constructed out of sight of the walls, turned out to be too short, to the embarrassment of all concerned. Groping through the darkness of the aqueduct, the soldiers nearly lost their way, for there was nothing to tell them how far they had come. Finally they reached a place where the roof had caved in. Close by stood a dilapidated house inhabited by a single, poverty-stricken old woman, and an olive tree growing within reach gave the troops a way to scramble down. It is one of those rare moments when the modern reader comes within touching distance of antiquity. This casual vignette of a crumbling aqueduct, a ruined house, an olive tree, conjures up an image of Italy with which the traveler, especially in the south, is still familiar.

So Naples was taken by storm after a siege of some twenty days, and Belisarius displayed his clemency by restraining his army from indiscriminate slaughter. Three hundred cavalry were left to hold the conquered city, and a further detachment sent to Cumae; Belisarius now held the only two fortified cities in the district. On the heels of their success an invitation arrived from Pope Silverius in Rome: if Belisarius brought his army, the city would be yielded up to him without a struggle. The blandishment was persuasive. Up through Italy the army marched, and found that one thing at least had not succumbed to time: the Roman roads were still as good as ever. Belisarius followed the Appian Way northward, and Procopius, the eyewitness, comments that the stones had not slipped out of joint, worn away or even lost their polish. This road, he says, is one of the wonders of the world. Such testimonies to the excellence of the old builders continue to appear throughout his story. Some time later the Byzantine army, while besieging the city of Auximus, fails embarrassingly to destroy an ancient cistern and cannot even prise one pebble from the structure. "The artisans of old had taken great pride in their work, and had built so well that their construction would not yield to the ravages of men or time."[5]

Thus the army reached the gates of Rome. Somewhat surprisingly in view of the shiftiness of later papal negotiations, Silverius' prophecy turned out to be cor-

rect. As Belisarius marched in through one gate the
Goths marched out through another. "And so," says
Procopius, "after sixty years, Rome was for the Romans
again."

What sort of city was Rome then? One from which
most of the glory had departed; which had lost not only
its power and wealth, but its desire to regain them.
When Alaric had entered through the Salerian Gate on
August 24, 410, he had burned the houses there. They
still stood half-burned in Procopius' time. When, forty
years later, the Vandals had plundered the city, they
had torn off half the roof of the Temple of Jupiter on the
Capitol. Nothing had been done to replace it. Aurelian's walls were crumbling; the streets and *fora* were
no longer showplaces for the world; *rus* was beginning
to appear *in urbe*. Procopius tells a casual anecdote
which brings this changing Rome vividly before our
eyes. A herd of cows is passing through the Forum of
Vespasian. The Temple of Peace is down, struck by
lightning, but there is still an ancient fountain there
and a Greek statue of a heifer, so realistic that one of
the cattle leaves the herd and wanders over toward it.

This shabby Rome still owns its wonders. There are
the Christian wonders of the martyrs' shrines, particularly the basilicas of St. Peter and St. Paul. Both were
notable centers of pilgrimage. Around the former the
beggars congregated to accost the visitors, while inside,
devout Catholics lowered prayers on threads to the
apostle's grave. There are the pagan wonders, real or
manufactured. Procopius was obviously as gullible a
tourist as any wandering through the Forum today,
staring dutifully at "the tower where Nero played his
fiddle." He breathlessly relates the story of the statue of
Domitian, assembled like a jigsaw puzzle to illustrate

the way his body had been butchered by his enemies. He writes that he has seen the house of the historian Sallust; he has seen, housed in a special museum by the Tiber, the original ship of Aeneas—120 feet long, twenty-five feet wide, the keel and ribs not artificially joined, but all of a piece, like the trunk and branches of a tree. It goes without saying that this preposterous relic is never mentioned in classical literature. The later Romans were already alive to the value of the tourist trade.

Immediately upon his arrival in Rome, Belisarius set about refortifying the walls, which had fallen into ruin in many places, and prepared to resist the inevitable Gothic assault. The enemy had given way too easily and was bound to return. Winged merlons were constructed on the battlements and a moat dug round the wall. Grain from Sicily was stored in the public granaries and kept under close guard. The Romans were ordered to bring in provisions from the country; the city was preparing for a siege. Meanwhile, Belisarius sent out portions of his army to scout through Tuscany and engage with the enemy where they met them. They were victorious, but word came back of the imminence of a large Gothic force, including mailclad horses, and Belisarius thought it best to call his army in.

In time the Goths arrived as promised, and drew up near the fateful Milvian Bridge. This, though not the only way to cross the Tiber, was certainly the most convenient; and Belisarius, playing for time, had fortified it with tower, gates and garrison. They were of no use. The soldiers posted at the bridge deserted, the Goths crossed without impedance, and the next day Belisarius, making a sally out, met them face to face. In the ensuing cavalry action Belisarius, with a panache equaled only by his stupidity, fought in the front ranks like a common soldier, riding a gray horse with a white face and offering a perfect target. Finally, after some inconclusive fighting, the Goths retreated to the protection of their infantry and the Byzantines to the fortifications of Rome. In the contretemps that followed, the Romans in the city refused to open the gates, fearing that they might let the Goths in too. They failed to recognize Belisarius in the fading light, for he was covered with blood and dust; besides, the rumor had gone out that he was dead. Thus the army, stranded between walls and moat, began to panic, and the Goths, seeing their plight, closed in to finish them off. Belisarius in desperation attacked first, and the Romans were encouraged by this sight to throw open the gates. Fires burned all night along the walls, and the city watched and waited.

There were fourteen large gates in Rome at this time, and several smaller ones, each a danger point which had to be defended. Belisarius had walled them up—as much, it seems, to stop the Romans' getting out as to stop the Goths' getting in. The Gothic army was divided into several camps. Most were on the left bank of the Tiber, though one was entrenched on the right, not far from the Basilica of St. Peter and what was then called the Cornelian Gate. Over the river too, apart from the main body of the city, though still fortified with its own walls, was the hill of the Janiculum, where the water mills turned busily in the streams brought down by the aqueducts, grinding flour for Roman bread.

They stopped turning when the Goths cut off the water. Belisarius blocked the aqueducts with stones, fearing the same trick that he had played at Naples, but he could not turn the water on again: no mills, no flour, no bread. Improvisation saved the day. Belisarius lined up pairs of boats below the Aurelian Bridge, with water wheels between them. They turned in the force of the current, and the Romans could still grind their flour. A macabre struggle now took place over these floating mills. The Goths threw dead bodies and fallen trees into the Tiber to jam the wheels and break them. Retaliating, the Romans stretched chains across the river to fend off floating objects. So the mills continued working, but the Romans had another complaint. Their cherished public baths had run dry. It must have seemed like the end of the world.

The next phase of the siege began with the Goths' making massive preparations for an assault on the walls. They built huge siege towers drawn by teams of oxen, scaling ladders, battering rams and bundles of faggots to throw into the moat. In the city the Romans built their own machines which they mounted on the turrets. When the Goths moved to the assault, the Romans disabled their siege engines by the simple process of picking off the oxen as they came within bowshot. The Goths, who had overlooked this eventuality, retired disconcerted and turned to other means. Much of the fighting took place around Hadrian's Tomb and the Basilica of St. Peter. A colonnade connected the basilica with the Aelian Bridge, and the Goths were able to use this as shelter for their assault on the tomb. Hadrian's monument, however, proved an impregnable fortress. Its great drum shape made a natural defense-work: it had been further protected by the extension of the walls, and, when all else failed, the defenders started to prize the statues from the top and hurl them on the enemy below.

There was desperate fighting elsewhere in the city. Near the Pincian Gate lay a stretch of broken wall. The inhabitants had forbidden Belisarius to rebuild it, claiming that it was under the protection of St. Peter. It apparently was, for the Goths were unable to force an entry. They did manage to penetrate the walls round the Vivarium, the Roman zoo, but they were soon repulsed and their siege engines burned. The day ended with the massed Romans on the walls singing hymns of triumph and claiming 30,000 Gothic dead.

Yet it must nave been clear to Belisarius that the struggle was far from over. He wrote to Constantinople for reinforcements and meanwhile cleared the decks for action and increased his food supply by evacuating all non-combatants from the city. Women, children and servants were packed off to Naples. Some went by boat from Portus, the harbor of Rome, a few miles off; others by foot along the Appian Way. They were happily unmolested, for the Goths did not have sufficient men to invest the whole city. Even so, the refugees suffered considerable hardship, and their unease spread to those remaining when Pope Silverius and others were suspected of treason. Belisarius was forced to change the locks on the city gates at frequent intervals and to keep a nightly watch for deserters. Soldiers with guard dogs patrolled outside the walls.

Psychologically the Romans were ill-prepared to withstand a siege. Their city had been too long impregnable, too remote for centuries from the scene of actual fighting. Now, whenever the enemy beat at the gates, the Romans all too rapidly broke down. During Alaric's assault there had been rumors of cannibalism; they were to be heard again during this crisis. Spiritually, too, the Romans showed their weakness. Under stress they were inclined to forsake their recent Christianity for the reassurance of a traditional paganism. This is not surprising: in many parts of the Empire, Christianity, even after two hundred years, was still only skin deep. When Julian the Apostate was traveling through Ilios in the Troad, he found not only that the people were worshiping a statue of Hector, but that the practice was defended by the Christian bishop Pegasius, on the grounds that the locals had as much right to worship their heroes as the Christians had to venerate their martyrs. And it is clear that, long after Julian's time, residual pagan practices were to be found throughout the Empire. Although, after the fourth century, pagans no longer played an active role in politics—Theodosius had explicitly deprived them of such rights—their continued existence is proved by Justinian's legislation, which sought religious uniformity, and Alexandria, in Egypt, was to remain a pagan stronghold for some time afterward.

In such a context it is hardly surprising to find the Roman patricians consulting the Sibylline Books, the renowned collection of oracular sayings that had advised Rome from time immemorial. Whatever dubious connection with actuality this rag-bag of prophecies may once have possessed had long since disappeared. The first collection had been destroyed in the Capitol fire of 83 B.C. The second had been burned by the Vandal Stilicho in A.D. 405. This was now the third collection, which Procopius claims to find totally incomprehensible: it has no apparent form or order, he says, but jumps about in space and time. Some citizens also attempted to open the Temple of Janus, resurrecting another cherished pagan custom. This small bronze temple stood in the Forum to the right of the arch of

Septimius Severus as you look towards the Capitol, just in front of the Mamertine Prison. In earlier times the door had traditionally stood open in time of war and had been closed in time of peace. "But the Romans," says Procopius, "who were as strong for Christianity as anybody could be, no longer used to open these same doors, even in wartime."[6] Now, in their fear, they tried to do so, only to find that the doors had rusted fast.

The battle now shifted downriver and brought new evidence of the decay of antiquity. The Tiber, in its lower reaches, divided in two. The left-hand channel led to Ostia, Rome's earliest port and, through much of imperial times, its most important. By now, however, it had been superseded by Portus (whose name means simply "harbor") on the right bank, and Procopius writes its gloomy epitaph: "a city of great repute in the old days, but now not a wall is left standing . . . the road from Ostia to Rome is abandoned to the woods and trees; it does not even run beside the Tiber any more."[7] Without a towpath the river was useless, for goods were brought upstream on barges hauled by oxen. But the towpath on the other fork was still in good shape, as was Portus itself, and there were many barges there prepared for river service. Portus thus became a natural target for both Goths and Romans. Whoever held the port controlled the lifeline to the city.

Portus fell to the Goths with disgraceful ease. At one stroke they had made it impossible for Rome to be provisioned by sea. Ostia was useless, for ships were not even able to put in there any longer; the nearest harbor was now Antium (Anzio), a day's journey down the coast. Even then there was great difficulty in transferring the cargoes to Rome, because of the scarcity of men. Then, fortunately, the hoped-for reinforcements

—Huns and Slavonians—arrived and Belisarius was able to turn to the offensive. In a lucky encounter a sizable Gothic force was encircled and destroyed. Taking heart, the Romans clamored for a decisive engagement, and Belisarius, against his better judgment, was forced to agree. His plan was to drive a wedge between the Gothic forces, divided on both sides of the Tiber.

In the early morning, battle commenced. Until midday it remained a shooting engagement, with the Roman archers driving the enemy back upon their own camp. In the Plain of Nero also things were quiet until noon. Then the Romans began their main onslaught. But the army was even more unmanageable than usual, a heterogenous force including many sailors—presumably refugees from Portus—and the servants who still remained in the city, none of whom had proper armor. Lacking the experience and intelligence to follow their attack through or even to destroy the Tiber bridges, they stopped to plunder the Gothic camp. Observing them so engaged, the Goths regrouped, charged and slaughtered them. Elsewhere, too, the Goths made a sudden recovery, driving the Romans back against the walls. There ensued a dismal repetition of the earlier scene, with the soldiers outside howling to be let in and the populace inside too terrified to open the gates. A massacre was prevented only by the fact that one side was as lackadaisical as the other. The Goths simply grew bored, turned their horses and rode away.

After this, enthusiasm for a pitched battle rapidly diminished. The two sides watched and waited, venturing out in occasional skirmishes. One brief engagement took place in a disused stadium outside the walls, perhaps the stadium of Caligula. A party of Goths was ambushed in the arena, and the Byzantines, shooting from the cover of the surrounding streets, picked them off at will. There was some fighting also when the imperial paymaster landed at Taracina and Belisarius had to give him an escort into Rome. But it was not money the army wanted as much as food, and by the next campaigning season the plight of the besieged was critical. With the coming of spring the city was devastated by plague and famine. There was still some grain left for the soldiers, but civilians went hungry. At least the plague kept the Goths away; they contented themselves with a discreet blockade. To the south of Rome, between the Appian and Latin ways, were two aqueducts which met and crossed at Torre Fiscale. A little nearer the city they recrossed, thus enclosing with their arches a considerable stretch of ground. This the Goths transformed into a fortress, walling up the lower arches and installing a garrison of 7,000 men. It was now impossible to provision Rome either by sea or land.

The siege of Rome now reads like the siege of Paris. As hunger increased, prices soared, and a flagrant black market sprang into being. As long as there was still corn growing outside the city walls, the more venturesome soldiers would gather what they could by night and sell it at exorbitant prices. The poor lived on herbs, or sausages made from dead mules. When even this source of grain dried up and the rich were going hungry too, the Romans clamored that Belisarius should stake everything on one last, desperate battle. But even as he debated, the people's mood changed. Rumor swept through the city that a relief force had arrived, that supplies had landed in Naples. Roused from his lethargy, Belisarius became a new man. Procopius too at this moment came into his own. He was dispatched to Naples to find ships, load them with men and as much grain as he could, and sail them into Ostia. The Romans would bring them up-river somehow. While he was gone, Belisarius, in his new burst of energy, began to turn the tables on the Goths. He would harass *their* food supply. A garrison marched out to Taracina, another to Tibur (Tivoli); a stockade went up round the Basilica of St. Paul, outside the Ostia Gate (now the Porta San Paolo), which was at this point still unfortified, though like St. Peter's it was connected by a colonnade to the city. Procopius notes that for Christians and Arians alike, the buildings kept their sanctity still; throughout all the vicissitudes of the siege, the services at both basilicas continued undisturbed.

Procopius talks happily of his participation in these events. We are reminded of Xenophon and the march of the Ten Thousand ten centuries before; again the chronicler assumes command. Arriving in Campania he made haste to carry out his orders. He collected 500 men, loaded "a great number of ships" with grain and made ready to return. He was still in Naples when Vesuvius rumbled, and so added his name to the long list of chroniclers of that angry mountain. Vesuvius had already become part of Byzantine lore. During the eruption of 472, ashes, so they said, had been carried as far as Constantinople. Procopius, however, is less concerned with the violence of the mountain than with its healthful propensities. It is, he notes, a popular resort for consumptives; doctors have been sending their patients here from remote times. Of Pompeii, of course, he makes no mention. It had been buried for five hundred years and forgotten nearly as long.

Fortune decided to favor the Byzantines for a while. As Procopius was preparing to move his force out, still more reinforcements—consisting of 3,000 Isaurians and 800 Thracian horsemen—arrived. This large force, with plenty of provisions, embarked for Rome. How to get them in? On land, Belisarius flung open the Flaminian Gate and launched a diversionary movement. Procopius contributes the gruesome detail that one Trajan, an officer, had the iron barb of an arrow embedded in his face, and it was still working its way out three years later. Under cover of the fighting the fleet arrived at Ostia. It was difficult to transport the goods up the Tiber for the reasons already mentioned. The towpath had fallen into disuse, the meanderings of the river made the use of sail all but impossible, and rowers would have to fight the current and the Goths at the same time. Nevertheless the Byzantines managed it. All the ship's boats were reinforced with palisades of planks. They were then loaded to capacity with freight; archers and sailors went on board; and as soon as the wind was favorable, the little fleet began to creep upstream, with the army proceeding along the bank in support. Inch by inch, by sail or oar, they made their way toward the gates of Rome; and the Goths, presumably staggered by this ingenuity, offered no resistance whatsoever.

The positions were now reversed. It was the Goths who were going hungry. Though still in possession of Portus, they were denied the use of the harbor as long as the Byzantine fleet commanded the sea. They were also compelled to abandon the port of Centumcellae (Civita Vecchia) further up the coast, because they could no longer get provisions through. Despondency was rife. Belisarius, increasingly venturesome, sent out detachments into the surrounding districts. Tentatively, the Goths began to sue for peace, sending envoys to the Emperor in Constantinople. And the Christian Church was once more turning militant. Datius, a priest of Milan, came galloping into Rome to declare that with a few men he could recover not only Milan itself, but the whole of Liguria for the Emperor.

Finally the news of yet another army marching into Italy withdrew the pressure from Rome. Through Pisenum it came, skirting the towns like Auximus and Urbinus (Urbino) that contained large Gothic garrisons, but picking off the more susceptible targets. Learning that their base at Ravenna was threatened, the Goths made ready to withdraw from Rome, and the citizens, looking out over the ramparts in the first light of morning, saw only the smoldering embers of the abandoned camps. Belisarius lost no time in pursuing. Once more the Milvian Bridge became the site of a pitched battle, in which the Goths panicked and did themselves more harm than they suffered from the enemy. Many fell into the river. The rest, the tattered remnants of the army, struggled off toward Ravenna.

This, then, was a sort of victory. But there was still no peace, only a pause for breath, disturbed by random campaigning and desultory negotiations. There was dissension in the Byzantine high command. Narses, the dwarf and eunuch who had led the relief army, insisted that the war was as good as won, while Belisarius claimed that there was much fighting still ahead. Neither of them seems to have considered whether the fighting was worth the effort. Northern Italy was a blasted land, a husk from which the traditional way of life had departed, exhausted by the endless progression of armies. Procopius recounts the gloomy catalogue of stories: of the goat who, taking its cue from the legend of Romulus and Remus, suckled an abandoned child; of the utter desolation of Aemilia, with the people of besiged cities reduced to eating hides soaked in water. Refugees who fled to Tuscany found little comfort there, for famine was everywhere in the land. The Tuscans ground a sort of flour from acorns, but this induced disease; in Pisenum alone, more than 50,000 died, so dehydrated that their skin was cracked and blackened like charred wood. Some turned cannibal: there was a legend of two women in the country above Ariminum who had killed and eaten seventeen people. Everywhere the corpses lay unburied, so emaciated that even the carrion birds passed them by.

Against this background the heroic speeches rang more than usually false. There is a note of desperation in Belisarius' description of Rome's rival: "This city of Milan, which has outgrown every other in Italy; which has the most citizens within its walls; which of all cities has been most smiled upon by fortune; which, leaving all things else aside, is a bastion against the Germans and the other barbarians; which is, we well might say, the outpost of the Roman Empire."[8] So far had the Empire shrunk that Milan was now its furthest outpost; so far had Milan shrunk that its sole value now was as a fortress. Yet even this outpost was soon to fall. The spokesmen of the Church had been too optimistic. Milan, so briefly Roman, was forced to surrender to the Goths again; its entire male population, to the number of 300,000, was killed and the women were taken off to slavery. The Byzantine army intended for the relief of Milan turned tail and marched back to Rome again. More negotiations followed, terms were struck, and Belisarius returned briefly to Constantinople with a group of Gothic nobles. Procopius records his popularity in the city—the unfortunate popularity which antagonized Justinian and deprived him of a full triumph:

It was the popular diversion in Byzantium to watch Belisarius as he made his daily progress from his home to the agora and back again. It was a spectacle of inexhausible attraction, for he was never alone: an enormous procession of Vandals, Goths and Moors was continually at his heels.[9]

But Belisarius was not destined to remain long in Byzantium. Changing events brought him back to Italy to continue the dreary war and to participate for the second time in a siege of Rome—this time on the outside, trying to get in. The most pressing of these changes was the shift of Gothic leadership: Totila, who now assumed the rule, was fiercely hostile to Byzantine interests and lost no time in reopening the campaign. In rapid succession the Byzantines lost Florentia and threw away a chance to take Verona, because, as usual, they were too busy counting the spoils. Totila swung through Tuscany, capturing cities right and left en route; but he prudently skirted Rome and headed for the south, where he razed the walls of Beneventum and laid siege to Naples. Two expeditions were sent out from Constantinople to draw him off; both failed because of wasted time, bad luck and habitual mismanagement. The fleet which might have saved Naples was held at sea by a ferocious storm. And so Naples surrendered to a victor who treated her with surprising clemency; her citizens were nurtured from starvation after the siege and permitted to depart for whatever destination they wished. Restraining his soldiers from reprisals, Totila contented himself with leveling the walls of the city, so that Naples might never be re-armed against him.

This was the Italy to which Belisarius returned. He landed, as Totila soon discovered through his spies, with a small force only, nor was there hope of finding local reinforcements. Procopius quotes the general's letter to Justinian, couched in a tone so far removed (as Gibbon saw) from the usual circumlocution of Byzantine rhetoric as to suggest that, for once, the biographer is quoting his subject verbatim and setting down the plain words of a desperate man:

> Greatest of Kings, we have arrived in Italy. We have no arms, no horses and no money; and these are things of which a man needs a good supply if he is to wage war adequately. Though we scouted diligently through Thrace and Illyricum, we collected only a handful of men; and these are of poor quality, having no weapons of their own and being altogether inexperienced in the art of war. As for the men who were left behind in Italy, they are too few to be of any use and terrified of the enemy besides; they have been beaten so many times that their spirits are broken. They did not merely break ranks and run. They threw away their weapons in their panic; they left their horses on the battlefield. And then there is the money. There is none forthcoming out of Italy; for Italy belongs to the Goths again.[10]

As usual, Constantinople maintained a discreet silence. Belisarius, faithful to his command against all obstacles, proceeded to move on Rome, whose inhabitants, again blockaded, had rediscovered the agonies of starvation. Their position now in fact was worse than it had been before. This time the Goths held Naples and the sea-route; with a fleet of light craft they could hold the whole coast to ransom. What was more, the Goths now held Tibur, up-river from Rome. It was no longer possible to send in supplies from this side. Belisarius could only watch and wait, deprived of action till the

reinforcements came. At long last more troops arrived
—though led by his old enemy, the eunuch Narses—
and Belisarius made haste to reinforce Portus, in the
hope of keeping that harbor clear for any supplies that
might manage to get through. Sallies were made
against the enemy, but with no effect. One of them
went so disastrously that the Byzantine commander of
the Portus garrison and most of his men were killed.
One disaster spawned another. Pope Vigilius, now safe
in Sicily, had sent a fleet of merchantmen with grain.
The convoy managed to penetrate the blockade and
made for Portus. Seeing the ships approaching, the
Goths laid an ambush on the shore. On the walls of
Portus the remnants of the beleaguered garrison
waved and shouted, trying to warn the vessels off, but
the sailors took the noise for greeting and sailed straight
into the harbor, to be captured en masse. Among the
prisoners was a Bishop Valentine, who was first interro-
gated., then had his hands chopped off. Pope Vigilius,
hearing of the fate of his fleet, made for the safety of
Constantinople.

Within the walls of Rome, all was despair. The starving population pleaded with the military either to feed
them or, in charity, to kill them. With more logic than
compassion, the generals replied that the first was impossible and the second a sin in the eyes of God. Yet the
true horror of the situation was that these men were
lying . There was grain in the city, but it was reserved
for the garrison; while the officers did their best to
appease the population by affirming that Belisarius
must send relief before long, the soldiers happily
revived the black market, selling off the military supplies at seven gold pieces a bushel. Those who could not
afford it lived off bran. Oxen captured in sallies outside

the walls fetched fifty gold pieces; the poor had to be content with dead horses and worse. A large proportion of the population was picking nettles "such as grow in abundance about the walls and among the ruins in all parts of the city" and boiling them to make the only food they had. Many died of starvation or committed suicide. Procopius records a Roman father of five who jumped into the Tiber as his family looked on, because he could no longer bear their cries for food. The black market itself could not survive when the stores were depleted. When the gold currency gave out, citizens brought their household goods to the Forum in barter. Finally all but the commander himself had run out of grain, and nettles became the staple diet for the city. The military authorities were compelled to let the citizens depart if they could; but the refugees were too weak to travel and either died on the road or were captured by the enemy.

In a desperate attempt to retrieve the situation, Belisarius sailed round the foot of Italy and headed for the port of Rome. The Goths made haste to close off the Tiber with a wooden bridge at the narrows. At each end was a fortified watchtower of stout timbers, and as a first line of defense, some way downstream, an iron chain was stretched from bank to bank. Undeterred by these elaborate precautions, Belisarius constructed two floating siege-towers, each higher than the enemy fortifications and lashed to a pair of skiffs. In addition he strengthened some two hundred sailing boats with wooden walls, manned them with soldiers and loaded them with grain. The bizarre fleet set sail upstream, towing the floating towers behind. A message had been sent to Rome appealing for a diversionary sally from the walls, but no help was forthcoming. Bessas, the commander-in-chief, was the only person happy with the siege. He was selling off his own hoarded grain at record prices.

The fleet inched its way up-river. In the event, the iron chain proved no obstacle: the guards were easily put to flight and the obstruction lifted out. As the boats hove into sight, the Goths rushed from their watchtowers to mass on the bridge. Now was the time for the floating towers. They were pulled into position, with a skiff on top of each. The skiffs were set alight and dropped onto the enemy's watchtowers, burning all their occupants alive. Appalled by this disaster, the rest took to their heels, but once again the Byzantine lack of discipline snatched defeat from the jaws of victory. Seeing what had happened, the remaining forces were so exhilarated that they charged without orders. The dreary pattern of the campaign repeated itself: taken by surprise, the Goths ran before the asault; then, while the Byzantines engaged in plunder, returned and slaughtered them. Belisarius, finding his rear threatened and no sign of help from the city, was compelled to return to Portus.

In Rome, Bessas continued to grow fat on the black market and to neglect the defense of the city. The population had been reduced to virtually nothing, no proper watch was kept, and officers had abandoned their regular rounds. Four of the guards, Isaurians, turned to treachery. Sliding down ropes from the walls near the Porta Asinaria, they brought in a small Gothic force to show how vulnerable the city was. Totila was at first suspicious and sent several parties in to reconnoiter, but was finally convinced and brought a detachment up to the walls by night. Four Goths selected for their strength and couraged climbed the walls, hacked

through the wooden beams and flung open the gates to
the invaders. As Totila's troops poured in, the surviving
defenders panicked. Most of the soldiers fled with their
officers through another gate. The rest took refuge in
the sanctuaries: the Basilica of St. Peter was crowded
with them. Deaf for once to pleas for mercy, Totila gave
his Goths license to plunder. Rome had become an
obsession in his mind, a thing of hate; he was fully determined to raze the city to the ground and pasture sheep
upon its wreckage. Some of the principal buildings
were about to fall when Belisarius, to his eternal credit,
came with the voice of reason to stop him, pointing out
that Totila would merely be demolishing his own prosperity.

Totila had reason to be sorry, for in this shuttlecock
war it was now Belisarius' turn. Totila pressed on with
his campaigns elsewhere and left a garrisoned Rome
behind him. Making one last spendid sally from Portus,
Belisarius retook it. About one-third of the walls had
been torn down by Totila before he left, and there was
no time to replace them, only time to heap the fallen
stones together and protect them with a wooden pali-
sade. In less than a month the city was refortified and
reprovisioned by boats which, in the enemy's absence,
could ply safely up the Tiber from Portus to Rome. As
soon as he heard the news, Totila turned about to smack
the city down. There had been no time and no artisans
to repair the broken gates, and it was in these gaping
holes that the fighting was fiercest. One wave of barbarians after another failed to retake the city, and their
frustration caused dissension in the ranks. Totila's
standard-bearer was killed, a bad omen, and his com-
rades began to call him a fool for not having destroyed
the city while he had the chance. And so the heart went

out of the attack. The Goths shambled off toward Tibur, contenting themselves with tearing up all the bridges except the Milvian.

But the heart had gone out of the defense too. The endless months of campaigning had brought lassitude and satiety. In 548 Justinian finally sent another army, and Belisarius was relieved to campaign in the south. From there, and cruising aimlessly up and down the coast, he watched the slow erosion of all that he had so painfully won. He finally returned ingloriously to Constantinople and retirement in Panteichion (Pendile) on the Asiatic shore; but his enjoyment of his rich estate was curbed by the continuing suspicion, and finally the outright hostility, of Justinian.

Few people, except Belisarius, came out well from this conflict, and even he, one suspects, gained much of his luster by comparison with the incompetence and corruption of his colleagues. The Christian Church, as an institution, survived with honor; Totila himself, after his triumphal entry into Rome, went straight to St. Peter's to pray. Some individual clerics emerged with their dignity intact, notably Deacon Pelagius, a figure of towering humanity in the besieged city, who gave all his wealth to the starving poor, tried continually but vainly to mediate with the attackers, and pointed out to Totila, as he was about to ravage the city, that he would merely be destroying his own property. Other members of the Church do not come off so well. The record of papal irresponsibility is appalling.

And what of Rome itself? The city was captured and recaptured five times during the reign of Justinian, finally by the eunuch Narses (who took up quarters in the Palatium) in 552. Each change of hands had left its mark. Totila had burned large portions of the city, par-

ticularly along the Tiber. A third of the walls were
down and had never been properly replaced. Fields
had been planted within the walls to eke out the food
supply of the starving population. And the population
itself, by the end of the war, had been reduced to a
mere 40,000. The city was little more than a sea of
rubble, above which reared the surviving monuments
that would soon be used as castles by contending parties. If the Theater of Marcellus had any virtue now, it
was not as a place for drama and song; Romans prized
it for its command of the bridge across the Tiber. That
Rome did not disappear from sight altogether is a tribute no less to the cohesive force of the Christian
Church, which continued to pull a steady stream of
pilgrims to the mother city, than to the continuing
magic of the ancient name.

Ravenna remained, and with it some memory of
grandeur. Its people looked upon themselves as heirs to
the authentic Roman spirit, as the name of their district, the Romagna, testified. Secure, it flourished
through Justinian's time and after: the building Emperor adorned it with the work that is its greatest glory.
The Church of San Vitale, though begun in 525 when
the Goths still controlled the city, was not consecrated
until 548, when Italy for a while seemed Byzantine
again. It is roughly contemporary with the church of SS.
Sergius and Bacchus in Constantinople, and poses a
similar structural problem: how to modulate a poly-
gonal interior into a dome? The mosaics recapture the
radiance for which we search in vain in the Eastern
capital. Even on a gray day San Vitale shines. Flanking
the altar is the imperial court, picked out in vibrant
colors set on gold. On the one side, Theodora with the

ladies of her retinue, attenuated, kohl- and almond-
eyed, exotic, oriental—though it was said that no picture could do justice to her beauty.

> The artist made a fair shot at her eyes.
> But that is all. The texture of her hair,
> Her glowing golden skin—these are not there.
> To picture Theodora you need one
> Skill and one alone—to paint the sun.[11]

The Empress waits beneath a sea-green, iridescent
dome, among striped awnings, by a running fountain.
Facing her across the altar is her husband with his
guards and courtiers.

On Justinian's left hand, his name labeled in large
letters, is the Archbishop Maximian, during whose ten-
ure the Church was consecrated. He is worth noting,
for in many ways he is typical of the political church-
men of his time. He attracted stories. Once, it is said, he
discovered a buried treasure chest:

> He took counsel with himself; and since he could not
> now hide it, he ordered a large ox to be brought to him,
> and when it had been slaughtered, filled the gutted belly
> with gold coins. At the same time he ordered shoe-
> makers to come before him and had them make him a
> pair of great goat-skin brogues. These he filled with solid
> gold. All that was left over he took to Constantinople and
> offered to Justinian. When the Emperor saw it, he rend-
> ered thanks and then questioned him closely to find if
> there was more. But Maximian swore to the Emperor,
> "So may God protect you and your immortal soul, there
> was nothing left over but what I spent on my belly and
> my boots.[12]

For his reward he was given the archdiocese of Ravenna, and he spent his hoard in buying the affections of a populace at first little disposed to like him. Once in Ravenna he fought loyally for its interests. Another story concerns a typical battle for the possession of sacred relics, waged by every church of substance with an enthusiastic disregard for honor and fair play. The churches of Byzantium were built literally on the blood and bones of martyrs. The Empress Helena, mother of Constantine, had made relic-hunting fashionable when, on a journey to the Holy Land, she had discovered the True Cross. Constantinople had the skull and arm of John the Baptist. The city of Edessa for a long while claimed to possess an autograph letter from Jesus, explaining that He was too busy to come to cure the local ruler of his gout. Now Maximian, a great builder himself, tried to appropriate the body of the apostle Andrew for Ravenna, but was forestalled by Justinian who ordered him to bring it to Constantinople instead.

Justinian rejoiced when he saw it and said, "Father, do not take it too hard. The first Rome possesses one brother, the second Rome the other; the brother apostles to the sister-cities. I cannot bring myself to yield him up to you, since where the seat of empire is, there too should the apostle's body be." But the blessed Maximian answered him, "Lord, let it be as you command. Yet this one thing I ask of you: that tonight my priest and I may sing a service of psalms over his body." To this the Emperor willingly consented. They kept their vigil throughout the night, and when the rites were accomplished, Maximian took up his sword, delivered an oration over the body, cut off the apostle's beard at the chin. . . . and took it back with him to his own seat.[13]

After Maximian's death the Ravenna churches continued to flourish, for Justinian bestowed on his successors all the ecclesiastical property of the Goths. As the center of the exarchate, Ravenna headed those few portions of Italy that still kept faith with Byzantium—cities mainly in the south, Lecce, Bari and others, where Byzantine buildings may still be seen in the streets, and whose influence spilled over into Sicily. It must have been easy in that small enclosed world to imagine that the Roman empire still lived. Some time toward the end of the seventh century, an anonymous clerk of Ravenna compiled a gazetteer of the known world. On the one hand, it is a testimony to the bastard culture that Ravenna represented, a fusion, like its architecture, of Roman, Gothic and Greek: the sources come from all three, and more often than not a Roman place-name is cited in a Greek form. On the other hand, it takes for granted to perpetuation of the world in more or less the same form as the Romans had left it, mutated a little perhaps, admitting new influences here and there, but given a new cohesiveness by the spirit of Christendom.

> There is an island in the western sea called Britain. It appears to be settled now by Saxons, a race who accompanied their chieftain, Anschis, from the former kingdom of Saxonia.

But so far as the compiler is concerned, these Saxons are newcomers, *arrivistes:* Britain is still a Roman island, though the last Roman army left its shores in Theodosius' time. Even the names of former Roman estates have become embedded in the local consciousness as town-names.

In time Ravenna fell to other enemies, not least of which was the rot from within. The Langobardi (Lombards) occupied Venice and pressed Ravenna hard. Gothic monuments, including a number of notable statues, were destroyed or carried off elsewhere. One of the worst offenders was Charlemagne, the Emperor who came to dinner following his coronation in Rome, made light conversation with the nervous clergy and took back to France, as a memento, a handsome statue of Theodoric. Stripped of its importance, Ravenna degenerated into a medieval town. We hear of gang warfare in the streets, pursued with vigor as a Sunday pastime and looked forward to throughout the week. When Galla Placidia died, it was written, a star burned in the heavens for thirty days. When Charlemagne departed, there was an eclipse of the sun, and men saw strange sights and wonders. It was one more in the long series of Ravenna's deaths and resurrections.

5. THE CHURCH OUTGOING: MERCHANTS AND MISSIONARIES

By the end of his reign Justinian could, at least in his own estimation, look upon an ordered and harmonious city at the center of a world reunited by his achievements. His Constantinople, surrounded by a twelve-mile circuit of walls, rose in beauty to the pinnacle of the imperial palace, crowned in turn by Haghia Sophia. Its streets were wide and spacious, with colonnades running the length of them; its buildings were limited by edict to a hundred feet—no shambling Roman tenements here—with their ground floors windowed with translucent marble or alabaster. The harbors were thriving. Byzantium could boast that Mede and Celt alike must come to her to trade:

> The Indian, bringing elephants and pearls,
> The man from Carthage, bending servile knee;
> All means of livelihood derive from me.[1]

As the foreigners sailed in, the Byzantines went questing out:

> Now Spring unveils her face to sniff the breeze,
> And there is beauty in green fields again.

Ships leave their beaches now; the cables sing
That haul them down the shipway to the sea.
Go with good heart about your voyage, sailors.
See, the sails swagger in the breeze. You go
To gentle labor, happy merchantmen.[2]

They went out to a world that, at least in theory, held
no more terrors:

Now Roman traveler, go your way in peace
And bounding joy. From inmost Scythia
Through the forbidding woods of Sousa go
To India beneath. If you should thirst
Upon your journey, drink Hydaspes' streams
Bound to your service. Walk safe in the dark
Past sunset, through the Herculean gates.
On the sandy shores of Spain, stretch at your ease
Above the lovely threshold of the sea
Where Africa and Europe, grazing horns,
Frustrate the landbound voyager. Pass by
The tip of Libya, Nasamanes' land
And reach the Syrtis, where the shelving sea
Is driven by the south winds from the shore
To make an ebb-tide pathway, shifting soft
Beneath the feet, where vessels sailed before.
Never will you be on foreign soil.
Go east, west, south or north, these lands belong
To our great Emperor, who in his wisdom
Embraces all the world in his domain.[3]

The testimony of his flatterers was supported by Justinian's enemies, who complained that there was no
limit to his ambition:

The whole wide world will not satisfy this man. For
him, it is not enough to rule over all mankind. He casts

his eye on heaven too, and searches out the dwellers
beyond Ocean, with a mind to creating a new universe.[4]

Flattery aside, however, the Byzantines could for a
while sail with a fair degree of safety. There were of
course natural hazards: a particularly alarming one for
several years was a whale whom the Byzantines nick-
named Porphyrios. He used to frolic in the harbor and
menace the shipping until, while chasing a school of
dolphins, he ran aground and stuck hard and fast. The
people came down and dismembered him with axes.
And there were the old hazards of bad winds and un-
charted reefs that had always made the coastal waters
of the Mediterranean dangerous to travel. It is through
them that we know a good deal about the ships the
Byzantines sailed in—too much, perhaps, for the classical archaelogist, who would rather find more Greek
and Roman vessels and fewer from the later period.
One of the most interesting and best documented of
these wrecks was found off Yassi Ada, a small island
near the southern tip of Turkey, lying between the
Greek islands of Cos and Calymnos and the town of
Bodrum on the mainland. Like Schliemann's Troy,
Yassi Ada was full of wrecks: the underwater archaelo-
gists found at least fifteen in this submarine graveyard,
ranging in time from the third century B.C., through a
Rhodian vessel of early imperial Rome, to a nineteenth-
century warship and a local caïque of the 1930s. All had
fallen victim to a reef some 150 yards west of the island,
a centuries-old menace to the important trade route
down the island-strewn coast.

The Byzantine wreck was the third in chronological
sequence. Discovered in 1958, it was subjected to a
series of investigations over the next six years: these

have become, in many ways, models for underwater procedure and have made it possible to reconstruct in virtually every detail a small trading vessel of the seventh century A.D.

The ship was built about 615, perhaps as far north as the Black Sea. It was a forty-tonner, riding on a forty-foot keel. The hull construction shows how shipyard practices were changing. It was traditional in the Mediterranean to employ the monocoque method, in which the hull was built up from strips of planking (strakes) connected by a series of mortise-and-tenon joints. Only after the hull was completed was it strengthened with ribs nailed on from inside. This was in contrast to the method of northern countries, which was to build the skeleton first and then apply the strakes over it. The Yassi Ada vessel is interesting for two reasons. First, it shows a tendency to economize on the old, laborious mortises and tenons. Instead of running the whole length of the plank, they are used only at three-foot intervals. Second, the over-all structure is a compromise, with monocoque construction below the waterline and the northern method above. We can see here the shipbuilders of the Aegean and its neighbor waters responding to growing pressures of time and money, and also to new ideas infiltrating from places hitherto unheard-of.

When completed, the ship was about sixty-three feet long, with a seventeen-foot beam. There was a single central mast, and projecting deck beams for the steering oars (the rudder had yet to be thought of); while most of the below-decks space was reserved for cargo, there was a galley at the rear, its tiled roof projecting above the deckline, which seems to have doubled as ship's mess and captain's stores. Here, in his cramped eight feet of space, the cook labored over an open fire made up on a bed of tiles and belching out smoke through a small hole in the galley roof. The excavators found his pots and cauldrons, which he stood to heat on an iron grill; they found, too, the red plates off which the crew ate, and their wine jars. There cannot have been many hands on board. We know the captain's name, because it was punched on his bronze balance in the galley: Georgios Presbuteros, George the elder, or perhaps George the Elder of the Church (for all this, the balance is ornamented with a figure of Athena). We know there was a ship's carpenter, for he kept his tools on deck—hammers, files, drills and punches for working wood and metal, with lead for patching. Besides these two and the grumbling cook, there were probably only a few seamen. Normally every member of the crew had a financial share in the venture, depending in size on his importance. In this case there may have been a separate backer in addition, a trader who came on board to keep an eye on his investment: the name Joannes has been found on a lead seal.

What was the ship carrying, and where was it going? In the hold were over nine hundred amphorae. With painstaking care the excavators plotted their positions on an underwater grid, then popped them to the surface with a puff of air. A reasonable guess is that the ship's home port was near Constantinople and that the jars that formed the cargo were destined to be filled with wine in one of the Greek islands, Cos, Cnidos or Rhodes, whose vintage was as good then as now. Resin was found on board; perhaps it was used for ship's repairs—the planks were coated with it—or perhaps to save money by lining the amphorae en route.

So we can imagine this little ship, brightly painted

like most of its kind, creeping down the coast, putting in from time to time to buy provisions, fill the water casks or take a passenger on board. We are told that Belisarius' wife kept water fresh by burying the jars in sand in a dark cabin, but such a method was for bigger ships and longer voyages. The coast-hopping would also have given the crew a chance to stock up with firewood.

Dropping anchor was a tiresome business. The ship had six, because anchors at that time carried no chains. Captain George would also have kept a wary eye out for pirates. By the mid-sixth century the menace that the Romans had suppressed, and that Justinian had kept at bay, was reappearing. This time it was the Arabs. Having solidified their land power across the Mediterranean, they were beginning to make sporadic attacks with their fast ships. With the Arab capture of Alexandria in 641, a new fleet was introduced into hitherto safe waters. George's ship was unusually small and slim for a merchantman. Perhaps it had been built with just such an eventuality in mind.[5]

The Byzantines retaliated with a new kind of navy. Earlier practice had been to maintain large naval bases, like Classis, with sizable fleets that could move to any crisis zone. Faced with the urgency of the Arab raids, the authorities had to find a defense that was more mobile and less ponderous. The new pattern was to recruit and control forces locally, with the naval authorities often becoming identified with the civil administration. An Arab historian gives an insight into Byzantine recruiting practices. Each household in the coastal regions paid a tax of two denarii. From this fund, twelve denarii were paid to any man who enlisted in the navy. After this he was expected to be self-support-

ing, living off what he could wrest from the enemy—
except that, as usual, the sale of captives and merchandise was an imperial monopoly.

For the most part the Byzantine navy policed the
waters with dromones, long ships driven by oar, like the
Greek triremes whose lineal descendants they were.
Dromon has a variable meaning, and it is usually safer
to translate simply "ship of the line." It could refer to
a monster vessel with a complement of 300 men or
more. Usually, however, the dromones were smaller,
designed for speed, maneuverability and the deployment of a particularly vicious weapon.

> Do not make your dromon too massive in construction,
> or it will handle sluggishly. Do not err on the side of
> lightness either, or it will be too fragile to withstand the
> force of the waves or collision with the enemy. . . . The
> dromon's equipment should be complete in every respect, with spares for everything: tillers, oars, ropes,
> blocks and tackle, masts, bulwarks and all else necessary
> for a ship to function. See that it carries ribs, planking,
> ropes, pitch—both solid and liquid—enough and to
> spare. There should be a ship's carpenter on board with
> woodworking tools, ax, auger, saw and so forth. There
> should be a nozzle mounted forward on the prow, as
> usual, to project combustible material on the enemy.
> Above it there should be platforms built of planks and
> fortified with the same, holding mariners to repel attacks
> from the enemy forecastle, or to attack the enemy with
> whatever weapons ingenuity can contrive.[6]

"Greek fire," as the terrifying substance came to be
known, seems to have been first used by the Byzantines
during the siege of Constantinople by the Saracens in
673. Inverted by a Syriac Greek, it functioned as an

early type of flame thrower, spraying the enemy with a mixture that ignited on contacted with water and therefore could not be extinguished by any ordinary means. To prevent accidental conflagration, the dromon's woodwork was covered with hides. In its time Greek fire was a closely guarded state secret, and so has defied modern analysis. Scholarly conjecture has suggested saltpeter, quicklime or petroleum products as the chief ingredients. Powerful in resisting the Saracens, as well as the Arabs when they besieged Constantinople in 717, Greek fire was to prove its worth on several similar occasions thereafter, as this account of a battle in 941 shows:

> There is a people living beneath the northern sky called Rousioi, Russians, by the Greeks because of their physical characteristics, and Nordmanni, Northmen, by us from their geographical location. . . . This people had a king called Inger [Igor], who sailed against Constantinople with greater than a thousand ships. When the Emperor Romanus [I] heard the news, he was greatly exercised in his mind, since his fleet was committed to the Saracen wars and guard duty on the islands. While he lay tossing night after night on his sleepless bed, the whole coastline was at Inger's mercy. Then word came to Romanus that there were fifteen galleys lying where they had been abandoned, old and half-rotted away. When he heard this he ordered . . . the shipwrights to be brought to him and said, "Prepare these ships for action with all the speed you may. But do not mount flame throwers on the poops alone. Place them on the stern and amidships too." [With God's help the Byzantines were granted the necessary calm.] So they took up station in the middle of the Russian fleet and shot out a ring of fire. When the Russians saw what was happening, they

threw themselves overboard, preferring death by drowning to cremation. Some, loaded down with armor, plunged straight to the bottom and were never seen again. Some were burnt alive as they swam. The only ones who got away with their lives that day were those who managed to escape by land. The Russian ships, with their low draft, were able to sail into the shallows, where the Greeks, who drew more water, could not follow.[7]

Under such protection the Byzantine merchantmen had a degree of safety. In many cases, though the countries they visited were now independent, they still found a residual Roman influence. In the forests of Germany were Roman "lost colonies" composed of the descendants of legionnaires who had once served on the Gallic frontier. Unable to return to Rome, they had gone over to the Germans, but had preserved their national identity. Their children's children still kept up legionary customs and dressed as Romans from head to foot. There was reputedly one such group as far away as China.

Yet the world was opening up, and there was still much that was mysterious and exotic. Particularly exciting was the Far East, the routes to which had long been known but were now more frequently traveled. Metrodorus, a philosopher of the time of Constantine the Great, is said to have traveled to farthest India with the intention of circumnavigating the world. He brought back jewels as a present from the King of India to the Emperor of Byzantium. We catch an early whiff of this traveler's world—half hard fact, half romantic invention, a blend of magic and merchandise—from a retired trader who, toward the end of his life, sat down in the Egyptian city of Alexandria to write his memoirs.

His name was Cosmas. He was probably a dealer in spices, since he seems particularly interested in the pepper trade, and as such, he should have made a fair fortune, for spices were costly and in great demand. Years of voyaging had taken their toll. Cosmas complains of stomach trouble and failing eyesight. But old age had not dampened his spirit. Against the mind-numbing mass of official Byzantine literature, with its panegyrics, rescripts and hairsplitting theological disquisitions, the work of Cosmas stands out as refreshingly individual and endearingly eccentric. This is not to say that Cosmas is not concerned with religion. He is indeed, to the extent that some scholars have believed him to have turned monk in his autumn days. This is unlikely, for he complains that the world is too much with him. He is still, however, a fanatic; but a fanatic who pushes his obsession to the point where it becomes diverting, the sort of man whose modern counterpart writes books to prove that the English are descended from the lost tribes of Israel, or that the Great Pyramid, properly interpreted, will unfold the secrets of the universe.

Cosmas is the archfundamentalist. He takes the Bible literally to the point of trying to deduce where Paradise may be, and after some discussion locates it at the source of the Nile. He knows that the account of the Red Sea crossing is true, for he has visited the site and seen the evidence:

It is located in the region known as Clysma, on your right as you go toward Mt. Sinai. There you can still see the wheel marks made by Pharoah's chariots. They are visible from a considerable distance inland right up to the water's edge, and have been preserved to the present time as a sign and a warning—not for the true believers, but for those who do not believe.[8]

He has seen, too, as he tells us, inscriptions dating from Moses' time; and his sense of the immediacy of the Bible story is betrayed in his writing when, in describing the Israelites' journey through the wilderness, he continually strays into the present tense.

The main thrust of Cosmas' book is to demonstrate his idiosyncratic view of the nature of the universe: namely, that its shape is represented in microcosm by the Ark of the Covenant, which he describes and illustrates. To this end he devotes the greater part of his narrative to an exhaustive analysis of the Old and New Testaments. His theology is naive, repetitious and dull. His geography, however, is fascinating, and when Cosmas illumines his account from his own experiences as a merchant mariner, his book springs to life and offers a rare insight into a period when myth, science and Christianity fused into a heady mixture.

When Cosmas wrote, most educated people would have followed the early Greek geographers in asserting that the world was round. They would have added, however, that only a portion of the globe was inhabited; that the world was split into two or perhaps three continents; and that the whole was bounded by the great stretch of water known as Ocean. Procopius sees the world as bisected by the Mediterranean, which is an outflow of Ocean; it would take a year, he says, to journey round the Mediterranean's perimeter. Cosmas, typically, is a flat-earther. He takes the part for the whole, insists that there is nothing beyond the traditional inhabited world, and sees the earth as a flat disk tilted in relation to the sun. The east and south are low and hot, so the people there have black skins. The north and west are elevated and further from the sun, so the people have pale skins. Cosmas believes, like everyone else, in the ultimate boundary of Ocean, and all the more strongly since he has seen it with his own eyes. It is "a place forever prohibited to sailors because of the multitude of currents there, and the mists and vapors darkening the sun; because, too, the distances are so immense."[9] Cosmas himself once nearly was sucked into that watery void:

One bitter day, in the sea lanes leading toward farthest India, we observed that the sky was full of flying birds—albatrosses, men call them, as big again as kites, perhaps even larger. On top of that, the air in this region is not good to breathe. The whole ship's company took fright. Sailors as well as passengers, all who knew anything about navigation, insisted that we were near Ocean and kept up a clamor to the helmsman, "Steer to port! Steer for the gulf! Or else the current may drag us into Ocean and to our deaths!"[10]

Where had Cosmas been? When he feared the pull of Ocean, he was probably somewhere off the coast of Somaliland. Certainly he knew parts of Africa well. He had made a voyage to Adoulis, an Ethiopan port on the Red Sea, and writes knowledgeably about that region. While there he saw two eclipses of the sun, which help us to date the work—February 6 and August 7, 547. With his professional interest in spices he talks of the land of incense, located at the farthest extremity of Ethiopia, the route of the Queen of Sheba when she brought spices to Solomon. He knows the Valley of the Blue Nile, "rich in gold mines"; he describes the stockades built by merchants when they come to sell their wares, though he may be confusing these with the permanent fortifications of Ethiopia's southeast frontier, still in existence in the sixteenth century. He has seen unicorns—not living, but in bronze, at the royal palace at Axoum. His biblical observations attest to his presence in Palestine; and we may assume that his principal activity was port-hopping through the Red Sea basin, with side trips where his business or devotion took him.

It is here that fact and fantasy begin to mingle. Cosmas writes as if he had gone further, to visit India and Ceylon, and this tradition has become so indelibly associated with him that he has been known since the Middle Ages as Indicopleustes, "the India sailor." Most scholars now believe, however, that he never made the voyage personally, but is merely repeating travelers' tales picked up from others. Stories of Indian voyages had appeared in Greek literature from the time of Alexander, and Cosmas could have acquired a second-hand knowledge of the subcontinent from sailors he met around the Red Sea. There seems to have been no direct trade route between India and Byzantium, and the Ethiopian ports offered a convenient meeting-ground. The difficulty is that Cosmas supports his narrative with such a wealth of corroborative detail that it is hard to determine how much is eyewitness report and how much hearsay. Some of his statements are demonstrably false. Others might well be true.

Cosmas offers an account of the internal politics of Ceylon.

There are two kings on the island, mutual enemies. One controls the dark interior and one the rest, where the market and the harbor are. The inhabitants have a great

market there. The same island has a Christian church for
resident Persians, with an elder and a deacon elected
from Persia and a complete church liturgy. There are
many holy places on the island, and in one of them, built
on a height, there is a ruby said to be fiery red and as big
as a spinning top.[11]

This stone was later known to Marco Polo and became
a favorite legend of the Middle Ages. Cosmas also describes Indian ports and what he says are Indian animals, though some of these are dubious in the extreme.
He specifies the buffalo, the giraffe—which we know he
had seen in Africa—the yak (though only by report),
which does live in India, and the musk-deer, which
inhabits the mountainous region between Tibet, Siberia and China. Could he really have seen it? And
what of the sea life he talks of—the *choirelaphos*—
whatever that may be—seal, dolphin and turtle? What
are seals doing in these waters? Cosmas is sure that they
exist, for he has eaten one.

Even at this late date we find ourselves entertained
with a Herodotean delight in the unfamiliar world. On
one aspect of exotic geography, however, Cosmas can
be trusted: the spread of the missionary Christian
Church. The center of activity was Persia, where con-
versions had been swift and impressive.

> Isbozetes is my name.
> Once I was a magus, with some fame
> Among the Persians. In deceit and lies
> I put my trust. A fire came; and the cries
> Of my citizens were answered—not by me.
> Another quenched the flames. A Christian, he.
> But though I was defeated in men's eyes,
> I lost the battle, but I won the prize.

From Persia Christian influence spread rapidly into the East. We have already noted the Christian Church and clergy of Taprobana, Ceylon.

In the land named Malé, where the pepper grows, and in Kalliana, there is even a bishop ordained in Persia. And it is the same in the island called Dioskorides, also situated in the Indian Sea, with Greek-speaking inhabitants from the colonies established by the Ptolemies. Clerics are ordained in Persia and sent into these regions, where Christians may be found in great numbers. It is the same among the Bactrians, Huns, Persians, other Indians, Persarmenians, Medes and Elamites; in Ethiopia, Axoum, Arabia Felix, Arabia proper and Palestine; in Phoenicia, the whole of Syria from Antioch to Mesopotamia, Nubia, the Sahara, Egypt, Cyrenaica, Mauretania as far as Gadeira in the south; in Cilicia, Asia, Cappadocia, Colchis, Pontus, Scythia, Hyrcania; among the Eruli, Bulgars, Greeks, Illyrians, Dalmatians and Goths; among the Spanish, Franks, Roman and other peoples. Thus we see that the words of the prophets have been fulfilled throughout the entire world.[13]

As a trader, Cosmas was naturally interested in silk, the most important luxury commodity of his time. In a real sense, he orients his whole world around the silk trade. His map takes a line passing through Byzantium and Alexandria as its line of longitude, and the 36th parallel approximately for its line of lattitude: this corresponded to a trade route of crucial importance to a number of peoples.

Certain Indian philosophers, named Brahmans, state that if you stretched a cord from China through Persia to Romania, you would bisect the world with mathemati-

cal accuracy. They may very well be right. . . . So, if you
measured the earth's length, taking China [Tzinista] as
your starting point and proceeding due west, as with the
cord, you would find it to be approximately 400 days'
march of thirty miles a day.[14]

China, the origin of silk, was a land of mystery.

[Beyond the Great Wall] the Chinese lead a quiet life.
They have never known what it is to carry arms or fight.
The tranquil mind loves ease above all things, and so
they never interfere with those who live on their borders. They enjoy a mild and healthy climate; in China
the skies are always clear, with moderate winds. Most of
the countryside is spaciously wooded. The trees exude a
substance which can be worked with frequent applica-
tions of water, like raw fleece. By mixing the wool-like
fibers with water they produce a thread of extreme
delicacy, which they spin into a fabric called silk. This
used to be a prerogative of the aristocracy; but even the
lowest orders enjoy it now, without discrimination.[15]

From China the silk moved west through Persia, to
be sold at the great trade fairs. Ammianus Marcellinus
tells of one

where every year the beginning of September is a great
occasion. A vast crowd of every walk in life comes flock-
ing to the market, bargaining for goods from India and
China and every kind of merchandise that comes by land
or water.[16]

The name of the commodity reveals its history. Silk was
called Media by the Greeks, who knew it only through
the middlemen: then, as China grew more familiar, it

was called Serica, "the Chinese stuff." Obviously the
Persians were anxious to monopolize this profitable
trade as long as possible and prevent direct contact
between Byzantium and the source. The legend of the
naturalizing of the process has become one of the most
famous stories in European literature. Justinian, desperately anxious to break the monopoly, was fortunate
enough to receive two monks who claimed to have
spent years in China and to have learned the secret of
manufacturing silk. They smuggled out silkworm eggs
in their hollow staffs, hatched them, and the Western
silk industry was born. In Byzantium the process became an imperial monopoly, placed under strict regulations for manufacture and sale. In the Book of the Prefect, promulgated by Leo VI in 911 or 912, we find a
collection of regulations governing private guilds in
Constantinople. The City Prefect was Minister of Eco-
nomic Affairs in the capital, and the rigid control of the
silk trade was entrusted to his hands. Raw silk dealers
were to confine themselves to this alone, and practice
no other trade. All their dealings had to take place in
the open market; they were not to front for richer back-
ers. They had to observe strict controls on whom they
might employ, and for how long. They were not to spin
the raw silk into the finished article—in a regulated
economy, the lines of demarcation were firmly drawn.
They were not to sell to Jews or other merchants for
resale outside the city. For breaking these regulations
a merchant could expect a beating and a shaven head.

The mention of Jews reminds us again of the growing
importance of this community in Mediterranean trade.
Although silk production was now a Byzantine affair,
there were other valuable markets to be sought between Constantinople and the Muslim East, and in

these the Jews took a prominent part. An Arab document from the late ninth century praises their skill in languages: the Jewish merchants could do business in Arabian, Persian, Roman (which could mean either Latin or Greek), French, Spanish and Slavonic. From the West they brought eunuchs, slave girls and boys, brocades, beaver skins, furs and swords. Disembarking in Egypt, they proceeded by camel train and boat to India and China. On the return journey they brought musk, aloe wood, camphor and cinnamon to trade in Constantinople.

If the Arabs represented a new threat to the south, an equal danger to the north was offered by the Slavs. They were latecomers to the European scene, receiving no mention from the historians before the sixth century. Though their origins are obscure, it is now generally agreed that they emerged from the Pripet basin, expanding with such vigor that they were soon strong enough to attack Thessaloniki and Constantinople itself. A Byzantine writer describes the sturdy independence of their national character:

> The Slavs, as a nation, resembled the Gauls, both in culture and in temperament. Their love of freedom made them unwilling enough to recognize authority when they were still living in their own territory across the Danube. After their forced migration here, when they were compelled to live as subjects, they would take no orders from foreigners, but only from their own kind. They would rather be misused by their own than admit the authority of Roman law.[17]

The Slavs, however, were not recalcitrant in all things. We are told of their simple kindness toward strangers, and their reluctance to treat prisoners harshly, and of the extreme faithfulness of their womenfolk, who "think that they have died, when their husbands die; and suffocate themselves, because they cannot face a widowed solitary life."[18] Above all, like many peoples from the north, they were softened by the chastening force of Christianity.

> From Georgia and Armenia
> These tribesmen, hungry to accept God's word,
> Bowed to our mighty emperors
> And knelt in homage to their matchless sword.[19]

In the case of the Slavs, the establishment of friendly relations was due mainly to the activity of two missionaries, Constantine, who was later to call himself Cyril, and his brother Methodius. These men have become legendary figures in the work of the Church, and accounts of their lives are preserved in a number of manuscripts; these, though inclined to err on the side or miracles, are credible in the main and present a fascinating picture of life on the fringes of civilization in the ninth century.

Constantine and Methodius (who may have been baptized Michael) were born in Thessaloniki to distinguished parents and were apparently destined for high office. Methodius, the elder, born about 815, went into the civil service. While still a young man he was appointed governor of a district in Macedonia and served in this position for ten years. Constantine went to the capital to study and progressed with the amazing speed that was to mark his accomplishments all his life. *Persona grata* in the imperial palace, he finally became secretary to the patriarch. After a short retreat to a monastery he was persuaded to accept the chair of philosophy, teaching lay students, and in 855 was a member of a diplomatic mission to the East. His expertise in argument made him a natural choice. On his return he rejoined his brother, who had himself spent some time as a monk, and togehter they went on a mission to the Khazars in the Crimea. Their purpose was diplomatic rather than missionary, being more to safeguard the interests of Christians already living there than to make new converts; and, according to the tradition, they gained enormous prestige by the discovery of the relics of a notable martyr. St. Clement had been the third successor to St. Peter in the see of Rome. He was supposedly banished to the Crimea in the reign of Trajan, and had so infuriated the authorities by the success of his preaching that he was tied to an anchor and thrown into the Black Sea. The angels built him a miraculous submarine tomb, said to reappear from time to time among the waters; but the relics themselves waited seven hundred years for the coming of Constantine, who, ⸺

hearing that St. Clement still rested in the sea, betook himself to prayer and said, "In God is my faith and in St. Clement my trust. I shall succeed in finding him and bringing him from the water's depths." So, when he had constrained the archbishop, they took a boat and, with a company of clergy and true believers, journeyed to that place where the saint should be. On their arrival the sea grew calm and still, and they commenced to sound the depths, singing as they did so. Suddenly they became aware of a powerful aroma of oil and incense, following which the relics of the saint rose into sight.[20]

During this visit Constantine's rhetorical skill was again put to the test.

> The Jews who stood around him said, "Tell us now how a mortal woman can enfold God in her womb—the God she cannot even see, much less bring to birth?" But the learned man pointed to the Khagan and his first minister, and said, "If someone told you that the first minister could not receive the Khagan; and if that same man were to add that the Khagan could be received by the least of his subjects; what would we call him, do you think? A man of sense or a fool?" They said to him, "A great fool, certainly." Then the learned man said to them, "Of all creatures that are seen on earth, which is superior to all the rest?" "Man," they replied, "for he has been made in God's image." Then the learned man answered, "How can we not call stupid those who would deny that God could ever be contained in man? For God is in the sea and in the clouds; yes, He entered into the storm and smoke, when He appeared to Moses and to Job."[21]

Returning to Constantinople, the brothers were soon, at the encouragement of the Emperor Michael, dispatched on another mission. Ratislav, the prince of Moravia, had requested instructors who could teach his people Christianity in their own language. The problem was that at this point there was still no Slavic alphabet. Constantine, with the speed which his successors regarded as miraculous, created one. There has been some unprofitable argument as to which this was. The present Cyrillic alphabet, as used in the Slav languages, bears all the hallmarks of adaptation from the Greek, preserving Greek letters for all sounds that the tongues have in common. On the other hand there exists another early Slavic alphabet, Glagolitic, which is also a patently artificial creation. Which came first, and who invented them? The details will probably never be known, but there seems no reason not to credit Constantine—Cyril with the alphabet that bears his name. Armed with this invention, the brothers won many converts among the Slavs, who before this time had been primarily nature-worshipers, honoring the sun, the wind and the four seasons. Methodius distinguished himself by a disturbing gift of prophecy:

A man of great wealth, a counselor, married one of his own relatives, his stepsister, and Methodius, despite all his sermons, exhortations and warnings, could not bring about a breach between them; for others, self-styled servants of God, seduced him in secret, flattering him to profit themselves and destroy his allegiance to the Church. Methodius said, "There will come a time when these flatterers can aid you no longer; and then you will remember my words, when it is too late." Without warning, when they had turned away from God, catastrophe struck them, and it was impossible to find the place where they had been, for the tempest had carried them away like dust and scattered them.[22]

After their work with the Slavs the brothers visited Italy, where they had a mixed reception. Many clerics insisted that only three languages, Greek, Latin and Hebrew, were sanctioned for theological studies, and regarded their work in the vernacular as akin to blasphemy. When Constantine was in Venice,

the bishops, priests and monks flocked round him like crows round a falcon and said, "Tell us, man, how you made books to teach the Slavs, when none before you has discovered the means—not Gregory the Theologian, nor Jerome, nor Augustine himself? . . . ." But the philosopher replied, "Is not the rain sent by God to fall on all alike? Does not the same sun shine on all the world? Have you no shame, to settle upon three languages only, and ordain that all other people, and all nations else, must be deaf and dumb forever?"[23]

In Rome, by contrast, they found an enthusiastic welcome, for they brought with them the relics of St. Clement. They were met by the Pope and a procession bearing candles. Miracles attended their arrival: a paralytic was healed, and jailers, moved by the sight, released those of their prisoners who invoked Christ and St. Clement. Liturgies were sung in Slavonic at St. Peter's, St. Paul's and other churches, while the relics were laid to rest in St. Clement's basilica. Wall paintings in the underground church show the whole story from the martyrdom to the happy return.

The only note of discord came in the debate between Rome and Byzantium as to who should administer the new Slavonic see. Rome won, and sent out bishops, but the dispute was a symptom of the growing breach between Catholicism and Orthodoxy. Constantine ended his days in a monastery, where he took the name of Cyril. He was buried, appropriately, in St. Clement's. Methodius lived for some years longer, returning to Constantinople to work on his Slavonic translation of the Bible and going on an expedition to the Magyars. He died "on the 6,393rd year from the creation of the world"[24]—884 A.D.—and his funeral mass was celebrated in Latin, Greek and Slavonic. A tablet in St. Clement's bears witness to the continuing loyalty of the Slavs to their first missionaries. It records that "in the

year 1935, on the 1,500th anniversary of the death of
St. Methodius, a number of Catholic Slavs performed a
celebratory mass."

The far north was originally no less a place of romance and mystery than the Far East. The Romans
barely knew of it; the Byzantines knew little more.
Procopius tells a story about Brittia, which is Denmark.
There is a wall across it dividing the country into two
parts. One side is healthy and habitable, the other pesti-
lential and full of poisonous snakes. Also from this fabulous country comes the story of the fishermen who,
from time to time, obey a mysterious and intuitive call,
and go out into the night to ferry the souls of the dead
through the swirling mists to their last resting place.

In the course of time the Northmen became more
familiar, both as traders and soldiers. The questing Vi-
kings found their way down the Dnieper rapids, which
in spite of its hazards remained the favorite route between Constantinople and the north.

The dugout boats which come down from outer Russia
to Constantinople are from Novgorod . . . also from the
post at Smolensk, from Teliutz, Chernigor and Buse-
grad. They all come down the Dnieper and assemble at
the post of Kiev. . . . In June they move off down the
Dnieper to Viticher . . . and wait two or three days till
all the ships have come. Then they move off down the
said Dnieper River. First they reach the first rapids,
called in Russian and Slavonic Essoupi, which means,
stay awake! The rapids are no wider than a polo ground,
and there are jutting rocks anchored in midstream
which stand out like islands. The water rears up and
breaks over their crests with an ear-shattering, terrifying
roar. Not daring to pass between them, the Russians put
in to the adjacent bank, disembark their crews onto dry

land, and leave the rest of the cargo on board. The men
then strip and edge the boat along the bank, fending off
the rocks with their feet. Some take the prow, some sit
amidships, while others punt from the stern.[25]

So the Russians proceed down the series of rapids, each
with its special dangers or attractions: at the fourth,
there are pelicans nesting in the rocks. Where the water is too rough, they resort to porterage, followed by
their chain gangs of slaves. Armed to the teeth, the
merchants fight off hostile bands of Pechenegs and give
thanks for their salvation by sacrificing live cocks under
a tree. The settlements they pass are the first signs of
emergent Russia—a stockade, a few houses, a pagan
shrine, a Christian church; and they bring furs, wax,
honey and slaves to trade in Constantinople.

In the city the Russians had a special quarter, the St.
Mamas district, where they were compelled to live by
law. Many joined the army, as did the Scandinavians
who came down the Dnieper with them, forming a unit
which came to be known as the Varangian Guard, and,
from the first half of the eleventh century, served as the
imperial bodyguard. At first they were chiefly Iceland-
ers, Danes and Norwegians seeking their fortunes: the
Byzantines described them as from Thule, that is, the
legendary countries round the North Sea, and the
Northmen knew Constantinople as Miklagard, the fairy
city, the place of enchantment. Then Englishmen were
added to their number, and Danes who had left their
countries after the Norman conquest. They fought for
Byzantium against the Normans in Sicily and defended
Dyrrachium with great bravery in 1084. Their great
plumed double axes were famous and notorious; the
Englishmen had a special graveyard in Constantinople,

near the Adrianople Gate, and their name survived in Turkish folklore for centuries. Outside the Arsenal at Venice stands a row of stone lions, pillaged from various parts of the Greek world—from Apollo's lion terrace on the island of Delos, from the ancient harbor of Piraeus. On the back of one lion is a runic inscription, the testimony of one of the Varangian Guard who chose to leave this brief memorial of himself so far from home.

6. THE CHURCH INGOING: MONKS, MANUSCRIPTS AND IMAGES

Byzantium's natural posture was one of defense, a fact of life which her territorial acquisitions only occasionally concealed. As these were gradually stripped from her, the city of Constantine stood revealed for what she was: a precarious survivor from another age, perpetuating behind her walls a way of life that had long since run its natural term. Constantinople looked inward and backward. It is not surprising that this exclusiveness transmitted itself to the people, and that the habit of retrenching to preserve, combined with the national obsession with religion, should have resulted in one of the most clearly defined characteristics of Byzantine culture: the zeal for the monastic life. We may see its power, its pleasures and its hazards in the life of one man, Theodore, whose name was to be inseparably associated with that of the monastery whose head he became, Studium, and who was later still to be canonized. His career is well documented and his own writings are considerable: to study him is to study not merely a vital aspect of Byzantine society, but also some of the burning religious and political issues of his time.

Theodore was born in Constantinople in 759. It was the city's fate to be ruled, at her crucial moments, by men called Constantine. There had been one at her birth, and there would be another at her fall; Constantine V, who reigned when Theodore was born, presided over one of the city's greatest crises, for he was the last ruler who could claim, in any sense, to have jurisdiction over the combined Greco-Roman world. Eight years before the birth of Theodore, the exarchate of Ravenna had finally succumbed to the Lombards. Constantine's activities during his reign were to exacerbate the differences leading to a cleavage of spiritual, as well as temporal, domain. And finally, the controversial coronation of Charlemagne in Rome on Christmas Day, 800 removed the government of Italy from the Mediterranean to northern Europe. Not since the first Constantine built his city had there been such disruption of the established pattern.

With these things the young Theodore as yet had little to do, though he was to feel their impact later in his life. He was born into a distinguished family. Photinus, his father, was an official of the imperial treasury. His mother, Theoctista, was a woman of fashionable society who, like many of her contemporaries, carried her piety close to fanaticism. When she died, her son delivered a eulogy which remains as a detailed record of the life of well-bred Christianity. We see a leisured lady with a passion for the proper use of time, rearing her family, attending to her children and her charities, looking askance at the mundane amusements of common men; we see the formidable piety which must have made Theodore's childhood home an uncomfortable place to live in:

When she gave birth to us, she did not mouth the usual women's clichés, nor did she listen to the devil's prompting and do what women customarily do, that is . . . hang amulets and talismans about their children's necks. It was enough for her to unite us in the sign of the cross, and with this protect us as with a suit of armor, an invulnerable shield.[1]

In a world which still prized the domestic rather than the intellectual virtues in woman, Theoctista had schooled herself:

As the love of God grew in her heart, she plunged into books and learning, and taught herself, since she had been left unlettered, as an orphan. In the shortest time she had her Psalter by heart, and word-perfect. And how did she accomplish this? There was no time in her day for learning; she had no wish to inconvenience her husband or be found wanting in her household tasks. Therefore she studied diligently by lamplight every night before she went to bed and every morning as soon as she arose. . . . She wore no jewelry; she never swore and never lied; she abstained from meat almost totally, particularly during Lent. When invited to a wedding breakfast she would make a pretense of eating, but leave the meat severely alone. When taken to a play, she preferred to sit with averted eyes. She was as modest as a woman can be. There was one man in her life and one man only, her husband; and when they no longer lived as man and wife, she disciplined her mind till carnal thoughts no longer troubled her.[2]

Theodore comments particularly on his mother's insistence on chastity, even within the bonds of marriage. What Photinus thought is not recorded; one has the impression that he was not asked. Theoctista was as

strict with her children as she was with herself. She had
a daughter

> whom she guarded diligently from men's eyes. She
> never permitted her to look at jewels or rings or cloth of
> purple; rather, she urged her to be pious in the sight of
> God, educated her in the sacred writings, taught her to
> be charitable to the poor and forced her to wash the
> sores of lepers with her own hands. . . . When her chil-
> dren lay down to sleep, she never retired to her own bed
> without making the sign of the cross over them. And
> every morning, at the time of rising, she urged and bul-
> lied us and drove us to our prayers, so that her sons might
> equal her diligence in God's service.
>
> About her treatment of her household, both men- and
> maidservants, there is a good deal I could say, if I wished.
> I could tell you how she gave them food, and drink, and
> clothes; you could not ask for a more generous employer.
> Her liberality did not confine them to their daily allow-
> ance of bread, salt pork and wine. On many occasions,
> especially on high days and holidays, she would augment
> this fare with fresh meat, fish and game, and ale to drink,
> since she had little use for such things herself. But I am
> bound to say this too: she would admonish and correct
> her servants, going so far as to slap them (whether this
> be a virtue or a vice, I know not) to teach them to be
> honest and keep their hands from picking and stealing.
> . . . But after administering a beating, she would retire
> to her own room, shaking at the knees and telling herself
> she should be sorry; then, full of contrition for her action,
> she would call in the maidservant she had just beaten, go
> down on her knees before her and beg her forgiveness.[3]

Such was the environment of Theodore's childhood.
He studied, we may assume, in the libraries of Constantinople, of which there were several by this time: Con-

stantine, traditionally, had built the first, and succeeding emperors had added their own. He would have read mainly in the Christian authors, for the time for the full resurgence of classical Greek and Latin studies was not yet. Every day he would have returned to a house where all the offices of prayer were read, as in a monastery; where life was hardly less rigid than in a monastery; and from which it was but a small step to a monastery itself.

This step, too, was taken at the urging of Theodore's mother. His uncle Plato had earlier gone to Bithynia to become a monk. Now the whole family followed his example. Theoctista was adamant with backsliders. She told Theodore's brother, who was reluctant to bid farewell to Constantinople, that unless he went voluntarily she would drag him on board ship with her own hands. She was equally severe with friends and relatives who tried to dissuade them. Thus the family divided. Theodore joined his uncle Plato, whose spirit he found congenial and whose way of life he admired.

Theoctista, to her credit, was as stern with herself as with others.

> She would eat only once a day, about sunset, and then a light plain meal, without oil or wine. She had taken the vow of poverty and renounced all personal possessions. She had no maidservant, no gold, no silver, none of the things of this world; only her shifts and two threadbare robes which she bequeathed to her descendants.

This extraordinary woman had a powerful effect on her son. There can be no doubt that she shaped his life. Theodore's eulogy ends with a moving tribute to her influence.

And now, Mother, whom I revere above all other
women, for whom I long above all other things, I turn
my speech to you. It is sweet labor, and a cherished
name. O vision of delight, my mother and my daughter
both: who twice gave birth to me, twice gave me life: for
what land have you left us? Where do your feet tread
now, to what place have you been translated? Whose
faces now do you look upon each day? . . . When my own
days are done, I pray that with my followers I may come
again under your parental care; and that I, the least of
your sons, may be so blessed as to stand with you at the
right hand of Jesus Christ, the son of God.[5]

There had been monks for nearly as long as there had
been Christianity, in both the Eastern and the Western
empires. The impulse toward religious isolation had
come through Egypt and manifested itself strongly
among the rocks and deserts of the Near East, where
the terrain was particularly appropriate to the solitary
life. In the East, too, monasticism tended to assume a
different shape and purpose. Where the Western monasteries were differentiated according to the interests
of their founders, and committed to the ideal of service,
their Eastern counterparts were united by their common function, which was to pray. Other interests were
admitted and occasionally even encouraged, but the
Eastern monk was expected to spend the greater part
of his days and nights at his devotions. For Theodore
and his family, therefore, the transition from city to
monastery life would have been swift and comparatively painless; it represented merely an increased
refinement of the way in which they had already been
trained to spend their days.

Many of the once-popular monastic sites have now
disappeared from view. Where they still exist, they are

difficult of access for the casual visitor. Fortunately, their pattern has been perpetuated nearer home. The traveler in Greece need go only a few miles out of Athens to find the sort of monastery in which Theodore spent his days, a community patterned after establishments in Syria and the Near East generally, whose buildings have been preserved, though they are no longer inhabited. This site is Daphni, one of the more spectacular survivals of Byzantine Greece.

Like so many early Christian sites, Daphni was built deliberately to efface the memory of a pagan past. It stood on the Sacred Way that led initiates from Athens to Eleusis by the sea, there to celebrate the mystic rites of Demeter and Persephone. There had been a temple of Apollo here—the name Daphni is connected with the bay or laurel, Apollo's sacred tree—and some stones survived to be built into the Christian church. Apollo met the same fate as the goddesses of Eleusis: his temple, like theirs, was destroyed by the Arians who followed Alaric the Goth on a foray through Greece. It was replaced by the first Christian foundation during the reign of Justinian, who further contributed to the demise of pagan culture by the closing of the ancient philosophical schools of Athens.

The first impression of Daphni is not of a monastery but of a fortress. It stands at the foot of a steep hill, surrounded by and lost among the pines. To one side runs the modern road, noisy inheritor of the Sacred Way, hot and dusty from the trucks and buses that rattle down the Isthmus to Patras and beyond. Another wall is flanked by a vast and spreading campsite, one of the unsightly blotches that are symptoms of the current Mediterranean disease. Yet Daphni manages to preserve her chastity behind her formidable walls—walls that could be defended by an army, as indeed from time to time they were. The original enclosure was approximately square, reinforced at various points with massive guard-towers. Even today, though the walls have shrunk and the entrances have shifted, one has the impression of penetrating a castle keep. Proceeding down a long, narrow passageway, the visitor is suddenly thrust out into a sun-burned courtyard, fringed with small arcaded buildings and closed off at one side by the Byzantine church. The courtyard is a vestige of its former self, the arcades are a modern restoration and the church dates only from the eleventh century. Only the atmosphere has not changed: the Daphni that we see now recalls the site at its beginnings.

Originally the monks' cells, in two stories, followed the line of the walls, enclosing the central space. To the north was the refectory, *trapeza*, where they gathered for their simple meals; it was not permitted to eat in private. The foundations of the refectory still survive, set apart and barely visible. It was originally a building of some pretensions, decorated with frescoes like a church and furnished with stone seats where the monks ate to the accompaniment of readings from the sacred texts. Details can be fleshed out from the monastery of Kaisariani, another Athenian foundation on the slopes of Mount Hymettus and only slightly less accessible than Daphni. Here the refectory still survives, with its dome and tall, handsomely decorated chimney. At Kaisariani too there is a bathhouse for the monks, a luxury by no means common in the monasteries.

Dominating the small group of buildings was the church, *katholikon*. At Daphni this was originally a basilica. During the barbarian invasions of the ninth and tenth centuries the monastery fell into ruin and decay, and the church was eventually replaced, at the bequest of an anonymous donor, by the octagonal building which may still be seen today. The church of Kaisariani is of similar date but of cruciform style: this spurt of building testifies to the resurgence of the religious life under the later Byzantine emperors. Inside, the walls were rich with frescoes and mosiacs, of which considerable portions still survive. At Kaisariani the old exclusiveness of monasteries is perpetuated by the modern authorities, who fiercely and pointlessly resist photography. Daphni, more liberal, displays a powerful head of Christ—bearded, following the inspiration of the Syrian East—glowering down from its accustomed position in the dome. Byzantine shepherds, frozen into formal astonishment, watch the Nativity from the arid hills, while St. Anne prays before a fountain whose living, playing image now graces the courtyard of the Byzantine Museum in Athens.

A less splendid wellhead marks the center of a modern courtyard. As the monks declined in number, the monastery shrank within its enclosing walls. The cells presently seen belonged to Cistercians, who were given the site after the Frankish conquest of Greece in the thirteenth century. Three hundred years later the Orthodox monks returned to use the monastery at least until the War of Independence. After their departure it fell into disuse, until excavations at the end of the nineteenth century revealed the line of the original foundations. Only one of a number of small monasteries round Athens, Daphni remains the best known and most frequented: it shows how monks lived and died (they were buried inside or outside the walls according to rank), not only here but in most parts of the Byzantine world.

From the Near East, Theodore returned to Constantinople and the more prestigious monastery that was to be forever associated with his name. This was Studium on the Marmara seacoast not far from the Golden Gate. It had begun life as a church, founded in 463 by an expatriate Roman named Studius. During his long residence in the Eastern capital, the donor's benevolence was attracted by a monastic community originally established on the River Euphrates. Its brethren were known as *akoimatai,* "sleepless ones," because they were divided into shifts to hold eternal prayer and vigil, and they displayed a certain doctrinal intransigence which was to become well-known in Constantinople. Studius offered them his financial support and made them part of his foundation. The Church of St. John of Studium has the distinction of being the oldest surviving church in Constantinople, though little of the original basilica now remains. The church itself is a shell which has suffered the customary transformation into a mosque. Some of the original capitals lie scattered outside, used, as one historian laments, by Turks for rifle practice; others, following the Elgin Marbles, found a distant home in England and now grace the lawn of a Surrey church. The monastery has completely disappeared. In its time, however, Studium was the home of an independent, closely-knit and highly disciplined community, which made its mark on the city in more ways than one.

Theodore himself reveals how tight this organization was. In his writings he has left a good deal about administrative matters—not least, a series of short poems describing the officials of the monastery of which he was abbot. They combine a list of duties with a moral homily, and usually end with a promise of reward in the life to come. By way of proem, there is a description of the delights of the monastic existence:

> Far from the shoals of life here let us find
> Safe water. Haste to follow Christ our guide,
> And breast the flood of mortal cares and strife.
> This is the one care of the monkish life,
> To find a harbor on that quiet shore
> Where toil is done, and hardship is no more,
> Where men can sing hymns to their God in peace,
> Where all constraints and persecutions cease.
> Is there for any man a better choice
> Then to forsake all things, and bear the Cross?

There follows the list of functionaries. At their head is the abbot, the *hegoumenos*, with his second in command. After him, scarcely less important, is the steward, responsible with his assistants for the smooth running of the domestic economy:

> Yours Stephen's work, who wears the martyr's crown.
> You have assumed these duties as your own,
> To offer to Christ's flock their daily bread
> And minister to their wants as they should need.
> Render your labor up each day to God
> And serve this body, as is best you should,
> By nourishing each limb. Bear this in mind.
> Let all stand equal. Be not overkind
> To one, and too closehanded with another.
> Anticipate their need, and let each brother
> Have what is good for him before he asks.
> If with a stout heart you perform these tasks,
> When your race is run you'll find your true reward
> And go with clear conscience in the sight of God.[7]

There follows a long list of minor officials: the *epistemonarchoi*, to whom any disputes among the monks are entrusted for arbitration; the supervisor of church music; the taxiarch, responsible for ordering the processions and other ritual; and, far from least, the *epitaktoi*, sinister functionaries whose job was to report any breaches of discipline. They are the abbot's spies among his flock, though never openly described as such; their existence shows the severity of monastic discipline even under so enlightened a head as Theodore.

You are my eyes among the brothers. See
All that they do, and note it carefully,
By dark of night or under noonday sun.
Let not the younger brothers, one and one,
Consort together and keep company,
For thence comes license and black infamy.
Restrain loose laughter. Angry words repress,
For these will turn our thoughts from godliness.[8]

We return to good humor with the cook and with the wakers-up who called the brethren to prayer when the wooden clapper, the *semantron* (a symbolic reminiscence of the building of the Ark) sounded the time of rising.

Who will deny you worthy of a prize
Who spend your days in servile offices?
A stringent labor, but a great reward:
This drudgery will take you straight to God.
You scour the pots, but scrub your sins as well.
Better the kitchen fires than fires of Hell.[9]

No little share of labor you must take
To rouse the flock when it is time to wake,

To call back to this world each sleeping brother
And bring them from their cells to meet together.
So, when the clapper sounds its wooden call,
Like angels go among them. Search through all
The drowsy cells and look in every bed.
Sleep's done. It's time for morning prayers instead.[10]

Finally, a reminder that not all of life's ills could be left at the monastery door:

To share the burdens of the sickbed is
To earn God's love. Be zealous then in this,
My son, since it is your appointed place.
Do the work willingly and with good grace.
At dawn's first light your sickbed rounds begin,
Dispensing kindly words for medicine.
Then fetch their food, their daily meal prepare
And give to every patient loving care.[11]

In the scanty time left over from the round of prayer, the monks' duties were simple and confining. Farming took some of their time, though animal husbandry was usually impeded by the fact that the female of any species was denied admission to monastic society. Theodore insists on this prohibition, and many communities took it literally. Of permissible activities, by far the most important and the most demanding was the copying of manuscripts, which in Byzantium was raised to the level of high art. We may look at an example which is particularly interesting because it is a scientific text, preserved for us by lucky accident as an early and beautiful example of this elaborate process.

The author of the work was one Dioskorides, a Greco-Roman who was born in the reign of Nero and died under Vespasian. A doctor, perhaps a military doctor, he compiled a pharmacological guide in five volumes, describing plants, herbs and poisonous serpents that might be useful in the practice of medicine. Drawn from his own knowledge and a picturesque imagination, it soon became established as a standard work and was still in currency centuries later. Our copy was made about 512, as a presentation gift to the Princess Anicia Juliana, whose father, Flavius Anicius Olybrius, had been for seven months Augustus of the West. Juliana herself, having narrowly escaped marriage with Theodoric the Goth, became the wife of the supreme military commander of Byzantium, to whom she bore an equally distinguished son. When she died at the age of sixty-five, she could look back on a life filled with devotion and good works. Having a keen intellectual interest in religion, she had enjoyed the friendship of some of the most distinguished theologians of her time. Liberal in her charities to the monasteries and the poor, she had founded a number of churches, including one dedicated to the Virgin Mary in what is now Pera. In token of their gratitude, the townspeople commissioned the copying of the presentation volume.

Juliana herself appears in a dedicatory illustration; it is the earliest such picture in the history of bookmaking. She sits among red cushions, on a throne of honor, dressed in the costume of a Byzantine patrician—purple tunic and dalmatica worked with gold, scarlet shoes, a scarlet scarf to bind her hair, earrings of gold and pearl. Her right hand is outstretched to heap gold coins onto an open book—the presentation book—which a naked winged cherub labors to hold up to her. To right and left of her stand other women, dressed in green and purple over skirts of white, with golden diadems gleaming in their hair. Surrounding them are allegorical figures representing the patronage of the arts. But this courtly dedication is not the only picture; the manuscript is rich in illustrations. At its head stands the peacock, the Byzantine symbol of immortality. Dioskorides himself is pictured in a portrait gallery of famous doctors of the past. Fact rubs shoulders with fantasy here: distinguished physicians of the Roman court with Chiron the centaur. These illustrations, like the text itself, probably represent a long tradition and had appeared in many books of medicine before.

More important, for our purposes, is a picture showing the actual process of book-illustration. The artist-author sits before a chunky easel, painting. At his knees are a wooden palette board and a row of shells that hold his colored pigments. A young woman labeled Epinoia, Inspiration, holds up plants for him to copy. Artistically, the text was hardly less demanding than the illustrations. For a list of the tools required we may turn to a poem written on the retirement of a scribe, one of several such poems to have come down to us:

> Callimenes, his eye grown dull and old,
> His hand arthritic, dedicates to you,
> The gay and laughter-loving Muses, this:
> The pencil lead that draws lines straight and true
> To keep the script in place, the wooden rule
> To guide those leaden lines, the pumice stone,
> The well of ink indelible, the sponge
> That in the gardens of the sea is grown,
> And this, his little penknife, sharp to trim
> The reeds.
> > Take these, in memory of him.[12]

The book which is the product of these combined arts has grown like a plant itself, sprouting annotations and scholia in Greek and Arabic, which grow densely round the text and climb the margins. The pictured plants, too, done with an incredible delicacy of color and line, are intertwined with their descriptions, so that a tendril may underline a phrase or a painted root sever a word in two. Thus we have *adianton,* the marsh plant, a useful specific for snakebite and tuberculosis and a cure for baldness besides, sprawled like a young squid in the center of the page, its fronds reaching for the corners. Thistly *adrantillis* has one stalk realistically broken. Smilax is rooted at the page's foot, and swarms over the sheet as if to cover it. A pointed leaf of *xiphium (gladiolus communis)* which is both aphrodisiac and depressant, depending on which part you take, punctuates a sentence. There are the hedgehog-like *oxyschoinos* and brownish roots which lie across the page like lizards; there are the lizards and snakes themselves, vipers intertwined about an orange tree, the horned *kerastos,* the *amphisbaina,* black and horrid with a head at either end, salamanders, beetles, scorpions and winged things. But the artist's pride and joy is clearly *mandragola,* mandrake, a root forked in a parody of human form. This has a large picture to itself. It shows the fabled digging of the root and the dog who has just found it lying dead.

Scientific sobriety asserts that, of the things described and pictured here, about half are accurate, while many are indifferent or fictitious. This treatise, in fact, is the medical equivalent of Cosmas' voyages. Yet the work as it has come down to us is a testimony to the Byzantine genius for preserving and adorning. These illustrations from the world of nature are done with the same care and precision that we see in the mosaics of the churches, and with as vivid feeling of the joy of life. We should have a different picture of Byzantium if more such things had survived.[13]

Such was the tradition to which Theodore fell heir. An expert calligrapher himself, he made a number of innovations in the art, and many believe that he decisively influenced the form that scripts were to take for centuries to come. Yet even in his still and cloistered life Theodore was not permitted to devote himself to such things undisturbed. Like monks everywhere, he was caught up in the major religious controversy of his time, a controversy that was to spread far beyond Byzantium and cause alarming political repercussions.

The dispute started in the use of icons, the painted images of the Holy Family and the saints which served not only to adorn churches but also as aids to domestic worship. In essence they were innocent enough, but in the hands of the superstitious soon came to represent what many regarded as an abuse of fundamental Christian principles. There seems no doubt that by the eighth century these harmless reminders were being addressed as if human and supplicated as if divine; were in fact creating a religion within a religion and offering a more convenient alternative to the proper use of the church and the Christian liturgy. In the popular mind, icons had assumed the status of talismans and magic charms; far from leading the worshiper to God, they threatened a new kind of idolatry.

About 726, the first edict against the use of images was issued by a troubled Emperor. His pronouncement was accompanied by ominous portents. Far away in the south, the crusted, volcanic island of Santorini erupted, as it had done periodically since its first outburst devastated Crete and marked the end of an empire. For the Byzantines on the island and elsewhere, this new manifestation had no connection with geology. Everyone knew it was a divine admonition. In Constantinople, however, the Emperor Leo was unimpressed. His workmen continued to pull down the great mosaic of Christ which decorated the Chalke gate of the Imperial Palace. In the other half of the world Rome was touched by the spiritual, if not the seismic, shock. In 731 Pope Gregory III summoned a synod of Italian bishops, who sprang to the defense of the images by threatening iconoclasts with excommunication. Once again, Constantinople took no notice: the whole controversy in fact was a demonstration of how foreign the city had become. An Eastern city, it could not be immune to Eastern ideas. The iconoclastic movement was supported fiercely by the army, which more than anyone had contact with the wide world to the East; and there was in it more than a hint of Islam, with its insistence that to represent the human form in art was blasphemy.

Worse was to come. In 741 Leo was succeeded by his son, Constantine V Copronymus, in whose reign Theodore was born, and who was as militant against the icons as his father, and more systematic in his persecutions. Once again a sweep was made among the orthodox, and once again they claimed to find a sign from heaven. This time it was the great plague which struck Constantinople in 749 and which Theodore records for us in his memoir of his uncle Plato. The symptoms that he notes belong less to the plague than to the religious hysteria of his age.

And at that time the wrath of heaven . . . fell on many cities and places . . . and most of all afflicted the state of Byzantium. . . . There suddenly appeared on each man's garments the sign of the living Cross, drawn in bold strokes as if by an accomplished hand. No such thing; it was formed by the finger of God. A man so taken was greatly disturbed in his mind, for death followed shortly thereafter. He could be carrying out the dead in the morning, and dead himself by evening. You could see two people being buried in the same coffin, four carried on one bier, the luckless dead piled one atop the other. From every side wailing greeted the ear, and beating of breasts; the mourners dropped with exhaustion, there were no longer enough undertakers to go round, houses were boarded up, whole districts deserted, cemeteries filled to overflowing; to such an extent that within the space of two months the most populous city in the world wore the look of a barren desert.[14]

If the army was against the images, the monks, by training and temperament traditionalists, came out no less strongly in their favor and thus brought down the wrath of the authorities upon their heads. Plato, embroiled against his will in politics, was imprisoned in the palace at Constantinople, and Theodore himself was sent into exile in Thessaloniki. The battle continued to rage about their heads. In 753 a council at Constantinople reaffirmed the inconoclastic decrees; a second council at Nicaea gave a promise of toleration, which turned out, too soon, to be delusory. In the sphere of international politics there were overtures for peace and the prospect of a dynastic marriage, but these too failed, and the spiritual rift between East and West grew only wider. Theodore, his own position uneasy, placed his considerable literary skill at the service of the icons, and composed a series of dialogues in which the arguments of the "heretics"—iconoclasts—were answered point by point. A God who cannot be comprehended, cry his opponents, cannot be depicted. "It is forbidden once and for all in Holy Writ to make any graven image." Certainly, Theodore replies, but this was written before God had manifested Himself in human shape, and when the people of old had still to be warned against the worship of pagan idols. "For He who had formerly forbidden idols now gave this instruction to His high priest, Moses"; and he goes on to quote the directions listed in Exodus for decorating the Ark of the Covenant, which involve making two cherubim of beaten gold.[15]

So the argument continues, point by point, in language hardly remarkable for its Christian charity. "What are we being shown here, the image or the reality?" "Fools! Christ is one thing, and his image another." This impassioned rhetoric had its counterpart in action. Not only was this a period barren of artistic accomplishment, for the forms in which the Byzantine artist had traditionally expressed himself were now denied him; it was an age of desecration, when many works of the past were defaced, the Byzantine equivalent of the Puritan revolution, whose tale is told all too clearly by the ravaged statues in the museums.

The tempo of the controversy heightened. In a supreme gesture of defiance a parade of monks marched through the streets of Constantinople on Palm Sunday. Each carried an icon, and Theodore strode at their head. He was imprisoned and flogged.

A new Emperor, Michael, came to the throne. Again there was a hope of tolerance, and again the hope was an illusion. There was indeed a restoration of the orthodox ways, but only outside the limits of the capital. This meant that Theodore, if he wished to keep his faith intact, would have to be excluded from his monastery. Intransigent, he retired to the countryside, and it took an armed rebellion to bring him back again. A pretender, Thomas, appeared upon the scene and took advantage of the disaffection to make a bid for power. Michael, fearing that the exiled monks might give aid and comfort to the enemy, had them hastily returned within the walls, and Theodore saw Studium again. It was as well; the whole city was sick with the dispute, and Byzantium's external fortunes showed the effects of the malaise. The frontiers were neglected and the enemy nibbled from all sides. Italy had already gone, with the exception of Venice, which remained a Byzantine fief of more than doubtful loyalty. Now the key islands of Crete and Sicily followed suit, and the power of the Franks spread throughout the Mediterranean.

The quarrel outlived Theodore. Christ's image, restored for a brief while to the Chalke gate, was soon torn down again, and the dissension penetrated to the heart of the imperial family itself. The Emperor Theophilus, known as the Unfortunate, took up his stand against the icons; his wife, Theodora, who had as much spirit as her great namesake, was firmly, though privately, for them. Though spies informed him of his wife's backsliding, Theophilus preferred to take no action, and after his death, Theodora triumphantly restored the icons to favor. It was the end of the last great heresy in an age that had bred many.

> The light of Truth shines forth again
> To blind false teachers' eyes,
> And Piety breeds progeny

While Error fallen lies.
Now blossoms Faith, and Grace grows strong,
For above the throne we see
The face of Christ blaze forth anew
To outlaw heresy.
And there above the doorway hangs
As in a holy shrine
The image of the Virgin, strong
To guard your ways and mine.
The Emperor and Patriarch
Who showed us what was true
Are set about the walls nearby,
Their fellow workers too:
The saints, disciples, martyrs, priests
And angels stand around
To guard what was the Golden Hall
And now is holy ground.
For here is Christ upon his throne
And Mary at his side,
The Twelve Apostles painted, and
St. Michael, wisdom's guide.[16]

Icons could be rehung, but the deeper harm could
not be eradicated. The breach between Rome and Constantinople, intensified by this long and pointless squab-
ble, reached its widest point in 1054. By this time the
Western Empire had left the family of Charlemagne
and become for all practical purposes German; Pope
Leo IX had suffered a humiliating defeat by the Normans at Civitella, and the Emperor of the East, Constantine Monomachos, was tactlessly enjoying the dis-
comfiture of his rival. The Roman liturgy was attacked;
so was the authority of the pope. Even at this late date
there was an attempt at reconciliation. Papal legates
arrived in Constantinople in a last-minute attempt to

patch up old misunderstandings. Met with insult and suspicion, they responded in the only way left open to them. Marching to Haghia Sophia, they deposited on the high altar a ban of excommunication on the Greek heresies. The Church was now officially two in Christ.

7. A SHOW OF KINGS

The years after the settlement of the iconoclastic heresy brought Byzantium to a new ascendancy. Under a series of astute and pugnacious rulers the Empire, albeit somewhat shrunken, prospered; the Macedonian dynasty pushed out the frontiers again, though the warriors often prospered at the scholars' expense, and the years fat in territory were barren of art. The men who ruled this enterprise lived lives as rigidly circumscribed, and subject to as many checks and scrutinies, as the humblest brother in Theodore's monastery: subject, too, to violence and sudden death, for the occupational hazards of ruling were severe, and few of the emperors died serenely in their beds.

We are able to reconstruct the public and private lives of monarchs in some detail, for the Byzantines loved gossip and loved history. The former was for them a way of life, the latter a major manifestation of literary art, part of the national concern with preserving the past. Of the histories that have come down to us, two at least are circumstantial, anecdotal and delightful. Covering a good part of the tenth and eleventh centuries, they paint a vivid picture of the trappings, pleasures and hazards of royalty.

The first is the *Chronographia* of Michael Psellus. Its author was a monk, though one whose connection with monastic life was at best tenuous; he preferred the life of court politician and occasional king-maker to that of the cloister. Baptized Constantine—Michael was his monastic name—Psellus was the son of a good bourgeois family that numbered patricians and consuls in its past. Brought up by a diligent mother—who seems, in her painstaking devotion to her family's well-being, not unlike Theodore's—he turned to the study of rhetoric, which was for the Byzantines what it had been for the Romans, a universal science, bringing every branch of knowledge under its sway. Rhetoric, he tells us in his work, is an exact discipline. It is both philosophy and art in one, in that it both formulates ideas and beautifies them. It encourages precise and logical thinking; it enforces concentration on the meaning of words, free of their conventional associations. To the rhetorician, all is grist to his mill. Psellus himself had read Homer, Hesiod, the Greek lyric poets and the tragic and comic dramatists; he had studied the Christian fathers; he knew and used for his own purposes the historians Herodotus, Thucydides and Xenophon, and the Attic orators. In a professedly anti-intellectual age, Psellus was a polymath who rose to high office, becoming secretary of state, lord high chamberlain, first minister and intimate of kings. He turned to the church, like others of his time, as a refuge from the political maelstrom: he writes frankly that he was none too firmly seated on the chariot of state and a sudden bump might throw him off. But his interest in religion was perfunctory at best. Always a politician at heart, he tells us the inside story of great events; in a cultivated, artificial Greek which is itself an attempt to recall the prose style of the past, he recounts the story of fourteen reigns (which tended, in Byzantium, to be short) and writes of events in many of which he participated.

Our second source is a princess and a *femme savante*, Anna, daughter of Alexius I. She too has studied, as she tells us, Plato and Aristotle, and hopes it is not bragging to say so. Delightfully prejudiced in favor of her father, she intends her work as a record of his achievements both before and after his accession to the throne. She writes to fix them in the public mind, to create a bulwark against the creeping erosion of time, and in the course of her philosophizing, lets fall domestic details that are not easily come by elsewhere. She is womanly in her interest in clothes—fortunately so, for of the emperors of Byzantium, if of no one else, Carlyle would have said, show me what you wear and I will show you what you are. If Psellus knows the staterooms and the conference chambers, Anna knows the bedroom and the parlor. What she loses in objectivity, she more than makes up in atmosphere.

The colors of monarchy were red and purple, and they attended the emperor from the moment of his birth. In the Palace was a special room to which the empresses were brought for their confinement.

From floor to ceiling-line it is foursquare: above this, it tapers off into a pyramid, looking seaward to the harbor where the stone lions [sic] and oxen are. This is the Purple Room. Its floor is paved with marble, and its walls faced with it—none of your ordinary marble, nor even the more expensive variety that a number of builders use, but marble that the kings of bygone days had brought from Rome. This stone is purple through and through, save for an occasional fleck of white, like a grain of sand on the surface. It is from the color of this marble, I believe, that our ancestors called this room the Purple Room.[1]

Hence, Anna several times tells us, the expression "born to the purple;" hence too the name Porphyrogennetus, carried by several rulers.

Born in the purple, the ruler was safe for a while, cosseted and guarded; his dangers would come later. Those born to the royal family, but not in the direct line of succession, were automatically vulnerable. The emperors disliked the threat of competition, however remote. A potential rival might be banished to the Princes' Islands in the Sea of Marmara—tourist places now, reached by casual airplane from Istanbul, but Siberia then, remote and formidable political prisons. The less fortunate might remain in Constantinople to be castrated, for no eunuch could ascend the throne— though women could and sometimes did, like the formidable sisters, Zoe and Theodora, whose court receptions, spiky with protocol, we shall see below. Or perhaps the princeling damned by noble birth would be blinded—the ultimate disqualification, though there was a time during the Fourth Crusade when a blind man sat upon the throne.

The legitimate heir proclaimed himself by his apparel and from the time of his accession was stamped with monarchy from the top of his head to the soles of his feet. He was crowned with the royal diadem,

made in the shape of a skullcap, lavishly adorned with pearls and precious stones embroidered on the surface

or pendant. Over the temples flaps of pearls and jewels
hung down to brush the cheeks; this is the distinctive
feature of the imperial dress.[2]

Over his body the emperor wore a purple robe, and
another of gold semé with pearls; and on his feet, hardly
less distinctive, were the scarlet or purple slippers
which were royalty's prerogative. Many were the battles of privilege fought over footwear. Constantine Porphyrogennetus, after his father's deposition, showed
politic haste to put away the scarlet slippers in favor of
more modest ones of black. As a mark of special regard,
he was allowed to replace those by others of varicolored
silk; and in the end his mother, jealous of her son's
rights—and doubtless to his considerable embarrassment—insisted that he have the scarlet ones again. Or
we may see Basil II the Bulgar-killer confronting the
rebel John Skleros and demanding that he divest himself of the outward symbols of authority:

> Skleros stripped himself of all the other insignia of
> power, but in his haste or forgetfulness failed to remove
> the purple slippers. Thus, when he approached the Em-
> peror, he was still wearing one of the distinctive marks
> of royalty. This caught Basil's eye while he was still a
> good way off. He shut his eyes in exasperation, refusing
> even to look at him until he was dressed completely as
> a private citizen. There and then, at the doorway of the
> tent, Skleros took off the offending slippers; and so he
> came under the Emperor's roof.[3]

The emperor's life was a constant show, brilliantly
costumed and choreographed as elaborately as a stage
production. His face pallid under make-up he sat in the
center of his court, the epicenter from which all things

proceeded. His every move was prescribed and codified by rigid etiquette. One of the books that has come down to us from this period is the manual of court protocol compiled in the reign of Constantine Porphyrogennetus, showing the fearful burdens under which the emperors conducted the simplest actions of life. There were officials responsible for the smallest details of procedure: one, for instance, had nothing to do but guard the scarlet ink used for the imperial signature when the ruler sent out one of his famous Golden Bulls. We are shown the sisters Zoe and Theodora presiding over a council of state, whose rigid and concentric arrangement reproduces in microcosm the structure of the Empire:

They both took their seats before the imperial tribunal, on a line which set Theodora slightly to the rear of her sister. Near them was the place appointed for the rod-bearers; then the foreign guard, with axes swung across their right shoulders. Beyond them was the place reserved for the highly favored and those with court business in hand. Encircling these was an outer ring of imperial guards selected for their unimpeachable loyalty. The eyes of all were deferentially lowered to the ground. After them came the senate and the privileged class. Then came personages of the second class, and finally the tribes, drawn up in ranks and spaced at equal intervals from one another. When these dispositions were complete, the court proceeded to the remainder of its business: the judgment of disputed cases, conflicts of public interest, contributions received, the reception of ambassadors, controversy and consensus, all the customary duties of the potentate. For the most part the ministers of the crown held the floor. If necessary the Empresses interposed their quiet but authoritative comments, or replied to questions. On some points they sought expert advice, and on others relied on their own judgment.[4]

Would-be usurpers laid claim to the imperial protocol, as they did to the imperial costume: the ruler had to manifest himself by show, and it would abate public confidence to forego one item of the ceremonial. Thus we see Isaac, who led a rebellion against Michael VI, sitting like a painted mummy in his tent, on a couch which stood upon a golden dais. His troops were ranged about him in concentric circles: the leading nobility, the front-rank fighters, the light-armed troops, the "barbarians"—Italians and Scyths—and finally the inevitable axe-bearing mercenaries, the northerners who performed the same function at the Byzantine court as the Swiss Guard were later to do at the Vatican.

Such courtly ceremonials were staged in buildings of appropriate magnificence. The Great Palace of course continued in use. Another went up by the Theodosian Wall, in the Blachernae district on the way to the Golden Horn: a palace in the suburbs, though the walls soon bulged out to accommodate and protect it. Of this structure, a treasured residence of the later emperors, not a single trace remains. Nearby, however, stood another palace, which has been rather better preserved; it is still known locally as the Palace of Constantine Porphyrogennetus, but was probably not built until the time of the Comneni. Because of its uncompromising rectangularity and its location hard by the fortification, it has been compared to a castle keep. Three tiers survive, faced with an elaborate interlacing of brick and hung with wrecks of balconies. Small boys play football in the disty road outside; rubbish tips on one side and a withered tree on the other mock the memory of lush and flower-filled gardens. For this was the baroque age of palace architecture, when the emperors landscaped Constantinople to surround themselves with parks and playgrounds. Many emperors loved to hunt in their own preserves. Another notable outdoor sport was polo, known and enjoyed from the reign of Theodosius II. The British were later to inherit it from India, and the vocabulary that we know was already familiar— though *chukka* transliterates outlandishly into Byzantine Greek. A private polo ground was laid out in the Great Palace and became a tempting venue for assassination, for here the emperor would be less well-guarded.

And then there were the follies, the prankish excesses of an imperial taste run to seed. Constantine IX, whose whims inclined to the bizarre, constructed a park that foreshadowed the aquatic hazards of Salzburg's Hellbrunn.

> Fruit of all varieties grew here in profusion. In the middle of the park he constructed a deep pool, its brim directly level with the land surrounding, and channeled water in to fill it. If anyone who did not know about the pool came in all innocent and unsuspecting to pick an apple or a pear, he took a tumble and a deep dive into the water and started swimming frantically when he came to the top. This gave the Emperor keen delight.[5]

Unfortunately the joke recoiled on Constantine. He used the pool for his own exercise and built a lavish bathing pavillion beside it; while swimming there, he caught the chill which killed him.

We have too few glimpses of these more intimate

moments, for privacy was a luxury which even the emperors were not rich enough to purchase. Occasionally we see the ruler relaxing at chess, or, like John Doukas, reveling in the hunt, which Psellus considers to be the one blemish on an otherwise admirable character; Doukas' particular obsession was pursuing bears. Anna gives us a picture of her father's sleeping arrangements. The palace bedroom was flanked by a chapel dedicated to the Mother of God and an atrium paved with marble. This chapel was left open to all comers—somewhat naively, one would have thought—at all hours of the day and night. Alexius once narrowly escaped death this way. But privacy for emperors was hard won, secured usually only by retirement, illness or death. Michael IV, who was subject to fits, sat on a throne surrounded by purple drapes. When the seizure took him, the drapes were closed and medical aid administered behind them. As soon as the fit had passed, the curtains were opened again and the business of state could resume.

When they moved outside the palace, the emperors abated none of their magnificence or formality. While campaigning or on royal progresses through their domains, they lived in tents which were virtually portable palaces, filled with rich and beautiful things. Psellus describes the pavillion of Romanus III, crammed with necklaces, bracelets, diadems, pearls and precious stones. Even a journey within the limits of Constantinople was a matter of formidable logistical dimensions, calling for special transport and a complex organization. The emperors had their private fleet, stationed in the Bosphorus and consisting of ten warships decorated in scarlet and black. In earlier, simpler days the emperor had traveled up and down the coast in a scarlet barge. Later rulers considered this too small, as it could accommodate only a handful of officials: the commander of the watch, admiral of the fleet, company commander, private secretary, secretary of petitions and, when he was in Constantinople, the commander-in-chief also; not to mention the court chamberlain, master of the wardrobe and grooms of the bedchamber as ordered. Obviously, no one could expect the emperors of a more grandiose period to go forth with so trivial a complement. The Emperor Leo therefore had two state galleys built, which lumbered through the water past the succession of royal harbors, and which, like all things in Byzantium, fell under the jurisdiction of a specially appointed official—in this case, the *protospatharius* of the basin, who commanded the fleet of barges and was responsible for settling disputes among the oarsmen.

As they journeyed through their city, the emperors could look on building projects designed to make past grandeur pale into insignificance. The masters of Constantinople were inordinately rich. Here is Basil II, the Bulgar-killer, squirreling away his surplus wealth into the bowels of the earth:

> In his reign, the assets of the imperial treasury accumulated to a total of 200,000 talents. As for the rest of his acquisitions, language is too poor to describe them. All the treasures of Iberia and Araby, the wealth of Celt and Scyth, the riches that had been amassed by every foreign land that borders on our own—all this was piled into the imperial treasury. But the vaults of the building designed for this purpose were not big enough. The Emperor therefore dug shafts deep into the earth that went

down in a spiral, as in the Pyramids, and stored a good part of his accumulated treasure there.[6]

This wealth went to finance grandiose constructions whose enormity and extravagance ominously recall the Götterdämmerung of the Roman Empire. Haghia Sophia was a perpetual provocation to the building emperors, a model, an inspiration and a challenge. Obsessed with the desire to surpass Justinian, Romanus III began to work on his own monument. Once more the world was ransacked for precious marbles, and the Church of St. Mary Peribleptos rose shudderingly against the skyline of Byzantium:

> The entire resources of the imperial treasury were made available to the enterprise, and gushed forth a river of gold. One by one the sources of revenue dried, and still there was no end to the work in sight. One tier rose, and then another tier above it: level upon level were destroyed together, and many times a new wall could be seen going up while the old one was coming down, the newer version slightly larger than the old, or with some extra architectural embellishment. . . . The project became an obsession with Romanus; again and again he came to glut his eyes with it, surrounding it with all the appurtenances of the imperial court, setting up thrones within its walls, adorning it with scepters, spreading it round about with purple tapestries. . . . Then an extension was added to the construction, and the church was turned into a monastery.[7]

The monastery in its turn succumbed to elephantiasis and became a vast complex holding swarms of monks; the world was ransacked for treasures to fill it.

But even this was surpassed by the great work of

Constantine IX, the Church of St. George the Martyr,
or St. George of Mangana. It neighbored the Imperial
Palace, and ancient testimony is unanimous in reporting the lavishness and extravagance of its construction.
Constantine, who had already enlarged and renovated
the dependencies of Haghia Sophia, was now determined to surpass his predecessor's work. And so we
read again descriptions of rare stones and costly decorations, of roofs covered with gold leaf and jewels encrusted in floral patterns on the walls, of "money pouring from the public treasury like a geyser welling from
unsounded depths."[8] With the building already halfway to completion, the concept was abruptly changed;
no objections could forestall the imperial whim. A new
scheme was adopted, with buildings ranged concentri-
cally about the church.

> And people came to wonder at each part of it and praise
> it to the skies: the size of the church, the grace and
> symmetry of its proportions, the way in which each de-
> tail contributed to the whole; the charm of contrast and
> the grace of unity; the streams of flowing water, the
> encompassing wall; the flower-filled lawns, the grass bes-
> pangled with the constant shower of waterdrops; the
> bath with its attendant pleasures; this place was jour-
> ney's end, perfected loveliness, a vision of sheer delight.[9]

Again and again this concentric pattern repeats itself
in the descriptions of the time: ring within ring around
the mystic core; tier within tier around the sacred presence of the emperor, who was all-wise, all-just, all-pow-
erful and all-pervasive. One of the most innocently sinister passages in Anna's memoir is her description of the
symbol of that power, the sculpture known to the peo-

ple of Constantinople as The Hands. Cast in bronze,
they reached out from the stone arch through which
every condemned criminal had to pass on his way to
execution. The victims watched them desperately and
dragged their steps as they passed, for up to this point
reprieve was still possible, while on the far side death
was certain.

> For this was the meaning of The Hands: that the Em-
> peror took men back in his embrace again, and held
> them with all his might, and did not release them from
> the hands of mercy. But if they passed The Hands, it was
> a sign that the Emperor rejected them with all the
> power at his command.[10]

For men who wielded such enormous power in life,
death did not come easily. Some tried to bargain with
eternity by renouncing worldly pomp before their time
was due. We see Michael IV, an adulterer and probably
a murderer also, leaving the court to consult with hermits and ascetics, bridging the fierce divisions that
were part of Byzantine life, seeking out these people in
their caves and hovels and changing clothes with them,
putting on their filthy rags while they took the imperial
purple. In an agony of abasement he bathed their tor-
tured bodies and pressed his lips to their sores; then,
returning to Constantinople, he set to work building
convents and monasteries to appease his conscience,
and a great infirmary, the *Ptochotropheion,* for the sick
and homeless of the city. Constantinople's prostitutes,
who seem to have been the first target of every reform-
ing emperor, listened to a fervent appeal to forsake
their evil life and enter the convent. According to Psellus, many did.

Finally Michael decided to turn monk himself. Even in this renunciation of the world there is a certain sensuousness and love of show which is never entirely absent from Byzantine writings:

> Disdaining the royalty from which he was in any case soon to depart, he placed himself above all worldly commerce and turned to God. To avoid harassment while he underwent this change of life and made his confession to the Almighty, he left the palace and made his way—or rather had himself transported by bearers—to the monastery that he himself had built [the Holy Anagyroi]. Arriving at this place of meditation, he fell to his knees on the floor of the church and prayed to God that he might appear as a willing sacrifice in His sight, and purified by the act of consecration. Having thus won the Deity to smile on him, he entrusted himself to the priests' hands, asking them to offer up the willing sacrifice of a happy victim. Standing in a circle about him, they chanted the opening prayer of the sacrifice to Our Lord. Taking his robe of imperial purple from him, they clothed him instead in the holy garment of Christ. They took the diadem from off his head and set in its place the Helmet of Salvation; his back and breast they girded with the sign of the cross, to ward off the powers of evil; and then they let him go.[11]

And then we see the monarchs who refused to let go: the men who struggled on to the last, their mortality growing daily more apparent within the gorgeous embroidered husk they could no longer fill. Such a one was the builder of St. Mary Peribleptos, Romanus III, whose particular misfortunes were an avid wife and a younger, lustier rival. Under the ministrations of his poisoners he shrank beneath his robes, a butterfly returning to a chrysalis. Scarcely able to stand up under the burden of purple and gold, he tottered through the palace like a walking corpse. His face was swollen with the pallor of the already dead; his breath came fast; the hair had fallen from his head, leaving only a few clinging strands of gray. As he took so long to give up the ghost, his enemies grew desperate and were forced to turn to sterner measures. On Good Friday 1034, Romanus was seeking respite from his pains in the palace pool; it was an easy matter to drag him under. He was buried in the same Church of St. Mary that he had built.

And even after death these emperors were builders. Their tombs and monuments were made of precious marble, surrounded by entire estates. Houses were laid out around them, and trees and parks, a court in architecture ranged about the imperial dead, whose memories were thus preserved in a reasonable facsimile of their life on earth.

We move from gaudy fact to factual fiction, from the kingdom of Byzantium to another kingdom that borders Byzantium on the one side, but the frontiers of the imagination on the other. At some time in the tenth or eleventh century—we do not know when—there came into final being a long and complex poem which is the Byzantine *Chanson de Roland* or its *Robin Hood*. About the sources of this poem and the stages of its growth, we can only surmise. It may have begun as one of a number of such poems fabricated over the years in the border country, where the races met and mingled, later to be shaped and polished by a city mind—perhaps by a monk—and retold with elegance and style. It is a folk-epic of Christian and Infidel, Emperor and Emir, set vaguely in the Middle East at the furthest reach of Byzantine influence, but really in the land of dreams. Sometimes its places and people have an urgent resemblance to actuality. Sometimes they exist by their own laws, pendent in an idyllic world. But the conflicts represented and the clash of temperaments are real enough; they sum up present history and frame the future.

In a terrain loosely patrolled—too loosely, as is soon apparent—by the Byzantine forces, we are introduced to an Arab who is the prototype of all sheiks of romantic fiction:

There was an Emir, nobly born, in this world's goods most blessed,
Who had his share of wisdom, who was every inch a man;
Not black, like Ethiops, but tawny-haired and good to look upon.
Fair was the beard that lately grew and curled upon his chin,
And thick the hair that matted hung across his noble brow.
His eyes were like a rosebed in the garden of his face,
Quick, frank and open; and his look was full of love.
He stood up like a cypress, trim, young, strong,
The kind of man that you would sooner see in pictures
Than living, breathing; and he had a strength besides
That recognized no rival. Every day he wrestled beasts
To try his courage, so that men might see his bravery
And wonder at the sight. And all that saw him marveled.
A paragon and terror to the young, this Emir.[12]

Our swashbuckling hero demonstrates his valor by a raid on Cappadocia, going so far as to pillage the Byzantine general's house. All the inhabitants are killed, and the general's daughter brought back as a prize. Returning to discover its loss, the family is full of grief, and the

girl's brothers band together to recover her. They find
their way to the Emir's camp and demand an audience:

The Emir gave the word, and they were brought before
him
Where he sat at the threshold of his tent, raised high
On a throne of gold, striking awe into their hearts,
With a throng of warriors in a circle round him.
The young men drew near, and he gave them audience.
Advancing on their knees to the third step,
They addressed him thus, with their eyes running tears:
"Emir, servant of Allah and prince of Syria,
As you hope to make the pilgrimage to the Holy Mosque
Of Palermo, Emir, and worship the Hanging Stone;
As you hope to be found worthy to adore the Prophet's
tomb;
Show your reverence to this, our prayer.
You have taken away a lovely girl, our sister.
Let us ransom her, servant of God in the highest;
We will pay whatever your heart desires.
For her father is mourning for his only daughter.
Without her, her mother has no will to live,
And we, her brothers, yearn for her endlessly
And are bound one and all by a fearful oath
To bring our sister back with us or die."[13]

The citing of names and places brings us into fleeting
contact with actuality and suggests a date for the poem.
Palermo, that open city which had already passed from
Phoenician to Greek, from Greek to Roman, from Roman to Byzantine, had fallen to the Arabs in 832; in 938
it became the capital of the Emirate of Sicily and
helped to contribute a pseudosaint to the Islamic calendar. Taking over so much that was Greek—not merely
in Sicily, but in Syria, where a late school of Aristotelian

philosophy had made its home—the Arabs found Greek
science and metaphysics sympathetic to their own intellectual bent, and venerated Aristotle as a polymath
of renown. It was through Arab commentaries and
translations that the Western world first rediscovered
several of his works, and Sicily, by virtue of its intellectual and physical associations, became a focus for such
activity. Palermo, which for long after its reconquest
remained half-Arab by association, became a clearing-
house for Aristotelian scholarship.

But to return to our brothers: the Emir, who speaks
"Roman" (Greek), offers to decide the matter by meeting one of them in single combat. Constantine is
chosen, and the ensuing tourney is tremendous. Greek
and Arab hack each other to pieces, but still each clings
precipitously to his saddle. At last the Emir's own people implore him to break off, for the "Roman" is too
much for him. Yielding the contest, the Emir gives the
brothers permission to seek out their sister. But where
is she? There is still room for oriental duplicity. The girl
is nowhere to be seen, nor is her body to be found
among the slaughtered prisoners piled up in a ditch.
Frustrated, they return to confront the Emir again. He
begins to be moved by their grief and questions them
more closely about their nature and provenance. In
Homeric style, they match genealogies:

From the Eastern Marches, patricians by birthright, and
Romans,
Our father is descended from the Kinnamades
And our mother a Doukas of Constantine's blood.
In our uncles and cousins we number twelve generals.
Such is the race we belong to—and our sister.
Our father was exiled on some stupid charge

Trumped up by fawning parasites and sycophants,
And none of us was present when you came attacking.
We were on the borders, with our own divisions.
Or else this would have been a different story,
And the road to our house would have been barred to
you.[14]

If the brothers' speech is a capsule summary of the
Byzantine condition—administration convuluted by
palace politics; overextension of an army which, though
well-trained, is too diffuse, too inaccessible—the Emir's
reply no less accurately sums up the ruthless Arab
march through the Roman world, the fierce young
power picking the bones of the old:

Chrysoverges was my father, and my mother Panthia,
Ambron my grandfather, Keroes my uncle.
My father died while I was still a baby,
And my mother placed me with my Arab kinsmen,
Who raised me in the True Faith of the Prophet.
They made me regent of the whole of Syria,
With thirty thousand hand-picked lancers under me.
After Syria was mine, I went on to conquer Kufah.
What I tell you now is fact, and needs no elaboration.
It did not take me long to wipe out Herakleion
And capture Amorion, as far as Ikonion.
I am the bandits' scourge, the slayer of beasts in the
forest.
There is no commander alive, no army that can withstand
me.[15]

Here the geography is problematical, but Syria, of
which the Emir is called *prótos*—"first man," "prince"

—had already been threatened by the forces of Islam while Mohammed was still alive. Damascus—where St. Paul had seen his vision, where stood a house which was traditionally that of Judas—soon became the seat of the Caliphate.

But the irrestistible Emir is not proof against a single girl. Unharmed, she is revealed to her brothers in the Emir's tent; overcome by her beauty, the Emir vows to turn Christian and marry her. The marriage takes place, and a child is conceived. But the Emir's mother, indignant at her son's apostasy, sends him troubled letters:

We are detestable in all men's eyes.
We have denied our faith and sinned against the law.
We have not hearkened to the teachings of the Prophet.
Whatever came upon you, child? And how could you
forget them?
How could you not remember the achievements of your
father,
All the Romans that he slaughtered, all the slaves he took?
Did he not fill his prison cells with captains and
commanders? . . .
And was he not tempted, as you have been tempted?
When the Roman army had him surrounded,
The generals swore by all they held most holy
That the Emperor would create him a patrician,
Make him Master of the Horse, if he surrendered.
But he kept faith with the commandments of the
Prophet.[16]

Again the fiction reflects the fact: the Byzantines preferred to buy off their enemies. Uneasy in his mind, the

Emir leaves his wife and child for a visit to his mother,
who continues her accusations in person:

And are there miracles in Romany, my child,
Like those that happened at the Prophet's tomb?
Yes—where I used to take you for your prayers.
Did you see any wonder such as those—a light
From heaven radiant, when light there should be none
At dead of night, to make the mansion glow?
The lions and the bears lie down together,
And wolves with sheep; beasts of all kinds, feeding
And in no way harming one another, but attending
Till the final prayer was spoken, when they bowed the
knee
And straightway went to their own lairs in peace?
What greater miracles has Romany to offer?[17]

The Emir replies:

Of all these things I have good understanding, Mother.
Before I was vouchsafed my share of light, I prized
Things of darkness and destruction, and accepted them
for true,
But as soon as God in the Highest—who for my sake
Was willing to assume the cloak of poverty and wear
My mortal weakness as his own—when this same God
thought good
To snatch me from the wiles of the voracious Beast
And thought me worthy of the waters of salvation,
I put all such things behind me, knowing them for lies
And fairy tales, that lead men to the everlasting bonfire.
Who shall believe such things and not be punished?
But he who puts his trust in God the Father
And in Jesus Christ Our Lord, the Word Incarnate,
Begotten of His Father before all ages,
Light of Light and very God in majesty,

Who for us men and our salvation
Came down to earth, born of the Virgin Mary,
And suffered on the cross;
He was buried in the tomb which you too honor,
On the third day rising from the dead again
As it was promised in the Holy Scriptures
To sit on the right hand of God the Father,
Almighty forever; and his kingdom shall be endless.
And with the Father, the Son and the Word
I acknowledge one baptism to remit our sins
And look forward to the resurrection of the dead. . . .
What does it profit us to gain the world
And lose our immortal soul? The hour will strike,
The Day of Judgment come, and God in Heaven
Will charge all men to render an accounting.
Then we shall hear a voice commanding us
To go into the outer fire, the fire of Hell,
There to abide with the Devil for eternity,
Since we have set ourselves against God's word.
But those who trust in Christ, as it is fit they should,
And have observed His holy ordinance,
At that hour they will shine forth like the sun
And hear the voice of their good master, saying,
"Come in, the Father-blest, to the inheritance
I promised you; yours is the Kingdom of Heaven."[18]

Thus the argument is polarized, and the debate that is to rack the last centuries of Byzantium—the insoluble debate between Christian and Mohammedan—is set out in poetic form. The years that had established Byzantium's greatness had also sown the seeds of her doom, for the reigns of Justinian and his successors had seen the birth and mission of Mohammed. At its inception Islam had seemed to have a negligible impact—had seemed so close to Christianity, in fact, as to offer little more than another heresy in an age that was am-

ply accustomed to them. But under the caliphs who
succeeded Mohammed the minor heresy became a
burning issue and a holy war, uniting peoples disparate
in race and temperament into a formidable unity and
providing the cohesive force that carried the Arabs to
military victory across the greater part of a continent.

The crisis of history, however, is still to come; that of
the romance is more easily and happily resolved. Over-
whelmed by her son's rhapsodical paraphrase of the
Creed, the Emir's mother allows herself to be converted, returning with her son and a large band of
followers to the Roman lands. The Emir

> Changed his apparel for the dress the Romans wear:
> A tabard wonderful to look upon, and powdered
> All with gold; his robes were violet and white,
> Layered with purple and embroidered griffins;
> On his head a shining turban, monogrammed in gold.[19]

So the family is reunited, and we are introduced to
the son who gives the poem its title, Digenes Basil Akrites: Digenes, "twice-born," because of the two worlds
represented by his parents; Basil, because it is a Greek
royal name; Akrites, "belonging to the border country," because this is his temporal as well as spiritual
domain. He grows up with his mother's grace and his
father's already-incredible strength increased tenfold.
On a childhood hunting expedition he breaks a bear's
neck, overtakes a running deer and tears it in two, and
carelessly lays the spoils aside while he fights a lion
singlehanded. Every inch a king, he inherits the dress
sense of the Byzantine emperors:

> He put on singlets thin and cool against his skin.
> The uppermost was red with golden borders

Hemmed with pearls, the neck of it perfumed
With musk and ambergris. Instead of buttons
Was a line of single pearls that matched with holes
Worked in gold thread. He wore a pair of leggings
Broidered with griffins. Jewels gleamed in his spurs.[20]

Digenes' snow-white horse has jewels and little tinkling bells plaited in its mane, and a saddle covered with a green and rose silk cloth. Its harness is plaited with gold and studded with pearls, and the rider brandishes a green Arcadian spear with a golden pennant.

Like father, like son: Digenes carries off a Greek general's daughter from a "mosaic house." Pursued by the entire Greek army, he wins the father's respect by his valor. A marriage is arranged, with the gifts and dowry representing the wealth and taste of two worlds in "twenty centenaries of ancient coins," hunting leopards, eunuchs, jeweled icons of St. Theodore, white turbans monogrammed in gold. The groom's fame comes to the ears of the Emperor, who makes him ruler of the border country.

The domain now ruled by Digenes is, at least most of the time, an idyllic land, a Camelot:

If months could name their king, that month is May.
May, the whole world's joy and ornament,
May, the eye of every growing thing,
The brilliance of the flowers, the spangled beauty
Of blushing meadows, and the breath of love
That blows to make men fond and wild. It turns
The earth into the mirror of the sky,
With daffodils and roses set as stars.
In such a month, so strange and sweet a month,
I took the road, with but my wife beside me,
The lovely daughter of the general Doukas.
We turned into a meadow, where every charm

Met to astonish us. I pitched my tent there.
A bed too for myself, within a bower
Of living green. The rushes towered high,
And from the meadow's heart cool water flowed
To every hole and crevice of the land.
And in that grove too there were diverse birds,
Peacocks walking tame, and swans and parrots.
The parrots hanging on the branches sang.
The swans browsed on the water, and the peacocks
Made feathered aureoles among the flowers
To answer nature with their own array.[21]

If Digenes is the apotheosis of the Byzantine prince, the castle he inhabits is a fairy-tale Byzantine palace. Stone-built and foursquare, it has a mosaic ceiling, columns and galleries; the pebbled floor is so intensely polished that it gleams like ice. Around the central hall are wings, retiring rooms, covered with mosaic depictions of Goliath, Achilles, Agamemnon, Penelope, Odysseus and the Cyclops, Alexander conquering the Indies, Moses and the plagues of Egypt. Digenes proves himself worthy of this company by finding his own monsters to destroy. A three-headed serpent is killed— does this, one wonders, derive from the serpent column in the Hippodrome? And when the old Emir dies, Digenes behaves with Odyssean propriety, bringing his body home and lodging it in the chapel of St. Theodore. But the hero too must follow nature's course:

There is no mistake, my darling. I am dying.
I, who have won each battle but the last,
With Charon. I must leave you, dearest heart, and go
To Hades; and I bear within the tomb my grief
That you must live out your life without a husband.[22]

The world has lost its hero, and a lonely monument, a purple arch, rises over the place where the Borderer's body lies. His life was not all fantasy. It speaks of a time when the forces of Christianity and Islam were, if not in harmony, at least in equipoise. If it has any precise historical correlative it is surely in the short-lived Norman kingdom of Sicily, where for a few years Byzantine, Arab and Frank lived side by side in peace, borrowing each others' traditions and strengths. It speaks of a racial propinquity such as we sense in the Church of the Chora, on the fringes of Constantinople, where the builder Theodore is mosaically depicted in a turban more Turkish than the Turks.

The Turks. It was they who were to destroy the idyll, to lay siege to Digenes' castle. The manual of imperial administration that Constantine Porphyrogennetus bequeathes to his son is already full of fear. The tribes of the north, it says, are warlike and rapacious; the Russians must be appeased with gifts of ceremonial robes and diadems; Mohammed is a blasphemous and obscene prophet who has seized the holy places of Jerusalem and whose soldiers "ride on camels, not on horses; nor do they put on coats of mail in wartime, but tunics colored pink; and they have long spears, and shields as big as a man, and enormous wooden bows that few men can bend, and then only with great difficulty."[23] A genealogy of the Turks is given, but it meanders into obscurity. They have come down from the north, and their sworn enemies are Pechenegs; but they seem to have restrained them, and they bide their time in Asia Minor, a silent threat.

As the Turks move closer, the Byzantine Empire weakens and shrinks. Psellus, in the midst of his parade of emperors, is gloomily prophetic:

I believe that when the first crack appears in the walls,
from this moment the whole house is doomed. The great
majority will pass unheeding by; but this is the beginning
of the evil, and it grows and spreads.[24]

Anna Comnena laments the extent to which the Empire had diminished by her day. Once, she says, it extended from the Pillars of Hercules in the East to the
Pillars of Dionysus in the West, from the Straits of Gi-
braltar as far as India; it reached from Thule in the cold
north sea down through Egypt to Meroe and the Tro-
glodyte country. And now, she says bitterly, what have
we left? The limits of Byzantium are Adrianople on one
side and the Bosphorus on the other.

It is perhaps symbolic that one of the fullest sketches
left by Anna of her father shows him founding a hospital. Its hub was the Church of the Apostle Paul, near the
acropolis. Round this, Alexius built a model city, "a city
within a city," as his daughter calls it, for the sick, the
aged and infirm. Food was provided at the Emperor's
expense, and grown on farms that Alexius had deeded
to his new foundation. Attendants were provided for
the poor and weak. Nor was their spiritual welfare neglected. A large body of clergy was appointed to St.
Paul's, and the church blazed with lights and rang with
hymns sung by a male and female choir antiphonally.
Attached to the foundation was a grammar school for
orphans of every race. "There you could see a Latin
furthering his education, a Scyth learning Greek, a Roman handling Greek texts, an illiterate Greek learning
how to read his own language."[25] It was the swan song
of a crippled culture.

8. THE SECOND CITY: THESSALONIKI

We have already been to Thessaloniki. We saw it as Galerius' city, one of the great centers of the Greco-Roman world, a powerful subcapital of the Tetrarchy. We must return to it now, for its importance had not diminished through the years. In the fourteenth century, as in the fourth, the Via Egnatia was still the great artery of the Empire from West to East; goods and travelers still poured into Thessaloniki, as they had always done, and, as it had played a part in the shaping of Constantinople, the city helped to usher in her fall.

In the last great persecution Thessaloniki, like nearly every city, had acquired its distinctive saint and martyr. This was Demetrius, a Roman of senatorial rank who rose to be proconsul of Greece while Maximian was still on the throne. Making no attempt to conceal his Christianity, he preached regularly on the west side of the forum, in the place called the "Brazen Stoa"; he apparently converted the heating chambers of the public baths into a chapel. In Roman eyes his zeal was culpable. Despite his high rank he was arrested and brought before Maximian, who had him imprisoned in the same rooms where he used to preach. The story goes that, at the same time, there was a Vandal called Lyaeus, a wrestler and gladiator of formidable reputation, who was taking on all comers at the stadium. This man was a great favorite of Maximian, who was addicted to the sport; the public recognized him as invincible. A young man named Nestor, scheduled for a coming bout, visited the imprisoned Demetrius to ask his help. The latter, eagerly awaiting his promised martyrdom, blessed him with the sign of the cross, telling him that he would not only win his fight, but become a martyr to God himself. All happened as Demetrius had promised. Nestor killed Lyaeus with a blow, and Maximian, furious, had the young man brought before him. When asked what witchcraft had produced this victory, Nestor replied:

"He fell by no magic—perish the thought! Nor was it any kind of spell that killed him. The God of Demetrius, the Christian God, sent down his angel to kill the offender in his pride, through the strength of this, my hand." At this, the Emperor was angry and gave orders that Nestor, being a Christian, should be taken to the western quarter of the city called the Golden Gate, and there be killed with his own sword by the imperial bodyguard Menutius. And so Nestor won the martyr's crown.[1]

Demetrius was murdered too. His servant Lupus dipped the martyr's headband in his blood and preserved it as a relic, while fellow Christians stole away the body and buried it deep out of danger. Later, when it was safe, they built a humble shrine to mark the spot. The next chapter in the story comes after Christianity had been established as the official religion of the Em-

pire, with the arrival of Leontius, prefect of Illyria.
Leontius was sick with an incurable disease, but was
healed immediately after venerating Demetrius's remains. In gratitude he built a church on the spot where
the saint used to preach, between the public baths and
the stadium. (It once was believed that part of this foundation remained in the crypt of the present church, but
this is no longer thought to be true.) Leontius, rejoicing
in his health, went on his way back home. Reaching the
banks of a river (said to be the Danube, but the geography is imprecise), he was held up by winter storms and
seemed certain to waste his journey. That night, as he
sat disconsolate on the bank, Demetrius appeared to
him and told him to attempt the crossing, trusting in
the power of the relics that he carried. Come morning,
Leontius did as he was bid holding the casket out in
front of him; and at his approach the waters grew calm
and still. On his safe return home his renewed gratitude
led him to construct a second church to St. Demetrius,
in Sirmium; and Demetrius in later years acquired a
great reputation among the Slavs and Bulgars, who
came to look upon him as their own protector.

But Thessaloniki still claimed him as her own, and the
church that Leontius had founded dominated the city.
Built in 412, it was basilical in shape, and the architect
utilized part of the public baths nearby for the crypt.
The notorious stadium was involved too, some of its
seats serving the new construction as steps. The Church
of St. Demetrius was an impressive building. Heavy
timber beams supported the roof. The interior was
decorated with mosaics and multicolored marbles, and
the long line of the nave, bounded by marble columns,
led the eye to the carved screen and the altar, beneath
which lay a vial of St. Demetrius' blood. In the mosaics,

some of which survive, one can trace the principal events of the saint's life. In one of them, Demetrius is shown standing between two men, one of whom is probably Bishop Iannes, his biographer, and the other Leontius, the founder. Underneath runs the legend:

Here you see St. Demetrius, and on either hand a famous builder of this house. He turns away the barbarians who come in strength by sea. He saves his city.

Demetrius saved his city many times. He was believed to manifest himself in time of peril. On one occasion, when Thessaloniki was under siege and the people were starving,

he appeared to one Stephen, a merchant captain, as he lay off Chios with a large cargo of grain aboard, making ready to sail to Constantinople, the queen of cities. The apparition was dressed as in the icons and was seen in broad daylight, when Stephen was about to raise sail and set course to starboard for Byzantium. Standing in the ship, he said to Stephen, "Listen to me, sail on the other tack. Make for Thessaloniki, and you shall have fair skies and fast sailing. For the city is in need of grain, and you can easily supply its wants with me to guide you." Stephen was beside himself at the wondrous vision of the martyr and stammered in reply: "But, Master, we have heard that Thessaloniki is taken by the barbarians. Why then do you bid me go there?" And he who was victorious in the fight replied, "In the eyes of men it may be taken, but not in the eyes of God. To God all things are possible. Go then, and proclaim to all the ships you meet that Thessaloniki has been saved by God's mercy." When he had so spoken, he went down from the ship into the sea and walked upon the surface of the water, saying, "Where you see me go before, there must you go also."[2]

A wall painting in the church, reduced by time and hazard to a blur, shows Thessaloniki threatened by just such an invasion. It was threatened in fact by most invaders in its time—Avars, Bulgars, Slavs, Franks, and ultimately Turks. St. Demetrius was best remembered for his role in the devastating naval blockade which began in 617 and lasted for two years. After a long period of siege the enemy moved in to the attack.

Three days so elapsed, and the Slav ships were cruising about two miles from the walls, searching daily for the more vulnerable sites where they might find the booty they desired. On the fourth day, at dawn's first light, the whole tribe of barbarians raised their warcry and made a concerted onslaught on the city from all sides at once. Some dragged catapults into position and started a barrage of stones. Others brought up scaling ladders to mount the city walls. Others hurled a shower of spears that fell upon the ramparts like a snowstorm. It was a sight to wonder at. The city wore an aureole of stones and arrows that shadowed the air, like a dustcloud passing before the sun. . . . Then all the people prayed to God, saying, "Lord, deliver us this day from the snares of the hunters, for if You do not, our enemies will cry, 'Where is their god, in whom they put their trust?' Help us, Lord, and we will cry to You, through him who was the victor in the fight. Our soul has been set free, we will cry, like a sparrow from the net of our besiegers. The net is broken, we are prisoners no more. In the name of God our help, who made both heaven and earth."

And then our champion and true patriot appeared, the martyr Demetrius in all his glory. He wore a white robe and was seen beyond all doubt, first atop the ramparts, then running on the surface of the sea. . . . At his coming all the ships were thrown together and collided. Some capsized, and the Slavs in them were thrown overboard. Swimming to the other ships to save themselves, they turned these over in their panic, and the crews fell into the water. The sailors on board hacked at the swimmers' grasping hands with their blades, and cut them about the head with sword and spear. In their anxiety for their own safety they turned on each other. And at that moment you could see the whole sea dyed red, recalling the drowning of Pharaoh and his Egyptians in the water.[3]

As well as a defender, St. Demetrius was a notable healer. His power transmitted itself through the miraculous aromatic oil that flowed unceasingly from his body. Its very quantity was amazing. When the Turks captured Thessaloniki, they tried for three days to pump the tomb dry and could not. There were some who disbelieved its powers, but they were soon converted. We have the tale of one Vitalius, a skeptic who was finally convinced by a dream. In it he was carried to Thessaloniki and the church of the saint. The doorkeeper asked him if he wished to view the martyr's body. Replying that he did, he was conducted inside the tomb to find Demetrius lying as one asleep, with a smile of peace on his face and the oil running in vast quantities from the gashes in his body. The vast majority of people, however, needed no such proof. For them the miraculous oil was irrefutable fact. It could be seen and touched; it was drawn from the saint's tomb and conducted through pipes to what is now the crypt of the modern church. The crypt is still accessible, and agreeably sinister. A broad stone staircase leads down from behind the altar to a series of low, dark, small arches. If you penetrate the right one, you emerge suddenly into a small chamber containing three stone basins which once held oil and holy water for the never-ending flow of pilgrims. The end of the pipe which fed these basins from the upper stories is still visible; recent investigations into the source of supply do not, unfortunately, exclude the possibility of a priestly confidence trick. By applying this oil the Thessalonians made themselves strong against their enemies and also cured disease. On one occasion it saved the whole city from the plague. On another it cured a military prefect of the bloody flux:

> Brothers in the love of Christ, what tongue can tell the magnitude of this miracle? What mind, by taking thought, could praise the martyr's great mercy as it deserves? When neither wealth nor family, medicine nor physicians could give him health, when charms and talismans had done but little good—for even these his family had not refrained from giving him (though they knew it was forbidden), since no cure seemed to work and they were desperate to try anything—the imitator of Christ, the city's true preserver, the victor through Christ, made him sound and whole, not only in his body but his soul, and gave his back his strength again.[4]

The church was burned down in the seventh century. It was promptly rebuilt on its original plan; the paintings and mosaics which survived the fire lived out the iconoclastic persecutions also, for the power of St. Demetrius was so strong that his people defiantly preserved his images through the century and more in which they were forbidden. When Thessaloniki was captured by the Turks, the church suffered the inevitable transformation into a mosque. In 1912 it became a Christian edifice again, only to be destroyed by fire five years later. For a second time it was restored according to the original plan. Although the tomb of Demetrius, walled with slabs of marble and covered with precious stones set in gold and silver, has completely disappeared, and the miraculous oil no longer runs, the church still stands as a facsimile of its own past, in its original site on the west side of the forum where the saint once preached. Garish in red brick and somewhat sneered at by the guidebooks, it still dominates the center of the city. It is faithful to the original at least in shape, and the reconstructed interior (though with concrete substituting for timber beams) is undeniably impressive. With the recent excavations of the forum at its doorstep, the visitor may see the heart of Thessaloniki as it was in an earlier day.

Around the Church of St. Demetrius the web of Christian Thessaloniki was spun. On October 26, the saint's day, the sacred oil ran over more freely than usual and special masses were said in every church. On the festival eve all the holy places were illuminated, and a long-candle-bearing procession wound its way down the Via Egnatia. Next morning High Mass was celebrated in the presence of the governor and occasionally of the Emperor himself. As in pagan antiquity, religion and trade went hand in hand, for the saint's day was also the occasion of the great trade fair for which Thessaloniki was famous. It ran from October 20 to the first Monday after St. Demetrius' Day, and was held outside the city wall, on the level ground leading to the River Axios. For the duration of the fair the plain became a city under canvas. Merchants came from all over the world, by boat or caravan, and particularly along the Via Egnatia. Many made the fifteen-day journey from Constantinople by the route that Theodore describes for us, alternating between coast-hopping boat and pack mule. The city was equipped to entertain its guests. There were numerous hostelries and caravanserais, one of which was still standing in Thessaloniki within fairly recent memory. The fair was a slightly smaller replica of the annual Constantinople fair. Cloth would have been sold here, dyes and spices, not to mention the wine for which Thessaloniki was famous; the modern *naoussa* is its not-unworthy descendant.

Though dominated by the Church of St. Demetrius, Thessaloniki was full of churches. Between the center and the waterfront, the great rotunda which may originally have been part of Galerius' palace complex was dedicated to St. George. A sanctuary and apse were added, and the whole vast dome—which may originally have been planned in emulation of the Pantheon at Rome, or Diocletian's palace mausoleum at Split—was covered with mosaics of the saints, listed according to their holy days. We see among others Philemon, whose flute was devoured by fire from heaven after he refused to play before the pagan idols; the healing saints, Cosmas and Damian, who cured an emperor, only to be murdered by their jealous rivals; and Ananias, whose fortitude against torture so impressed his captors that in the end his warder and seven guards had to be martyred with him. They stand theatrically posed, surrounded by peacocks and the Tree of Life, against backgrounds reminiscent of the classical Roman theater. The effect on the susceptible Thessalonians must have been stunning.

Near the center also Thessaloniki had its own Haghia

Sophia, built perhaps at the end of the seventh century. There was the Church of the Virgin too, containing an icon that came down straight from heaven untouched by human hands; and there was the trim, square Panaghia Chalkeon, standing in what was once the coppersmith's' district, now sunken amid the lawns and trim trees of a public park. Further west in the Old Town, where streets forget their modern symmetry and run berserk uphill, churches proliferate. The Church of the Prophet Elias, elaborate with striated brickwork, wearing its dome askew, was once probably the *katholikon* of Nea Moni, one of the most important monasteries of the city.

The church alone remains, trapped by apartment houses in a dusty square. Around two or three corners is Hosios David—founded, according to legend, by Galerius' daughter—with its mosaics of the visions of Ezekiel and Habbakuk and a young, beardless Christ. This was once the center of a monastery too—Moni Laotomos, the monastery of the quarrymen. And, crowning the whole city, with a splendid view across the rooftops to the sea, stands the *katholikon* of the Blattades monastery, founded, tradition says, by two Cretan brothers of that name who pursued their reclusive calling this far north. It is the center of a monastery still; the modern buildings, arched in concrete, reach out from the slope below. But the church itself is timeless, like the living peacocks, Byzantine symbol of immortality, who strut in a cage nearby. On the outer wall can still be seen the painted fragments of a liturgical calendar ordering a rite that has not changed across the centuries, while down the precipitous cobbled street walk priests, monks and nuns, whose robes would not be unfamiliar to the last Constantine.

These are the churches that are still visible, and by no means all. Beneath the soil lie many others, for Thessaloniki, during the last centuries of its Byzantine life, was covered with churches and monasteries. There were at least sixteen of the latter, including one dedicated to St. Clement, one to St. John the Baptist, and no less than three to St. Nicholas, one of them also serving as an orphanage. The monks and clergy enjoyed enormous power and privilege. Exempt from taxation, they reaped a fat profit from their vast estates. They owned businesses and hostelries; they owned slaves, like the Children of Demetrius who were dedicated to the patron saint. Not surprisingly, this prosperity provoked resentment, and in the fourteenth century this resentment was to come to a head.

The citizens who filled these churches, watched the archbishop parading through the streets, and grumbled at the privileges of the monks, were a mixed population. It was a large one too; Thessaloniki, like Constantinople, was *megalopolis*, the big city. By the early fifteenth century, because of the depredations of the Turks, it had shrunk to 40,000, but earlier figures must have been much larger. There was a sizable Slavic contingent. There were Jews, such as could be found in every city. Benjamin of Tudela, pursuing his rabbinical way around the world, noted that there were five hundred of his people in residence—more, apparently, than in most Greek cities of that time. They were engaged in handicrafts and subject to their own leaders, but were persecuted by the Greek majority. There was as yet no ghetto, but the Jews seem to have been forced to live in tumble-down houses; a complaint was made that some were occupying homes still decorated with Christian religious paintings. In addition there were

Italians from the burgeoning mercantile cities, Venetians, Genoese and Pisans. Of these the Genoese were most prolific; in other parts of Greece they had established virtual colonies.

These were the races that lived within the shelter of Thessaloniki's stout walls. Most of the original defenses can still be seen, enclosing the upper half of the town. Begun at the time of the Greek foundation, they were successively rebuilt and enlarged. In some places the signatures of Byzantine occupancy are still visible: crosses and inscriptions embedded in the stone. At the summit stood the Acropolis, separately walled and towered—now a dustbowl with a scattering of houses inside —while other towers protected the town perimeter. Their most striking survivor, the so-called White Tower of the waterfront, dates from the fifteenth century, its massive stones replacing a smaller fortress which had stood there previously. It may have been constructed by the Turks, or by the Thessalonians, uselessly, against them. A smaller curtain wall, as at Constantinople, surrounded the main wall for additional protection. The gates surviving on the west side are barely large enough for modern traffic to squeeze through. Thessaloniki could count herself well-guarded.

Within the walls, discipline was maintained by the governor, who flew the imperial standard over his palace. His garrison was reduced in peacetime and seems to have been made up mostly of local cavalry, who were quartered on the Acropolis. But there were also the police, who seem to have been addicted to brutality; they reinforce the picture of a noisy, squabbling cosmopolitan city where tempers run high and order must be kept forcibly or not at all. Thessaloniki has always been a violent city, from Theodosius' massacre in the Hippodrome through the Nazi purge of Macedonian Jews to the modern political turmoil of *Z* and its aftermath. The police met violence with violence, bludgeoning the citizens into unwilling respect:

> Their weapon is cruelty. They live the way that wild beasts live; every day sees them starting or pursuing some new quarrel. They steal the property of the rich, as in Athens at the time of the Thirty Tyrants. You can see men pledging their sworn oath and simultaneously breaking it. You can see them in the marketplace, using their fists on people's faces, knocking them down, raining blows upon their backs, dragging others along by the beard—yes, old men too—shouting insults and obscene threats. This is part of the regular way of life here. Such things happen all the time: public brawls that make the night streets hideous, honest citizens set upon by bullies, drunken and dissolute mobs roaming the alleyways, walls broken through, property stolen, houses ransacked, and all that sort of thing—no, worse than that: arson, stone-throwing, vicious assaults, a whole string of murders committed every day, knife and scimitar kept ready for instant action. They do not even take their weapons off to go to bed. You might well think they could not live without them.[5]

An explosive city, then, with an oriental tendency toward the violent and sensational that could be partly appeased, or at least kept dormant, by the gaudy ceremonies and elaborate celebrations of the church; a city that, like modern Thessaloniki with its industry on one side and its university on the other, embraced both the rarified intellect and the hard-bargaining commercial mind. Thessaloniki was to meet its doom in 1430, when the Turks marched in. But a century before that time, the second city of Byzantium was to see two great crises, one spiritual, one political, that between them signified the disbanding of an era.

The first began, harmlessly enough, in one of those spiritual explorations that characterized an age officially dedicated to emphasizing the soul over the body; in that obsessive concern with the flesh that drove the Byzantines either to decorate it or to mortify it. With religious interest so intense, the extremes of fanaticism were always liable to manifest themselves, and there were many who willingly accepted lives of the utmost rigor. For these, the self-abnegation demanded by monastic life was not enough. Byzantium produced a number of well-publicized ascetics whose remorseless austerity drove them to the limits of endurance.

Such a one was Simeon Stylites, first of the "pillar saints" and most famous of them all. Though he entered a monastery with the best intentions, he soon found himself unpopular with the other monks because he imposed on himself a discipline far more rigorous than their own. He could go for a week without eating, a feat which apparently made them jealous; his record in later life was thirty-nine days, but by that time he was beyond their ken. He bound himself, with ropes made of palm-fibers, so tightly that he bled, and sought solitude in the bed of a dried-up lake, from which he had to be brought back by force. Having finally abandoned monastic life as too indulgent, he settled on top of a column six cubits high, building it up by stages till he finally attained thirty-six cubits. He was fifty-six when he died, and his body, out of long habit, remained standing after the soul had departed from it.

Such men had a glamor which gave them widespread fame and attracted many converts, like Daniel, one of

Simeon's disciples. He too was a man who turned his back on the world at an early age.

> The early seed showed how the future tree would grow, and he who walked in the light cast the shadow of virtue behind him. As he grew older, it gradually became apparent that he was spiritually inclined beyond his years. When Daniel had reached the age of twelve, having not yet spoken a word to anyone of his intention, he had already turned away from his parents for the love of Christ, and from his family also. He despised this world and all that herein is. All these things he left behind him—his friends, his peers, the very place that saw his birth—and went off to join a community of monks.[6]

Here he was almost rejected by the brothers, who thought him too feeble to endure their life. He insisted on staying, however, and the abbot was so impressed by him that he eventually took him to Antioch to see the famous St. Simeon on his column.

> When they had arrived at the column, they contemplated the height of it, and the harsh, uncompromising countryside, and wondered that a man so delicately nurtured could bear the cold of winter and the summer's heat, the menace of the rain and the blast of the wind, and all the other demands upon his body. . . . Since the crowd at the foot of the column made so loud a noise, the great man looked down and said that they should bring up ladders and mount to him. Then it was possible to see the true state of their minds. One man claimed he had no strength in his feet; another, that he was suffering from kidney trouble; a third pleaded old age; all had some excuse for not climbing the column.[7]

Daniel made the ascent, however, and was blessed by the saint, who promised him a lifetime of hardship in God's service. Taking advice, he went to Constantinople, "the second Jerusalem," and established himself on a column there. Simeon's promise was fulfilled. The new stylite suffered every conceivable hardship, including harassment by the church authorities and the well-meant interference of his own followers, who continually entreated him to come down. On one occasion they almost succeeding in persuading him, but were so moved by the sight of his feet, swollen and ulcerated from years of immobility, that they let him remain where he was. Daniel also survived a storm which nearly uprooted his column and lashed it about like the branch of a tree. In recompense he attained healing powers and was constantly visited by an adoring public. When his death was imminent he delivered a farewell homily, dutifully heard by monks ranged on ladders round the column. He was buried at the foot of the pillar that had been his home for many years. When his body was lowered to the ground, his hair was found to have grown four cubits long; and three stars shone at his funeral, although it was bright day.

There were others, less well-known but hardly less spectacular. St. Makarios the Roman, having swatted a mosquito that had bitten him, was so overcome by remorse that he went to live for months in a mosquito-ridden swamp; when he emerged, he was so covered with suppurating boils that his friends could not recognize him. St. Joannikios had a passion for solitude which drove him to the limits of endurance. Leaving the monastery, which he found too noisy for his taste, he climbed to the top of a mountain, built himself "a rude shelter from the wind and rain," and shut himself inside. Finding that even here too many visitors came to disturb his "pleasant and familiar silence," he went down to the shores of the Hellespont, where the woods were thick and impenetrable, and

> dug himself a hole in the ground, deep and narrow, in which he took up his abode. He never ventured out; he did not even have, like Elias, a raven to bring him food. This office he entrusted to a passing goatherd, with the promise of greater benefits in return. Every month this man would bring him a supply of bread and water. And in this solitude he spent three years, singing hymns to God by day and night.[8]

These were the men who pushed to the extreme their desire to mortify the flesh, the elite or the lunatic fringe, depending on one's personal preconceptions. There were many, however, with equal aspirations but lesser stamina, who found the discipline that they desired within the confines of a monastery, and a number of settlements grew up which had a special appeal for such ascetic spirits. A monastery like Studium, located in a rich and powerful city, visited regularly and with ceremony by the Emperor, and involved, however involuntarily, in the politics of church and state, could hardly escape the taint of worldliness; inevitably, something would seep through the walls. But there were many places in the wilder regions of the Greek landscape where the world's temptations could be firmly repulsed. One of these was Meteora, in Thessaly, where the monasteries grew up on cliffs accessible only by rope and pulley. They are still there—though their populations have been depleted almost to extinction—decorated with paintings whose grotesquerie reflects the bizarre, distorted nature of the mountain landscape. More relevant to Thessaloniki, because closer at hand, were the settlements on Athos, the Sacred Mountain, which has been the breeding ground of controversies and divines for hundreds of years.

If you climb the White Tower of Thessaloniki and look out across the bay, you will see a distant smudge of land on the horizon. On the map this smudge extends and resolves itself into three fingers of land thrusting into the water, according to the Greek imagination, like the prongs of Poseidon's trident. This is the Chalkidike peninsula, whose easternmost arm rises to the mountain peak of Athos. The narrow neck of land was notorious for its storms, a familiar and dreaded navigational hazard. Xerxes, on his way to invade Greece, found it more practical to bypass it by means of a canal; some traces of this man-made waterway may still be seen. Athos seems always to have acted as a magnet for the superhuman and the grandiose. Two centuries later the architect Dinarchus conceived the project of honoring his ruler, Alexander, by carving the entire mountain into a colossal statue of the conqueror. The proposal was never translated into actuality, but in the eighteenth century the Austrian architect Fischer von Erlach sketched his own design of what this Greek Mount Rushmore might have looked like. He shows a mountain whose porportions ideally match those of the seated human form. Its summit becomes Alexander's head, while its flanks hold his bent arms; a township nestles in the crook of his elbow and a river spills from his lap down to the sea, where broken islands and black clouds provide a suitably theatrical if somewhat sinister frame. As an evocation of Athos it is powerfully in keeping with the spirit of the place.

Dinarchus' conception was never attempted, much less realized, and it was left to an even more powerful patron than Alexander to endow Mount Athos with glory. This was no less than the Virgin Mary, who, according to the legend, landed here in the company of St. John when they had been driven off course while on a companionable voyage to Cyprus. The Mother of God immediately claimed the peninsula as her own, and at her coming the pagan idols throughout the whole district groaned aloud and fell to the ground, lamenting their defeat. Scholarship has ingeniously connected this miraculous event with an earthquake which took place in 49 A.D. The Virgin was also one of the last women to set foot on a site which was soon to become—as it still is—an exclusively male preserve.

The beginnings of monastic life on Athos were sporadic, desultory and to a large extent, unwelcome. Attracted by the isolation of the mountain no less than by its reputation, austere spirits came to settle there. Once again, for lack of written records, we are thrown back on tradition, and we are told that sometime in the ninth century St. Peter the Athonite came to inhabit a cave on the mountain, subsisting wholly upon herbs and manna. He was later joined by St. Euthymius of Thessaloniki, almost as great a recluse as himself, whose habit was to go about on all fours eating grass. Euthymius' fame attracted a colony of disciples (forming a *lavra*), which so offended his sense of privacy that he followed historical precedent and betook himself to the top of a column. But the flow of visitors increased, the original *lavra* was joined by others, and the sacred mountain began to be occupied by organized groups. Where the hermits had once sought peace, whole settlements now arose. Protection was extended to them by the tenth-century general, Nicephorus Phocas, whose personality embraced the two extremes of the Byzantine character. In civil life distinguished by his involvement in the murder of the Emperor Romanus, whose widow he subsequently married—eventually to be murdered by her in turn—he still had close friends within the Church, and through the monk Athanasius extended his patronage to the fledgling Athonite monasteries.

Athos took its character from this moment. Rigid sanctions and embargoes were set up to immunize it against the tribulations of the world outside. Time stopped for Athos, literally as well as figuratively, for the monasteries still keep Byzantine time and the Julian calendar. On the Virgin's sacred mountain no woman is allowed to walk; even female animals are forbidden. Athos governs itself, maintains its own restrictive rules and fiercely resists interference even from the Church outside its borders. With few interuptions this precarious, artificial serenity has been preserved until the present day. Occasionally and roughly, the outside world has made its existence known. In 1261, as a political concession, Athos was forced into accepting the Latin Mass. In 1307 it was attacked by Catalan mercenaries. In 1430, after the fall of Thessaloniki, it surrendered to the Turks, but by doing so preserved its religious and political autonomy, for the conquerors only pillaged the places that resisted them. Today Athos is doubly secure by virtue of its position within a militarily sensitive zone for which special checks and clearances are required. Although its population is steadily declining, Athos maintains its status as a haven.

The communities that grew within its boundaries,

austere, dedicated and cohesive, provided a climate in which religious extremists could flourish. Orthodox monasteries were based on the principle of a communal life secured and advanced by brotherly love. It had been St. Theodore's particular contribution to develop an order which, while recognizing the primacy of the group, still tolerated some degree of individuality. In Athos, by virtue of its situation, the group at that time stood for more and the individual for less. In later Athonite history this ceased to be true: a number of monasteries went over to the idiorhythmic principle, according to which monks were permitted to eat alone, keep their private devotions and live their lives virtually undisturbed by their brethren—even, in extreme cases, turning into hermits within the colony, inhabiting caves on the mountainside and being fed daily by monks they never saw; but in the fourteenth century the community life was still the rule, and any idea which fired the community could rapidly develop an explosive potential.

The issue which swept Athos into conflict first with Thessaloniki and then with the world, and brought the basis of her whole existence into question, was a new movement masquerading under an old name. The name was hesychasm, meaning a seeking after spiritual tranquillity, which in itself was harmless enough: but its present manifestation carried alien connotations which made it offensive to certain powerful voices in the Church. Since the eleventh century there had been those who believed in a divine light, a radiance which had its own existence and was not merely a state of mind; that this was the celestial light which bathed Mount Tabor on the day of the Transfiguration; and that it could be rejuvenated, and experienced anew, by those determined enough to undergo a rigorous physical and mental preparation.Such was the discipline that hesychasm now implied. It recalls the practices of Indian fakirs—the mental awareness brought about by bodily discipline that we now associate with zen or yoga. Like them, it came from the East, having been imported to Athos by one Gregory of Sinai in the first quarter of the fourteenth century; like them too, it held a fascination for a certain kind of religious temperament, one which was already strongly represented upon Athos.

The disciple was required to enter a trance-like state through a form of self-hypnosis. This could be assisted, as in most such cases, by the repetition of a formula—in this case the name of Jesus, intoned to the rhythm of the heart-beat—and by eliminating all disturbances from the mind.

> Sit down by yourself in a corner, and diligently follow the instructions I shall give you. Close the door. Turn your thoughts away from all empty and transitory things. Then drop your chin upon your chest and, with all the strength your mind can command, turn your eye toward the midpoint of your belly, to your navel, that is. At the same time block the passage of your nose so that you can only breathe with an effort. Search within yourself. Seek for the location of the heart, which is the seat of psychic energy in man. Your first sensation will be of languor and obscurity. But if you persist in this and continue your efforts day and night, oh what marvels! You will perceive infinite joy.[9]

Many willingly performed these exercises, and the number of hesychasts rapidly increased. There was some opposition to the movement, even on Athos, but this was quashed by the emergence of a redoubtable and universally respected champion. He was Gregory Palamas, by birth aristocratic and by temperament devout. Educated at the court of the Emperor Andronicus II he had voluntarily embraced a life of poverty. Admired both for his learning and the simplicity of his life, he stood before the Thessalonians and delivered urgently-needed sermons on brotherly love and the avoidance of civil strife:

> All men are brothers, for we are all the sons of Adam, and we alone are created in God's image. But that is something we have in common with all the other races of mankind. Here we have added reasons to regard ourselves as brothers. We were born in the same region and cultivate the same soil. Above all, we enrich our common mother, the Holy Church, and the faith we share. For its beginning and end is Jesus Christ, God's true-begotten son, who thought it good that He should not be God alone, but our Brother and our Father too. . . . But who are these who make onslaughts against our city, who shake its houses to their foundations, who rob these houses of their goods and persecute their owners with outrage and fury, raising a blasphemous and beastly outcry against them? Surely not the people of this city? From whom this rage and fury, this angry roar, these alarms and incursions? . . . Oh, the pity of it, the catastrophe! It is a war in which the city locks arms with itself, wounds itself with its own heel, tears itself apart with its own hands.[10]

This was the gentle man who now became chief spokesman for the hesychasts, and there were many in Thessaloniki, monks and laymen both, who took him seriously.

There were others, however, who regarded the movement as a disturbing eccentricity bordering on mania, and their spokesman was a figure of another sort. His name was Barlaam, and though he was, like Palamas, a monk, he came from a wider world. Calabrian by birth, he was learned in theology and particularly in ancient philosophy. Petrarch, who was his pupil, remarks of him that he was erudite but humble, and (like all good teachers) learned more from his pupils than he taught them. Though eloquent in Greek, Barlaam was said to have some diffidence in Latin, a tongue in which he had trouble expressing himself. His surviving speeches do not give that impression. On the contrary, they reveal a man whose language is economical to the point of curtness, but pungent and forceful; who has no time to waste on the gloss of rhetoric, but tells the truth as he sees it, simply and powerfully. It was inevitable that such a man should make enemies in Constantinople. His virtues, however, were prized in high places, and he was chosen to represent the state in negotiations on the continuing and urgent question of Church unity. In 1339 he was sent to Avignon, to plead before Benedict XII—this was still the time of the divided papacy—on the nagging problems of doctrine that Rome and Byzantium continued to debate right up to the moment of the latter's demise. The mission was, as usual, fruitless, but the speeches show the man.

Most Holy Father, there are two ways in which this union may conceivably be brought about. One is by force. You may offer violence to the people of the Eastern Empire and constrain them against their will to enter your communion. But there is another way, a free way. Appeal to their minds. Win them over with the

eloquence of learning. Then they will unite with you of
their own accord. There are two ways then; and the
former, if it so pleases you, should be banished from your
mind. But the second way, the way of free choice, has
two sides to it. It is one thing to win over our learned
men. Overcoming popular prejudice is quite another.[11]

So Barlaam calls for a conference that will involve not
merely the heads of state, but the leaders of the Church
also—the Pope's representatives, together with the pa-
triarchs of Constantinople, Alexandria and Antioch
debating together in ecumenical harmony.

It is typical of Barlaam, however, that he sees the
docrtinal issue as subordinate to a larger and more
pressing danger.

And this also I advise you—no, I beg you—to consider.
In Turkey there are four large and prosperous cities
which in former times were Greek. But for our sins they
have long been betrayed into the hands of the ungodly.
Those who guard and maintain them were once Christians. They have been made Turks by force. And these
people, in their desire to become Christian again, have
sent word to my master, saying, "Come to us with an
army, and we shall deliver these same cities into your
hands." Our Emperor, doubting that his people could
succeed in this unaided, sent us to His Most Christian
Majesty of France, to ask for his help in the enterprise.
For if those cities could be taken and restored to us, the
Turks would immediately forefeit their whole strength
by sea. The hazards which now plague Christians on the
sea would cease. The towns and countryside which lie
between these cities and your own domains would be
handed over to you. And the door would be flung wide
open for pilgrimage again.[12]

Barlaam sees the internecine squabbles of Christianity as paltry beside the threat to Christianity itself.

> The Turks are making war on Greeks. Not for the simple reason that they are Greeks. Not because they are any different from you. They are making war on them because they adore the Cross. It is the Cross they are attacking. The fact that their victims are Greek is coincidental. Therefore if you go against the Turks, it is not the Greeks you will be defending, but the Cross. . . .[13]

In pursuit of this grand and, in his mind, essential design, Barlaam dismisses differences of doctrine as of no more than passing interest. Forget them, he urges; leave it to every man to pursue the form of worship that his own conscience dictates. There are more important things to worry about.

It was a sound, common-sense argument, that desperately needed to be heard. It was also one hardly calculated to endear Barlaam to the princes of either half of the Church. And it was an argument that summed up Barlaam's whole life; temperamentally, philosophically, politically, he was opposed to everything that a man like Palamas stood for. He was an activist, Palamas a quietist; he was practical, Palamas contemplative; he took the world view, Palamas sought the spiritual satisfaction of the individual. Barlaam wished to make one community of the entire Christian world; Palamas sought to establish a tiny group of the elect within a system already infinitely fragmented by the convolutions of Byzantine theology. It was inevitable that the two should clash, and the shock of meeting and opposing minds came in Thessaloniki, where Barlaam had come to escape the animosity of Constantinople and to found a school in the classical Greek manner, teaching the precepts of Plato and Aristotle to students in a garden.

The debate began in 1337 or the year after, with a courteous and dispassionate exchange of views. From this point the course of argument slid rapidly downhill. Random charges began to fly, facile labels to be attached. Barlaam professed to find the professions of the hesychasts absurd. His shout of "heretic!" was answered with the indignant cry of "blasphemer!" Well-known for his fondness for the ancients, he now found his classicism held against him. His opponents claimed that Barlaam knew more of Plato than of the Christian Fathers. He was a dangerous throwback, a neo-pagan. As was inevitable in Byzantium, religious controversy became political crisis. First the governor of Thessaloniki intervened, appealing to Barlaam for the city's sake to be quiet. The Calabrian was forced to leave for Constantinople, where he loosed another barrage of accusations, charging the hesychasts with breaking canon law. It had now become a matter for the ecclesiastical courts, and Palamas was forced to travel to the capital to defend himself.

In the synods that followed, each man fought with the weapons that suited him best: Palamas with mysticism and quotations from holy writ, Barlaam with deadly logic. Their auditors preferred the former; it had the comfort of familiarity. Barlaam lost his suit, but the contest was not yet over. There were strategic regroupings and shifting allegiances. A former disciple of Palamas, Gregory Akindynos, now turned against him on doctrinal grounds, and the hesychast was forced to attack him and Barlaam together. By this time the argument had degenerated into mere name-calling. Pala-

mas, defensively snobbish, cast aspersions on Akindynos' low-class origins. His opponents promptly retaliated by labeling Palamas a bastard. Another synod intervened, and farce turned into tragedy. When the dust
had cleared, the victory was adjudged to Palamas, more
out of piety than any just desert. In 1351 the Emperor
John Cantacuzene officially upheld the hesychast cause.
Barlaam and his followers were excommunicated, and
the name of the Calabrian still heads the list of those
anathematized by the Greek Orthodox Church.

In the eyes of history, the wrong side won. The great
debate between Palamas and Barlaam was more than
a clash of personalities, more even than a dispute over
religious doctrine. It was a clash of cultures. Palamas, by
virtue of his training and preconceptions, stands as a
representative of the dying Middle Ages, priest-ridden,
introverted and withdrawn. He preaches disassociation
rather than involvement, obedience rather than ex-
ploration. Against him Barlaam is seen as a precursor of
the Renaissance, exemplifying the explosive potential
that had still a century to go before it reached full force;
one of the first great humanists, whose active mind
could not be contained within the walls of a monastery.

The second conflict that shook Thessaloniki during
the fourteenth century also had implications that extended far beyond the walls of one city. On this occasion the issue was social rather than spiritual, although
the anti-hesychasts drew comfort from it in their time,
and we may see it as another instance of the same
phenomenon, the "cracks in the building," the upset-
ting of a traditional order by a new concept of society.

The Byzantine Empire by its nature had fostered a
feudal system which was probably the most pernicious
example of its kind in Europe. Society was divided be-

tween a small governing class, the *dunatoi* or powerful
ones, and the vast mass of the population, many of
whom lived on the edge of poverty. These are the people who tend not to be written about—official Byzantine literature, its attention fixed on loftier things, ig-
nores them—though from time to time the lives of the
popular saints drop hints of penury and squalor. St.
John the Almsgiver, receiving a warm and costly coverlet as a present from an admirer, reflects on the number
of those who have no coverlet at all; who go to sleep
cold and hungry on the mountain; who lie in the mar-
ketplace for want of a roof, exposed to the rain and
freezing cold. The hospitals and almshouses founded by
the emperors could hardly begin to alleviate the problem. Even in so prosperous a city as Thessaloniki the
gap between the rich and poor grew steadily wider,
with the added burden of an oppressive and heavily
subsidized religious establishment. It was only a question of time before popular indignation found a voice.

The opportunity came with one of the incessant disputes over possession of the throne. On the death of
Andronicus III, the succession hung between Anna and
the pretender, John Cantacuzene, who has already appeared in this story as the defender of the hesychasts.
In most parts of the Empire the nobility favored Cantacuzene, but this choice was not well received by the
mass of the population, who had a sentimental attach-
ment to the old regime, and who seized the dispute as
a pretext to revolt against their masters. Thessaloniki,
like most other cities, was divided. The nobles invited
Cantcuzene, whose troops were enjoying considerable
success elsewhere, to march in and take possession.
They found themselves, however, frustrated by the
party called the Zealots, who now stood out as violent

advocates of the popular interest. It was nothing less
than revolution. A cross raised on an altar gave the sign;
with the Zealots at their head, the people stormed
through the city and marched on the governor's mansion. There was little bloodshed as yet, but a number of
the houses of the rich were sacked, and the governor
was forced to leave the city.

Thessaloniki now went wholeheartedly into opposition. A democratic army marched down from Constantinople, and the harbor suddenly bristled with warships, seventy of them, sent down in support. With his
friends and allies abandoning him in droves, Cantacuzene apppeared to have no hope. Mercenaries were
brought in on both sides; for a while, one could see the
strange spectacle of a Thessalonian army with its ranks
swelled by Turks and other foreigners. Cantacuzene's
defeat seemed more and more inevitable, yet there
were strange delays, the expected final blow failed to
materialize and the pretender was allowed to linger on
among the bleak rocks of Macedonia, slipping away to
muster his forces and finally returning to besiege the
city that had rejected him.

Within the walls, the war now began to assume an
ugly aspect. A noble suspected of treachery was decapi-
tated and his body quartered; the segments were displayed over the city gates. Other suspects had their
noses and ears cut off. Food was running short, and the
citizens, looking out over the walls, could see their
farms and fields destroyed. Cantacuzene, who had
begun it all, had sense enough to leave well enough
alone. His successes were sufficient elsewhere, and he
withdrew without a fight, leaving a city which was still
independent, still under Zealot control and still smoldering with hatred against him and the nobles who
were his principal supporters.

It was a situation that could have no happy outcome. In theory, the structure of the government remained unchanged, for the nobles were still in control. In practice, the aristocratic governor had to recognize the leader of the Zealots as co-ruler. Both were proud and arrogant men, reluctant to relinquish any part of their authority. Suddenly, in 1345, animosity flared up into action; the leader of the Zealots was assassinated. Whether it had been deliberately planned or not, the citizens took it as a declaration of war against them, and their suspicions were confirmed when the nobles promptly assumed their former powers and publicly proclaimed their support of Cantacuzene. It was a foolhardy move. Even with a force of eight hundred men, the nobles could not hope to contain the resentment of the populace. All the city was astir. Along the waterfront, the sailors and the Zealots called upon the people to resist. Hounded from their homes and from the city center, the nobles scattered through the narrow streets and sought high ground, assembling in the false security of the Acropolis. From this position, fortified by its independent system of towers and walls, they hoped to dominate the city, but their expectations proved illusory, and their fortress turned into a prison. It was the work of a moment to lock the gates against them from outside. Cut off from any hope of support, with a maddened crowd between them and Cantacuzene's armies, the nobles were helpless.

A rumor spread that a relief force was in sight, and the mob went mad.

Fire was brought against the gates . . . and those inside threw open the doors to their assassins. . . . The soldiers were stripped of their arms, and the man whose lightest word had been law was now at the mercy of all and sundry. The slave no longer recognized his master. The learned judge of yesterday was the victim today. Slaves and paupers turned into rich men, with weapons in their hands; those who had enjoyed these things before they now afflicted with the lot of a slave, and threw them into prisons where they were barred even from the light of day. Falling upon their houses, they made a barren and a blasted place, where there had once been a city. And anyone who saw these things and wept, was promptly put to the sword by the ungodly.[14]

The onslaught turned into a massacre. In their panic, the nobles sought shelter everywhere. Some hid under their neighbors' beds; others dived into wells; many took refuge at the altars, but found no security there; some even forced their way into the tombs and lay among the corpses, cynically anticipating their own demise. Even the Zealots were unable to stop the slaughter.

Some of the victims were dragged out nearly naked, with only one poor garment to cover them. Those who had risked their lives on many occasions to keep these people and their city free were dragged along by halters round their necks, as if they had been slaves. Here was a servant pushing his master, there a slave doing the same to the man who had bought him. The peasant dragged the general, and the farmer dragged the soldier.[15]

The Zealots had accomplished their revolution . . . and for what? For a year or two, Thessaloniki was independent. Orders that came down from Constantinople were burned; the people even gave their city to the Serbs, rather than to submit to their own Emperor—

Cantacuzene, in fact, who by that time had won. But in the end submission was forced upon them. Even in its dying years, Byzantium could still keep a hold upon its own. It was then that Palamas' sermons on peace could be heard in the city, too late; and the lament of Demetrius Kydonis is not so much for Thessaloniki as for the whole Greek people, who have never been more brutal than when they turn upon themselves.

Cry then for the dead and for the dying; for those whose deaths are still to come and those who are left behind. For I think them no more fortunate than the dead. Those who have gone have found their bitter ending. Those who stay must listen to the recital of their shame. . . . Cry for the city, which was once a light and glory to its citizens and now enfolds them in deep and lasting dishonor. What shall we do when faced with our accusers? To hold our tongues is criminal, when our country is being slandered; to offer a defense is madness, when our guilt is so transparent. . . . Cry then for the sickness that came upon our hearts, the destroyer of reason, the great enemy of our common life. All we can do now is pray to God that He will stretch out His hand and let us start again; that He will let us make a city here again. He is our only hope; He alone can fill this empty place that once was Thessaloniki. For we are only men. We can only destroy or turn our backs on the abomination.[16]

9. ISTANBUL

The century which watched the crisis of the second city saw that of the first already far advanced. A hundred years before Thessaloniki had been shaken by her troubles, there had been a falling off of greatness in Constantinople. Up to that time, despite the vicissitudes of internal politics and the centuries that nibbled at her Empire, the mother city herself had contrived to remain proud, independent and prosperous. If you divided the world's wealth into three, it was said, you would find two parts at Constantinople. The rabbi Benjamin of Tudela, making his visit in the twelfth century, saw it as a city of enchantment.

> The Greeks who inhabit the country are extremely rich and possess great wealth of gold and precious stones. They dress in garments of silk, ornamented by gold and other valuable materials; they ride upon horses, and in their appearance they are like princes. The country is rich, producing all sorts of delicacies, as well as abundance of bread, meat and wine, and nothing on earth equals their wealth. They are well skilled in the Greek sciences and live comfortably, "every man under his vine and his fig tree."[1]

Benjamin was only one of the thousands of foreigners who poured annually into Constantinople and were, together with the tribute exacted from subject states, the principal source of her wealth.

> Great stir and bustle prevails at Constantinople in conse-
> quence of the conflux of many merchants who resort
> thither, both by land and by sea, from all parts of the
> world for purposes of trade. Merchants from Babylon
> and from Mesopotamia, from Media and Persia, from
> Egypt and Palestine as well as from Russia, Hungary,
> Palzinakia, Budia, Lombardy and Spain are met with
> here, and in this respect the city is equaled only by
> Baghdad, the metropolis of the Mahometans.[2]

Large numbers of these foreigners were now permanently resident in the city and assembled periodically
to do homage to the Emperor. Benjamin describes the
Christmas celebrations:

> The Hippodrome is a public place near the walls of the
> palace, set aside for the sports of the king. Every year the
> birthday of Jisho the Nazarene is celebrated there by
> public rejoicing. On these occasions you may see repre-
> sentatives of the nations, who inhabit the different parts
> of the world, and surprising feats of jugglery. Lions,
> bears, leopards and wild asses as well as birds, that have
> been trained to fight each other, are also exhibited, and
> all this sport, the equal of which is to be met with no-
> where, is carried on in the presence of the king and
> queen.[3]

In the palace, Christmas saw more decorous ceremonies. Each group of foreigners in residence sent its representatives; the Genoese, the Pisans, the Venetians,
the Varangians of course. Each in turn uttered the

ritual prayer that the Emperor might live many years, and each received the ritual reply, "Our Lord the Emperor bids you many years." The choir then sang a canticle by Romanos, whose poems were the staple of Byzantine hymnology.

A number of foreign communities had established permanent settlements along the waterfront, and the yeasty racial mixture which had long shaped the ruling dynasties—Greek, Roman, Syrian, Armenian, Amorite, even Turkish—now also helped to mold the rank and file. Merchants, from whatever source, were welcome; if they wished to stay, the city granted them commercial privileges and tax exemptions.

A number of Italian colonies were firmly planted on the banks of the Horn, in the area now framed between the railway station and the ferryboats, from Seraglio Point round the corner to the site of the two modern bridges. Here you could see Amalfi, Venice, Pisa in microcosm. Genoa went across the water, to the far bank of the Horn. Galata Tower, which still dominates the district in defiance of modern industrial competition, was built by the Genoese in the early thirteenth century. There had been something on the site before —perhaps a Roman lighthouse, perhaps a Byzantine castellation—but the thrusting tower with its steep-pitched, pointed roof marked out Galata as Genoa's own. It became the center and the landmark of a walled colony. The Turkish conqueror truncated it and turned the tower into a firewatcher's post; in the last generation, rebuilt with modern materials, it has at last resumed its original shape. The Genoese had their share in Constantinople's defense. From Galata stretched the chain which closed off the Golden Horn in time of attack and kept the landward flank of Con-

stantinople safe from siege. Its starting point, somewhere near the bridge, has been blurred by modern
buildings, but great chunks of the chain itself survive,
preserved in the Military Museum. Along the Bosphorus too the Genoese built their castles, which are
still to be seen crowning the hills that march northward
to Russia and the Black Sea.

But of all the foreigners who infested Constantinople,
the city found the Venetians most intriguing. The Byzantines had watched Venice grow, and leave us some
of the earliest records of its foundation and progress:

> Be advised, then, that when the Venetians, as they are
> now known—they were called Enetikoi in the old days
> —crossed the water to their present location, their first
> act was to lay out a city strongly fortified against attack.
> This is the same city that the Doge of Venice inhabits to
> this day. It is surrounded by some six miles of sea, into
> which open the mouths of half a dozen rivers . . . in time
> gone by this Venice was an empty place, a swamp where
> no human being ever set foot. The present Venetians
> were originally Franks from Aquileia and other Frankish
> places, and used to inhabit the mainland across from
> Venice. But when Attila, King of the Avars, descended
> on the Frankish lands and stripped them of their power
> and men, all the Franks from Aquileia and the towns
> nearby began to look to the unpopulated isles of Venice
> for a place of refuge. Such was their fear of King Attila.[4]

There may have been a handful of settlers on the
islands before, but the story which connects the founding of Venice with the advent of the Huns seems to be
largely true. Certainly there would have had to be
some powerful inducement to force a whole population
to abandon prosperous Aquileia for the dismal tufted

islands in the misted lagoon. With half-closed eyes, we may still see the site as it appeared to the first inhabitants, for by a quirk of history the traveler who sees Venice at its most modern sees it at its most primitive. Arriving by air, one travels southward from the airport by motor-launch, dodging the islets. There are the larger ones, Torcello, Burano, which still maintain some show of habitation, with the little gray streamers chugging aimlessly and endlessly among them. There are the tiny ones, aground in their own mud, exactly as the fleeing Aquileians must have known them. Occasionally one may see a line of broken wall or an abandoned boathouse, where some unlucky soul has tried to build and failed, but mostly the islands are left to the wind and the marsh birds. Even the double rows of stakes planted deep into the water to guide the launch down its appointed channel have a primitive look, as though they were waiting for a wattle hut to be planted on top of them and for coracles to bob nervously at their base.

For this is how Venice began, with poles and piles thrust down into the mud, and houses built on top of them. Cassiodorus, foreshadowing a modern poet, compared them to the nests of water birds. Gradually the process of building up the islands began. Today, the view from the campanile of San Marco is the most surprising in Venice, for you can see not a single canal, nothing but acres of red roofs stretching seemingly unbroken to the sea. But in the beginning every inch of building land had to be defended from the water. Bridges linked the islands, and the streams were banked and tamed; the nomenclature of streets, squares and canals testifies to the long, slow process of reclamation. The work was done with such thoroughness that it is only now, after centuries, that the water is beginning to fight back, and the Piazza San Marco regularly turns into an inland pool.

Around the islands, the lagoon still offered its protection against enemies. Any ships that ventured across were met by chains, like those of Constantinople, strung between the islands, and Venice started building ships of her own. First a dependency of Byzantium, falling under the exarchate of Ravenna, Venice gradually grew independent. With the Lombard invasions and Ravenna's fall, the dependency grew more and more nominal. The change of spirit was denoted by a change of saint.

Apart from an early chapel to St. James, Venice's first patron was St. Theodore, a figure as nebulous as the sea-mists out of which the city rose. He is almost impossible to disentangle now from the numerous saints and martyrs who bear that name; it is doubtful whether the medieval Venetians could have been more precise. It may be relevant that excavations have revealed a domestic church in Aquileia whose first bishop was one Theodore. Yet the saint in question—or saints, for they were at least two in one—seems to have come from the East, this being the only point on which historians agree. There are two claimants for the honor. One is St. Theodore Tiro, the Recruit—so called because of his standing in the Roman army, or because he was enrolled in the *cohors tironum*, "recruits' brigade"—martyred at Amasea under Galerius, Maximian and Maximin. Apprehended in his proselytizing activities, he was sentenced to death unless he renounced Christianity. The authorities, who should have known better, allowed him a short time to reconsider. This he turned to rather different advantage.

What did he do, you ask? I will tell you; and it will give you joy to hear. In the metropolis of Amasea stood a temple to the legendary Mother of the Gods, which the people of that time had constructed on the river bank in their blindness. Taking advantage of his temporary lack of restraint and endowed with timely strength, our hero burned it to the ground. There was a favorable wind, and it was soon in ashes. When those impious men, those unbelievers, came back for their awaited answer, this was what he showed them.[5]

Not surprisingly, he was promptly put to death—his sufferings are recorded in the windows of Chartres Cathedral—and, like most saints, went on to accumulate an impressive body of folklore.

It is here that the second St. Theodore enters the picture, also an army man, but this time *Stratelates*, general. He was a provincial governor, with his seat at Heraclea, and was beheaded by Licinius in 319. As late as 970 he was still highly regarded as a military saint: John I, who attributed to his patronage a striking victory over the Saracens, rebuilt his church and his final resting place was renamed Theodoropolis. It is disconcerting to learn that, in the opinion of most modern scholars, Theodore Stratelates is an invention, called into existence to take some of the burden of legend off Tiro's shoulders. So many works were attributed to the latter that even the medieval mind grew cautious and hazarded that there must have been two men of the same name. Confusion was worse confounded when the Theodores became involved in monster-hunts and tangled with the legends of those other well-known dragon-slayers, Saints Demetrius and George.

This was the Theodore who became the patron saint

of Venice, and whose church, supposedly founded by Justinian's eunuch general Narses, occupied the site of the present campanile when the Piazza San Marco was little more than a reclaimed swamp. Ruskin beautifully sketches the memory of the square, set in "a green field, cloister-like and quiet, divided by a small canal, with a line of trees on each side; and extending between the two churches of St. Theodore and Germanium, as the little piazza of Torcello lies between its 'palazzo' and cathedrals."[6] Another church to Theodore, known affectionately as San Toto, stands at the foot of the Palatine in Rome.

The remains of both Theodores (for even if one was fictitious, there were indisputable relics) traveled over a good deal of the Christian world, appearing variously in Alexandria, Brindisi, Constantinople and finally Venice, as the gift of the notorious Doge Dandelo, though unfortunately too late, when the saint had already been supplanted. But Theodore remained the minor patron of Venice after his deposition: his feast was still celebrated on the day of his martyrdom, February 7; his name was held to ward off storms; and his statue, posed above a crocodile, still looks down on the piazzetta. Why a crocodile? The obscurity deepens. It is one of Theodore's established symbols, along with a torch, a temple and a crown of thorns, but no one seems to know where it came from. For some, it is a symbol of evil; for others, a result of the confusion with St. George; and there are even those who claim that the statue is not Theodore at all, but George in person.

It was symbolic that this shadowy figure should have been replaced by a new patron who was not merely more luminous, but much more firmly rooted in history; by no less a figure than St. Mark, whose name was

ever after to be indissolubly associated with the city,
and whose lion became the winged symbol of Venice.
Post factum legend established an early connection between the gospeler and the city. It is said that Mark was
the first bishop of Aquileia and was washed up on his
later domain while it was still a damp and miserable
clutch of islands. As he inspected them from his boat,
an angelic voice called, "Peace be with you, Mark; here
shall your body rest," and it was prophesied that a great
city would later stand on the site. For a long time,
however, Mark's remains seemed destined to lie far
from Venice. Tradition took him to Egypt, where he
was arrested during a festival of Serapis and thrown
into prison. After his death the impious tried to burn his
corpse, but were prevented by a monumental storm,
with thunder, lightning and lashing hail. It lasted
throughout the day, demolishing buildings and taking
many lives, and the ungodly, taking the hint, left the
body alone.

> "Then came godly men, who took the relics of this ser-
> vant of God from the ashes, and set them apart, and sang
> prayers and psalms over them. They attended to his
> funeral as the custom was in that city, depositing his
> relics in a noble tomb of stone, keeping the saint's mem-
> ory alive with devout and solemn prayers. Alexandria
> holds nothing more precious than this tomb.

In the ninth century, however, came equally devout
and godly men to steal the relics from what was now a
stronghold of Islam. This is one of the gaudiest of Christian legends, noteworthy even in an age when traffic in
holy relics was fierce and cities bargained for saints'
bones as eagerly as the people of the Peloponnese had

once quarreled over those of Orestes. The inspired thieves covered their loot with slabs of pork, knowing that the Muslim *douanier* would never search under the meat which was anathema, and so smuggled the body into Venice. In the relic-hungry Middle Ages, it was a superb diplomatic coup. An obscure Byzantine saint had been replaced by an infinitely more prestigious figure of the Venetians' own choosing, and in a way which demonstrated Venetian enterprise and daring. The original church to St. Theodore came down— his remains are still in Venice, but have been transferred to San Salvatore—and that to St. Mark went up; a mosaic over the main facade shows the basilica in its early, simpler shape. In the twelfth century the familiar pair of columns was erected in the piazzetta, displaying St. Theodore and his crocodile and the lion of St. Mark side by side.

Venice and Constantinople eyed each other jealously. Venetian merchants living in the capital had no guarantee of safety. In 1182, when commercial rivalry flared into open violence, six thousand were killed. The riots died down, the Venetians resumed their trade, and life apparently returned to normal. But some things were not forgotten, and within a generation Venice took her cruel revenge. Her opportunity arrived with the Crusades, which had involved Constantinople, along with every other Christian city of importance, and were now to serve a whole state, as they already had countless private individuals, as an excuse to rob and plunder.

In 1096 the world had seen the First Crusade, played on the levels of bloody farce and high strategy simultaneously. While Peter the Hermit led his disorganized mob of amateurs to destruction by the Turks, a more disciplined force had been assembled by the major European powers with a view to systematic conquest. From northern France they came, from Flanders and Provence, from southern Italy, and made their gradual way to the Near East. Constantinople was their stopping place and their reluctant host; but if the Byzantines were unhappy, the forces of Islam were more so, for the Crusaders' ventures prospered. First the city of Nicaea was wrested from the Turks. This striking capture was followed in 1099 by the fall of Jerusalem. A new Christian dependency was established, that of Outremer, the Overseas Territories, embracing the principalities of Edessa and Antioch together with Jerusalem itself. But these were harder to retain than win. The fluctuating fortunes of Outremer called further expeditions into being and made Constantinople, the unwilling host of the First Crusade, the innocent victim of the Fourth.

In 1201, when the Fourth Crusade was being planned, arrangements were made to take the most convenient route, by sea, with Venice—whose control of the Adriatic was now firmly established—as the obvious port of embarkation. Venice, on her part, scented the possibility of vast profit and offered her services eagerly. Her Doge and chief negotiator was Enrico Dandolo, an implacable enemy of Byzantium, with all the qualities that the world has come to label Byzantine. Born in a tiny house on the Grand Canal—the house is still there, a few doors down from the Rialto Bridge, almost elbowed out by more palatial neighbors —he became the highest officer of a rich and powerful state; blind, he was the most farsighted general that his army could have wished; almost ninety, he displayed an ardor and vivacity that put young men to shame. His picture, by Paolo Veneziano, hangs in the sacristy of S. Maria degli Frari. It shows St. Francis presenting Dandolo to the Virgin and Child. Dandolo, kneeling, wears a thin and patronizing smile; it is clearly he who is doing them the honor. It was this man who now horse-traded with the French, and from whose usurer's hands the Crusaders found it impossible to extricate themselves with decency.

Under Dandolo's guidance Venice contracted for the carriage and provisioning of a substantial force. The city would build transports for 4,500 horses and 9,000 squires; there would be other ships to take the knights and infantry. Venice would add an escort of armed galleys; contracts were also signed for rations and fodder. To Crusaders still in the first flush of enthusiasm, this contract must have seemed the answer to their dreams. Much later, when the force assembled and was found to be only a fraction of the number originally planned, it looked more like a nightmare. Payment had been arranged on a per capita basis, and with so many defections it was impossible for the Crusaders to fulfill the terms of their contract. But the ships had been built and would have to be paid for, and the Crusaders found themselves forced to work their passage, transformed in all but name into a mercenary force of the Venetian state.

Their first, comparatively harmless duty, was to subdue the city of Zara, which Venice claimed as her own. Robert de Clari, one of the Crusaders and an ebullient tourist, describes the departure of the fleet:

> The Doge of Venice had with him fifty galleys at his own expense. The one in which he sailed was all vermilion, draped with a satin canopy to match. There was a fan-

fare of silver trumpets at her prow, and a merry rattle
of drums. All the grand folk, and the clerics, and the laity
of high and low degree, kept up such joy at the fleet's
departure that you had never seen or heard the like
before—no, nor such a fine fleet either. Then the pilgrims called on priests and clergy to mount the castles
at the masthead and sing *Veni creator spiritus;* and every man there, great and small alike, wept at his good
fortune and the joy which possessed him. . . . The people
of the city stood enraptured, marveling at the fleet and
the high nobility it carried; and they told themselves
again and again (and indeed it was true) that never had
a fleet so rich and fair as this been seen or assembled
anywhere on earth.[8]

Imperceptibly the purpose of the expedition
changed. From Zara it was sent against Constantinople.
The political pretext was one of the customary dynastic
squabbles, this one perhaps more sordid than most. Os-
tensibly the army was intervening on behalf of the Emperor Isaac, who had been deposed and blinded by his
rival, Alexius, and cast into prison with his son, also
named Alexius. The boy, brought out of Constantinople, was paraded before the soldiers, and extravagant
promises were made which went some way to appeas-
ing the Crusaders' consciences. The Eastern Church, it
was said, would accept the Latin rite. In any case, the
soldiers had little choice. There was no time to consult
the Pope, and they still owed some allegiance to Venice. In practice, many of the Crusaders were motivated
by the same greed that impelled their employer. The
world's richest city was about to fall before the jealousy
it had aroused in others.

For all its vaunted defenses, Constantinople was
easily taken. While the land army laid siege to Blacher-

nae, the sea force captured the Galata Tower and with it access to the harbor. Constantinople, after a ludicrously short struggle, now lay open to the invaders. The Crusaders kept faith with their professed cause so far as to reinstate blind Isaac on the throne. Alexius the usurper fled the city, and the French were offered the intimidating spectacle of the Byzantine court in full ceremonial array. Entering through the Blachernae gate, the emissaries were conducted to the presence.

> The Greeks had posted English and Danish guards armed with battle-axes along the road from the gate to the Blachernae Palace. The emissaries were thus taken to the inner sactum, where they saw the Emperor Isaac—so richly dressed that one would ask in vain to see a man more so—and by his side the Empress, his wife, a right beautiful lady and sister of the Queen of Hungary. There were other great lords and ladies besides, so many that there was scarcely room to turn round; and as for the ladies' dresses, you could not ask for anything finer. And those who had a day before opposed the Emperor were on this day his to command.[9]

If the spectacle of the Byzantine court had on the French the same effect as the Roman senate centuries before is said to have had on the invading Gauls they soon shook off their paralysis of mind and, like victorious soldiers of all times and places, went out to see the town. "You can be sure," says de Villehardouin,

> that many of the army went to see Constantinople, and the rich palaces and soaring churches that it possessed in such abundance—and its vast wealth, more than any other city in the world. No need to speak of all the holy

relics, for on that day there were as many in this one city
as in all the rest of the world put together.[10]

De Villehardouin is strangely reticent on the details
of what he saw. Perhaps he could not find the words
(though this would be strange for a man hailed as
the father of French prose); perhaps he was simply
overawed. The latter is more likely, and many of the
army must have shared his feelings. De Villehardouin came from the city of Troyes, not far from
Paris. It was one of the most prosperous French cities of its time, an original Roman settlement which
had long since outgrown its walls and spread out to
embrace new districts and an annual trade fair. Yet
for all this, what had Troyes to offer? Two main
streets, unpaved, with the rest of the town a network of cramped alleys; the River Vienne, so choked
and fouled with sewage and butchers' offal that a
new canal had to be dug to flush it out; a cathedral
school which restricted itself to Latin—no Greek, no
French even, let alone science, history or music.
Compared to this, Constantinople was a city of fabulous enchantment. De Villehardouin was merely anticipating the experience of the G.I. transplanted
from an Iowa farm to Paris. No wonder he was silent.

Mercifully, his fellow-traveler, Robert de Clari, is less
inhibited. He rushes everywhere, sees everything,
often with a less than perfect understanding and a tourist's gift for getting names wrong. But from his breath-
less narrative we get a vivid picture of a city overripe
and fit to fall, crammed to bursting with the wonders
of the ages. The tale loses nothing in the telling, for de
Clari exaggerates the already-marvelous:

When the city and its palaces had been taken, as I previously reported, and billets found for all the pilgrims, these same palaces were found to contain an abundance of treasure. There was the palace of Bouke-de-Lion;[11] how rich it was, and how constructed, I will tell you. This palace, now the property of the Marquis, comprised 105 mansions all of a kind, and decorated every one with gold mosaics. There were thirty chapels also, great and small. One of these they called the Holy Chapel. It was so rich and so magnificent, that all those things that are elsewhere made of iron—bolts, bars and so forth—were here made out of silver. The columns were of porphyry or jasper; every one was paved with white marble, gleaming and translucent and polished like a mirror. This chapel was so rich and magnificent that words cannot describe its grace and beauty. It contained some relics of singular virtue: two slivers of the Holy Cross, thick as a man's leg and some three feet long; the spearhead that was thrust into Our Lord's side; and the two nails that transfixed His hands and feet.[12] There was also a large crystal vial, filled with His sacred blood, and the tunic He was wearing that they took from Him on the road to Calvary. There was the blessed crown of thorns, as sharp as spikes; the robe that belonged to Our Lady; the head of John the Baptist; and so many precious relics that the tongue could not list them all, nor the mind believe them.

There were other relics in that chapel too, as we shall tell. In its center hung two vessels of costly gold, each on a silver chain. One held a tile, and the other a cloth. The story of their origin is as follows. Once upon a time there lived in Constantinople a holy man, who happened out of Christian charity to be laying tiles on an old woman's roof. While he was so engaged, Our Lord appeared and spoke to him. The good man had a cloth tied round his waist. "Give me that cloth," said the Lord. The good man gave it him. Our Lord wiped His face with it, and immediately His features were imprinted on it. He gave it back to its owner, telling him to carry it to touch the sick; and whoever he touched would be cured of his disease. The good man took the cloth and carried it away but before he did so, he placed it underneath a tile till evening. When evening came he took the tile away, but on removing it, found the imprint of Our Lord's face on this too. He took them both away with him, and many of the sick were cured.[13]

Here too is Haghia Sophia, boasting wonders that Justinian never thought of:

Its name means Holy Trinity in French. The church was built as a full circle, with internal vaulting supported on elaborate and costly columns . . . and there was not one of these columns but would cure you of some particular disease. One of them, if you rubbed it, would cure your kidney trouble. Another was good for backache. For other remedies, you went to other columns.

Some features of the great church remained unchanged: the gem-encrusted altar cloth, the chandeliers with little silver lamps. Others were new, like the magic tube that hung by the door,

about the size of a shepherd's pipe. It has the virtue I shall now relate. Whenever a sick man puts his mouth to it—say, for instance, he has a swollen belly—if he so much as touches it to his lips, the tube lays hold of him and sucks out the sickness and the poison through his mouth. It latches on to him so tight that he foams at the mouth and his eyes roll in his head, but he cannot break away till all the sickness has been drawn out of him.[14]

The equestrian statue of Justinian was still there, pointing toward the East—though de Clari or his informant believed it was Heraclius—and the herons built their nest undisturbed on it every year. There was the "Church of the Seven Apostles"—containing the column to which Christ was bound while He awaited crucifixion—"said to be the last resting place of Constantine, and Helena, and many other emperors besides."[15] He saw the gate called Golden and the Hippodrome with more carved beasts decorating the *spina*

so well made and so close to nature, that there exists no master craftsman, in Christendom or in the pagan lands, who could make them better. They were magic once and gave tongue; but they do not do this any more.[16]

There were looting and brawling in the conquered city. The promises so lightly given when the army's help was sought could no be kept, and Greeks and Latins began to fight. In the scuffle some anonymous arsonist set the city on fire.

The conflagration was so complete and so horrendous, that all attempts to put it out were useless. When the barons of the army saw it from their quarters on the far side of the harbor, they looked on with heavy hearts and wept to see the beautiful churches and sumptuous palaces collapsing into rubble and the spacious shop-lined streets glowing red with flame. There was nothing else they could do. Catching hold above the harbor, the fire passed into the most densely populated quarters of the city and down to the sea on the far side, within easy distance of Santa Sophia. It burned for two days and nights, and no hand of man could put it out. As it burned, its front measured half a league across. Oh, the pity of it:

there is no man among you that can reckon up the goods
and rich possessions that were destroyed there, or number the men, women and children who were burned
alive.[17]

There were more fights, another siege, another fire.
More houses were burned, they said, than existed in all
the cities of France put together. Over the rubble, men
fought for loot. French nobles took Boukoleon and Blachernae:

each set his own men to guard the palace that had surrendered to him, and placed a watch over his treasure.
Others scattered through the streets and gained a
wealth of booty of their own—gold and silver vessels,
precious stones, drapes of silk and satin, mantles of squir-
rel fur and ermine.[18]

The Crusaders congratulated themselves on having
beaten down the strongest city in the world, while the
people of Constantinople gathered in the streets to
read their doom in prophecies, too late.

There were two columns, each the width of three men
and thirty feet high. On top of each there lived a hermit
in a little cabin. There were doors in the columns,
through which one could ascend. On the outside were
pillars and inscriptions foretelling all the conquests of
Constantinople, all that had been and those that were
yet to come. But no one could read the future till it
happened. . . . And when this thing had come to pass, the
people came to muse upon the columns and found there
pictures of ships, with an inscription foretelling the coming of a people from the West, with cropped hair and
coats of mail, to conquer Constantinople.[19]

This almost surrealist vision of the destruction of the city, with the star-struck people shambling through the gutted streets and pillared hermits peeping from their aeries at the holocaust, seemed to write finis to Constantinople. In fact it was only the dress-rehearsal for catastrophe. The Byzantines, with the ease born of long practice, shrugged off the disaster, regrouped and recovered. For some time Constantinople itself remained in foreign hands. Doge Dandolo did not live long to enjoy his triumph. He was taken off by dysentery at Boukoleon, and his body lay for a while in Haghia Sophia, the church he had helped to desecrate. A stone plaque in the upper gallery still marks the spot. But his associates remained. Tommaso Morosini, a Venetian, became the first Latin patriarch and began to claim dominion over the churches of the wider Greek community, while the internal squabbles of Christianity continued to the point where Latin could burn Greek for heresy on the issue of unleavened bread. The conquering French nobles carved themselves estates out of the old Byzantine Empire. Banished from their former capital, the remnants of the imperial court sought refuge in Nicaea—seat of Constantine's first great Council—which for a brief period became the center of Byzantine life and letters. It was an empty, frustrated time. We hear the anger of the churchman-to-be, George of Cyprus, complaining that under Latin rule all good teachers have vanished from his own island, while Nicaea, for all its vaunted literary glory, proves a sad disappointment. It was touted as a second Athens; George found it full of pedants and windbags, who had nothing to offer but the threadbare superficialities of their art.

In 1261 the Latins had retreated, and the Byzantines

returned for a brief renaissance under the shadow of the final blow. The glories of Constantinople had been dissipated, and Mistra, just south of Sparta on a foothill of Mount Taygetus, became the seat of the imperial court in its last days. Its name, it is said, comes from *mezythra,* a kind of cheese; and it is also said, fancifully, that the place was so called after the lumpish castle built there in 1249 by Guillaume de Villehardouin, when the Franks were running wild in Greece. But Guillaume was captured by a Byzantine army in Macedonia and the castle ceded to the Emperor in part ransom. A town grew up around the castle, a Constantinople in miniature, and when, in 1349, the Morea was recovered from the Franks, it became the capital of the despotate. For the short time remaining, it was the *de facto* capital of the whole of Byzantium, acquiring an enormous population for its place and time; it survived the Turkish conquest of 1460, and when the Venetians took it in the end of the seventeenth century it held 42,000 people, vastly more than Athens. Mistra remained inhabited until the Albanian sack of 1779, and even then a few people clung to the site. Finally abandoned in 1834, it was resurrected by archaeologists sixty years later.

Mistra has been preserved as the Greek Pompeii, a cenotaph to a departed empire—for Constantinople, indelibly overbuilt, ineradicably Turkish, can hardly claim that honor. Brick-red and undisturbed, Mistra's remains spill down the hillside, neglected by the tourist hordes for whom Byzantium is a footnote to ancient history that can be safely skipped. Its streets and private houses have dissolved into a blur, but the churches, as always, stand out clear and strong. There are six still to be seen, including the Church of the

Peribleptos, dating from the mid-fourteenth century and partly carved out of the living rock; the Pantanassa, with its rows of nuns' cells; and the oldest of them all, St. Demetrius, the Metropolis, with the double eagle carved upon the marble floor, the Byzantine symbol that eventually passed to the Imperial Russian Court by marriage. In this church Constantine XI was crowned the last Emperor of Byzantium, before he went north to Constantinople and the looming menace of the Turks.

The final and conclusive threat to Byzantium came from the quarter to which Justinian had pointed. Christian apologists had long exercised their bitter and imaginative vituperation against the infidel. John Cantacuzene, preaching against Islam, had charged that its founder, "reeling and foaming at the mouth in an epileptic fit, had claimed that he had met the Archangel Gabriel face to face . . . had boasted that all the men in the world—no, more: all the spirits and all the angels put together—could never have written the Koran as he had done . . . that he came to give his law not through miracles, but with the sword."[20] It was the sword, and not the faith, that now perturbed the Byzantines. By the middle of the fifteenth century the Turks were knocking on the gates of Constantinople.

We have an eyewitness report of the last days from a foreign resident, one Nicolo Barbaro, a Venetian and a surgeon. His diary records the city's agony and death, from the moment when the invaders clamped their blockade upon the Bosphorus.

In March 1452 the Turk Mohammed Bey began the construction of a formidable castle, six miles from Constantinople on the way to the mouth of the Black Sea. It

had fourteen towers, of which the five in dominant positions were massive structures with leaded roofs. . . .
Work proceeded steadily on the castle through the
month of August 1452, and its sole purpose was the taking of Constantinople. It was strongest on the seaward
side, where rows of cannon mounted on the shoreline
and the walls made it impregnable. It was strong on the
landward side too, but not as much as by sea. The first
shot fired by the great cannon of the castle sank a ship
commanded by Antonio Rizo, in passage from the Black
Sea, because he refused to lower his sails. He was carrying a cargo of provisions for the relief of Constantinople,
and the date was November 26, 1452.[21]

The two Turkish castles, their teeth drawn, still pin
down the Bosphorus at its narrowest point. There had
been one on the eastern, Anatolian, side for some time.
Its western counterpart, Rumelihisari, went up, as Barbaro indicates, in a remarkably short time; the Sultan
himself, according to tradition, carried stones for the
construction. Rumelihisari is a museum now, a short
bus-ride from the center of modern Istanbul. Its inner
and outer rings of massive walls still bristle with cannon, though they are now pointed inward, and every
boat that passes up and down the Bosphorus must sail
in its shadow. Its construction made sea-travel impossible without Turkish permission. Captains were compelled to heave to and come ashore for a permit, which
cost them a considerable sum in duty. There were occasional daring blockade runners. Once, a galley came
down from Trebizond; while the captain was on shore
paying his respects, his crew took to the oars and hur-
ried the vessel triumphantly into Constantinople. What
became of the stranded captain is not recorded. The
sea-road to the south, through the Hellespont, was of

course still open. Eight ships came in this way with a cargo of wine from Candia, to cheer the spirits of the citizens who had little else to rejoice about. Most uneasy were the foreigners who had been trapped there by the rush of events. As usual, there were many Venetian traders and sailors in the city, as well as a contingent of visiting Genoese; there was also a religious delegation headed by the Cardinal of Russia, who had come with two hundred followers to pursue the thorny and interminable question of Church unity.

December 13, 1452.

The Union was affected in Santa Sophia with great solemnity on the part of the various holy orders. Also present were the Reverend Cardinal of Russia, representing the Pope, and His Most Serene Majesty the Emperor with all his nobles and the population of Constantinople en masse. Loud were the lamentations heard in the city that day. The purpose of this Union was to unite the Greeks and Latins as we Franks are, to put an end to schism in the Church and subscribe to one Law and one Faith. We Latins would be able to say Mass in the Greek churches, and the Greeks in ours.

The next months were punctuated by uneasy, furtive departures. Every foreigner was anxious to escape while opportunity allowed, whereas the state, fearing an erosion of matériel and manpower, sought by all means to retain them. There was great debate over the Venetian ships in harbor. Should they be permitted to leave or must they stay to help in the defense? The Venetians, more concerned for their merchandise than for Constantinople, agreed to a reluctant compromise.

Three galleys and two light vessels would stay. For the
rest, there was a general exodus.
February 26, 1453.

> Piero Duranzo slipped out of Constantinople harbor by
> night, bound for Venice. The same night also saw the
> escape of six Candian vessels, homebound with a cargo
> of cloth goods. There was a ten-mile-an-hour nor'easter
> blowing when they raised sail, so the seven ships got
> under way without trouble. These seven had been de-
> tained by the Council of Twelve, just like our Venetian
> galleys. What made them run away was their fear of the
> coming Turkish onslaught, expected daily. . . . A number
> of important personages escaped along with them, about
> seven hundred in all. They reached Tenedos unseen by
> the Turkish armada, and once through the Straits of
> Gallipoli split up and went their several ways. Six sailed
> to Candia, while Piero Duranzo made for Venice. All
> seven reached their home ports safe and sound.

The sailors unfortunate enough to be left behind
were seconded to land duty. Ditches were dug round
the palace and the weaker sections of the walls. Though
he did not, like his Turkish counterpart, carry stones
himself, the Emperor was present with his court to
urge them on. Elsewhere, the customary preparations
for defense were made.
April 2, 1453.

> His Most Serene Majesty commanded Master Barto-
> lomeo Saligo to stretch the boom across the harbor from
> Constantinople to Pera. . . . It was made of huge,
> rounded balks of wood connected with large iron nails
> and heavy links of the same metal. One end lay inside
> the walls of Constantinople, the other inside those of
> Pera, to afford the chain better protection.

Undeterred, the Turk began his approach on the landward side:

April 5.

An hour after daybreak, Mohammed brought a force of 160,000 Turks. They made camp about a mile and a half outside the walls.

April 6. The Sultan moved with half his force to a mile from the land walls.

April 7.

The Turk moved with a great part of this force to about a quarter of a mile from the said walls. His tents stretched in a line the whole length of the land walls, an extent of six miles.

The Turkish cannon were placed to command the gates. By sea, a fleet of 145 vessels came down the Bosphorus to within two miles of Constantinople, on the Asian side. In spite of this, four ships from Genoa managed to slip through. On land, the bombardment commenced. You could not see the ground, says Barbaro, it was so thick with Turks, the white turbans of the Sultan's personal slaves mingling with the red of the ordinary soldiers. Yet the walls held, until the stalemate was finally resolved by the most original and spectacular stroke of the war.

April 22.

The Sultan considered the situation and reflected that even a full-scale assault had been unable to do any damage on the landward side. Finally, the infidel's cunning mind evolved a scheme. It was essential for him to get part of his fleet, which now stood at the Columns, inside

Constantinople harbor. In this way he could fulfill his diabolical intent. Listen, and you will hear how the dog carried out his evil plan. Ordering all the crews to disembark, he set them to clearing the high ground overlooking Pera, from the seashore (that is, by the Columns, where the fleet was) to a point within the harbor limits, three miles distant. When they had leveled the ground to the best of their ability, the Turks laid quantities of rollers down this man-made passage, having first greased them thoroughly with fat. It was the Sultan's intention to start hauling a section of his fleet into our harbor. They began with one of the smaller ships. Placing it on the aforementioned rollers, a great crowd of Turks began to pull, and in a short space of time it had been drawn into the Pera basin.

Ship after ship came sailing on this landbound shipway, over the crest of the hill, until there were seventy-two Turkish vessels inside the boom. The Byzantines, in a last desperate measure, tried to destroy them with fire ships, but the Turks, forewarned by Genoese traitors, bombarded these with cannon and repelled them. Not only were the Turkish ships in harbor, but the Byzantines were trapped there too, bottled up at the far end of the Horn under continuous cannon fire. Now the Turks moved inexorably toward the final assault. A bridge of barrels, flung across the Horn, gave passage to the army. Mines crept underneath the city walls, while bonfires turned the night sky into day, and trumpets and castanets kept up a never-ending assault on the nerves of the defenders.

May 29, 1453.

Today was the last day of the fighting, the day on which Our Lord God gave his bitter final judgment against the

Greeks, the day on which He willed that the city should
fall into the hands of Mohammed Bey the Turk, the son
of Murad.... This judgment came from the heart of God
Almighty in fulfillment of the prophecies spoken of old;
and most of all that first prophecy delivered by St. Constantine, who sits on horseback near the church of St.
Sophia in this city. With his hand he prophesies, and says:
"From that direction shall my destroyer come." It is to
Anatolia that he points, in the quarter where Turkey lies.
He spoke a second prophecy also: that in time to come
there would be another emperor called Constantine, the
son of Helena, and that his reign would see the end of
Constantinople. And he made yet a third prophecy, say-
ing, "When the moon makes a sign in the heavens,
within a few days the Turks shall take Constantinople."
And all these prophesies were now fulfilled.

Waves of Turks came pouring into Constantinople,
crowding the streets, invading the churches. The Emperor Constantine fell fighting as the standard of Islam
rose above the Byzantine crescent. And all the while a
Venetian fleet had waited to give aid, detained first by
the ponderous deliberations of its masters and then by
a contrary wind. It waited still, while the city was systematically looted, street by street and house by house,
with flags marking the buildings already under occupation; and then, seeing that no more could be done,
turned round and sailed for home, to be joined by those
few vessels that had managed to escape from harbor.

Yet the conqueror was not wholly merciless. The city
changed its name to Istanbul, interpreted by some as
"the city of Islam," by others as a corruption of the
Greek for "to the city"—for Constantinople always was
"The City" to the Greeks. But by whatever title, it
remained an international settlement. Many Greeks

continued to reside there; there were 1,500 houses belonging to Jews; in Galata Turks, Greeks, Franks and Armemians lived side by side. It was the city's face that changed. Little by little the old Byzantine places were taken over. Around the Greek *strategion* grew up a new administrative center, soon to be known to the world as the center of Near Eastern diplomacy, the Sublime Porte. On the slopes of the Acropolis the Sultan built his first simple palace, soon to be dominated by Topkapi on the crest, laid out in a architectural recreation of the squared-off Turkish military encampments. Constantine's Church of the Apostles was razed to make room for the Mosque of Fatih; Haghia Sophia, though spared, became a mosque. While commerce continued on its traditional site beside the Bosphorus, the early years of occupation saw that infallible token of the orient, the nucleus of the Covered Bazaar. On the city limits, the Yedikule fortress grew new towers and swallowed up the Golden Gate. Wooden Turkish houses—only now beginning to disappear—crept up the coast toward the twin fortresses.

Other cities received, for good or ill, the Byzantine inheritance. Reluctant Vienna became the easternmost bastion of Christianity; her citizens would soon be singing *Ach, du lieber Augustin* as the armies of Islam prowled outside her walls. Over the water went the relics of saints. Paris acquired the Crown of Thorns, Venice a portion of John the Baptist. Venice took over the burden of Byzantine trade also, and flourished. The walls of San Marco, along with those of many private houses in the city, were already studded with fine marbles pillaged during the Fourth Crusade. Over the main door of the Basilica the four bronze hourses from the Hippodrome paused in their picaresque journey across the face of Europe. Positions were now reversed, for Venice cultivated its own Greek colony. Round the church of St. George, the longer-established Orthodox received new refugees and perpetuated a Byzantine style of religious painting marked by increasingly imaginative excursions into the morbid and bizarre: seventeenth-century views of the Last Judgement by Klatzes and Kavertos, showing the damned intertwined with snakes and the resurrected dead growing new flesh on their bones; a Noah's Ark by Teodoro Pulakis, in which the animals have human faces; St. Gobdelas and his tortures, painted in the eighteenth century. Byzantine peacocks flaunt themselves in the Cathedral of Torcello, and everywhere, among the streets and canals, one may see relics or memories of The City.

And the City still has not died. It lives as an ideal in the minds of Greeks who hope against hope that one day the Turks will vacate their conquered territory and Istanbul will become Constantinople again. It lives in the cultural history of Europe, to which it passed on a major portion of the classical heritage. Perhaps its best epitaph may be read in a letter written by Thomas Magistros to the Thessalonians:

> We must remember that it takes more than wood and stone to make a city; takes more than gymnasia, harbors, theaters, assembly-halls; more than the size and splendor of its buildings. It take citizens who agree together on all questions in their hearts and who preserve what has been accomplished in the past.[22]

FOOTNOTES

CHAPTER ONE

1) Zosimus, *Histories* I.49
2) Ammianus Marcellinus, *Histories* XV.12.1
3) ibid. XIV.4.5.
4) ibid, XVII.12.2
5) Julian, *Panegyric in Honor of Constantius*
6) Ausonius, *Catalogue of Famous Cities: Rome, Milan.*
7) ibid., *Trèves*
8) Eusebius, *Ecclesiastical History* VIII.6.9
9) ibid. VIII.7.1–3
10) Ammianus Marcellinus, *Histories* XVI.15–18

CHAPTER TWO

1) *Corpus Inscriptionum Latinarum* VI.1139
2) Eusebius, *Ecclesiastical History* IX.9.11
3) ibid. X.4.37–40
4) ibid. X.4.44
5) ibid. X.4.66–8
6) *Greek Anthology* IX.764

7) Zosimus, *Histories* II.37
8) ibid. II.31
9) Bell, Martin, Turner, van Berchen, *The Abinnaeus Archive*, I
10) Claudian, *Shorter Poems*, xx.1-7
11) Claudian, *Against Eutropius*, II. 335-8
12) ibid. 63-9
13) id. *The Sixth Consulship of Honorius*, 407-11
14) id. *The Fourth Consulship of Honorius*, 565-74
15) Ammianus Marcellinus, *Histories* XVII.4.14
16) ibid. XIV.6.18-20
17) ibid. XIV.6.25-6

CHAPTER THREE

1) *Greek Anthology* VIII.169
2) ibid. V.292
3) ibid. V.293
4) ibid. IX.653
5) ibid. IX.650
6) ibid. II.1.59-61
7) ibid. 79-81
8) ibid. IX.620
9) ibid. IX.682
10) Procopius. *History of the Wars* I.24.4-6
11) id. *Anecdota (Secret History)* 8.7
12) id. *Buildings* I.11.1
13) *Greek Anthology* IX.808
14) Procopius, *Buildings* I.5.13
15) *Greek Anthology* IX.663.1-2
16) ibid. IX.651
17) ibid. IX.656.1-11,19-21
18) ibid. XVI.62
19) ibid. I.8

20) Paul the Silentiary, *Haghia Sophia* 476–480
21) ibid. 186–92
22) ibid. 315–9
23) ibid. 337–43
24) ibid. 617–30
25) *Greek Anthology* VII.375
26) Procopius, *History of the Wars* XXII.1.30

CHAPTER FOUR

1) Paul the Silentiary, *Haghia Sophia* 168
2) George Gissing, *By the Ionian Sea: notes of a ramble in Southern Italy*
3) Procopius, *History of the Wars* I.1
4) Julian, *Panegyric in Honor of Constantius*
5) Procopius, *History of the Wars* VI.27.19
6) ibid. V.25.23
7) ibid. V.26.8
8) ibid. VI. 21.6
9) ibid. VII. 1.5
10) ibid. VII.12.3–6
11) *Greek Anthology* XVI.77
12) Andreas Agnellus, *Liber Pontificalis* II: *Life of Saint Maximian* I
13) ibid. IV

CHAPTER FIVE

1) Paul the Silentiary, *Haghia Sophia* 230–2
2) *Greek Anthology* X.15.1–6
3) ibid. IV.3.77–96
4) Procopius, *History of the Wars* II.3.42–3
5) A detailed report of the Yassi Ada excavation is given by George F. Bass, 'A Byzantine Trading Venture', *Scientific American* August 1971

6) Document of Leo VI quoted in A. Dain, *Nauma-chica*, pp. 19–20
7) Liutprand, *Antapodosis* V.15
8) Cosmas, *Christian Topography* V.8
9) ibid. II.29
10) ibid.
11) ibid. XI.445
12) *Greek Anthology* I.101
13) Cosmas, *Christian Topography* III.65–6
14) ibid. II.46–7
15) Ammianus Marcellinus, *Histories* XXIII.6.67
16) ibid. XV.3.3
17) Leo the Philosopher, *Tactics* VIII
18) ibid.
19) *Greek Anthology* IX.582
20) *Life of Constantine* 8
21) ibid. 9
22) *Life of Methodius* 11
23) *Life of Constantine* 16
24) *Life of Methodius* 16
25) Constantine Porphyrogennetus, *A Manual of Imperial Administration (De Administrando Imperio)* 9

CHAPTER SIX

1) Theodore, *Orations* XIII.2
2) ibid. 3
3) ibid. 4–5
4) ibid.13
5) ibid.14
6) id. *Iambic Poems* 3
7) ibid. 7
8) ibid. 9
9) ibid. 14

10) ibid. 16
11) ibid. 17
12) *Greek Anthology* VI.66
13) The original is now in Vienna; for American readers, a facsimile is available in the library of the Morton Arboretum, near Chicago. I am indebted to the Librarian for permission to work from this copy.
14) Theodore, *Orations* XI.3.4
15) id. *Antirrheticus* I.5.11
16) *Greek Anthology* I.108

CHAPTER SEVEN

1) Anna Comnena, *Alexiad* VII.2
2) ibid. III.4
3) Psellus, *Chronographia: Basil* II 27
4) ibid. *Zoe and Theodora* 3
5) ibid. *Constantine* IX 201
6) ibid. *Basil II* 31
7) ibid. *Romanus III* 14–16
8) ibid. *Constantine IX* 185
9) ibid. 187
10) Anna Comnena, *Alexiad* XII.6
11) Psellus, *Chronographia: Michael IV* 52
12) *Digenes Akrites* I 30–43
13) ibid. 93–112
14) ibid. 265–275
15) Ibid. 284–97
16) ibid. II. 56–62, 65–70
17) ibid. III. 137–149
18) ibid. 166–87, 204–17
19) ibid. 256–60
20) ibid. IV.220–229

21) ibid. V.4–26
22) ibid. VIII.124–8
23) Constantine Porphyrogennetus, *A Manual of Imperial Administration* 15
24) Psellus, *Chronographia: Constantine IX*.9
25) Anna Comnena, *Alexiad* XV.7

CHAPTER EIGHT

1) Anon. *Acts of Saint Demetrius* 2
2) Simeon Metaphrastes, *Miracles of Saint Demetrius* II.8
3) ibid. II.162–5
4) ibid.
5) Thomas Magister, *Letter to Metochites*
6) Simeon Metaphrastes, *Life of Saint Daniel Stylites* 4
7) ibid. 6
8) id. *Life of Saint Joannicius* 11
9) Instructions of Abbot Simeon of Xerocerkos, quoted by Demetrius Kydonis, *Against Palamas*
10) Gregory Palamas, *Homilies* I
11) Barlaam, *An Oration on Church Unity*
12) ibid.
13) ibid.
14) Demetrius Kydonis, *Lament for the Dead of Thessaloniki*
15) ibid.
16) ibid.

CHAPTER NINE

1) Benjamin of Tudela, *Itinerary* trans. A. Asher p. 23.1

2) ibid. p. 20.1
3) ibid. p. 21.1
4) Constantine Porphyrogennetus, *A Handbook of Imperial Administration* 27–8
5) Gregory of Nyssa, *Encomium Delivered upon Saint Theodore Martyr*
6) John Ruskin, *The Stones of Venice* II.4.3
7) Simeon Metaphrastes, *Life of Saint Mark*
8) Robert de Clari, *The Conquest of Constantinople* 13
9) Geoffroi de Villehardouin, *The Conquest of Constantinople* 38.185
10) ibid. 40.191
11) This is one of the names that the author gets wrong; he seems to want to make it mean "The Lion's Mouth." Note also the inspired mistranslation of Haghia Sophia below.
12) *Sic.* It is difficult to conjecture how de Clari imagined the crucifixion to have taken place
13) ibid. 82–3
14) ibid. 85
15) 87
16) ibid. 90
17) Geoffroi de Villehardouin, *op. cit.* 44.203–5
18) ibid. 55.249
19) Robert de Clari, *op. cit.* 92
20) John Cantacuzene, *Four Sermons Against Mohammed*
21) Nicolo Barbaro, *A Diary of the Siege of Constantinople*, references as dated
22) Thomas Magister, Gk. ms., Paris 2629 f. 129

INDEX

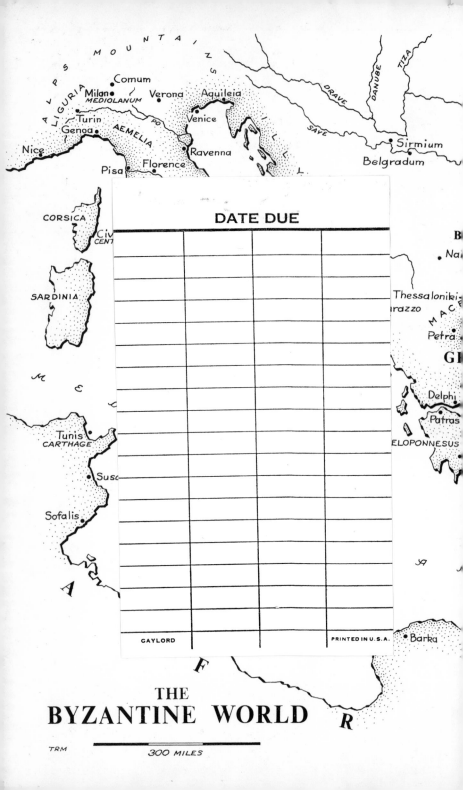

THE
BYZANTINE WORLD

TRM

300 MILES